Mapping Public Theology

Mapping
Public
Theology

Beyond Culture,
Identity,
and Difference

Benjamin Valentin

TRINITY PRESS INTERNATIONAL
A Continuum imprint
HARRISBURG • LONDON • NEW YORK

For five beloved friends and mentors

Catherine Keller

Anthony B. Pinn

Gordon D. Kaufman

Ada Maria Isasi-Diaz

Otto Maduro

Trinity Press International, P.O. Box 1321, Harrisburg, PA 17105
Trinity Press International is a division of The Morehouse Group.

Cover design: Brenda Klinger

Library of Congress Cataloging-in-Publication Data

Valentin, Benjamin
 Mapping public theology : beyond culture, identity, and difference/
Benjamin Valentin.
      p. cm.
Includes bibliographical references and index.
 ISBN 1-56338-391-8 (pbk.)
 1. Hispanic American theology. I. Title.
 BT83.575 .V35 2002
230'.089'68073--dc21

                                   2002009363

Printed in the United States of America

02 03 04 05 06 07   10 9 8 7 6 5 4 3 2 1

We must focus our attention on the public square—the common good that undergirds our national and global destinies. The vitality of any public square ultimately depends on how much we care about the quality of our lives together.

—Cornel West, *Race Matters*

Contents

Acknowledgments

It is my pleasure to thank a number of people who were essential in making this book possible. I would first like to thank the five beloved friends and confidants to whom this book is gratefully dedicated: Catherine Keller; Anthony B. Pinn; Gordon D. Kaufman; Ada María Isasi-Díaz; and Otto Maduro. My work on this project would have been impossible without their multifaceted support, encouragement, guidance, friendship, and kindness. I would like to thank my parents—Rev. Angel M. Valentin and Luz Belen Santa Valentin—for their unreserved love, help, and ideal example in life. I would also like to thank my beloved brother, Elieser Valentin, for his love incomparable friendship, encouragement, support, and energizing enthusiasm. Special thanks are also due to my dear sister Bethsaida Valentin, for her love, backing, and inspiration. Thank you always!

I want to extend a special thank you to the faculty, administrators, staff, and students at Andover Newton Theological School for providing an ideal academic community and supportive space in which to discuss and shape the ideas expressed in this book. Thanks for your understanding, warm embrace, acceptance, enthusiastic support, and manifold assistance. Thank you to the Hispanic Theological Initiative, and all those connected to the HTI, for community, support, and many-sided nourishment over the years.

I would also like to thank all the members and ministerial leaders of La Iglesia de Dios/The Church of God in New York City, and of La Congregacíon León de Judá/The American Baptist Congregation Lion of Judah in Boston for their love, "apoyo," and encouragement. Muchas gracias!

I would like to thank the following persons for their love, friendship, intellectual, emotional, moral, and editorial support: Mayra Rivera, Luis

Rivera-Pagan, Roberto Pazmiño, Mark Heim, Leticia Guardiola-Sáenz, Jerusa Carvajal, Justo González, Eldin Villafañe, Zaida Maldonado-Perez, Joanne Rodriguez, Efrain Agosto, Harold Recinos, Humberto Alfaro, Luis Pedraja, Melissa Valentín, Omar Soto, and Aidimarys Martinez-Soto, Samuel L. Caraballo, Miriam D. Martinez, Rev. Roberto Miranda and Mercedes Miranda, "los tremendos musicos/the great musicians" at León de Judá/Lion of Judah—Jose, David M, Gonzalo, Samuel, David, Uzziel, Elias, Eric, Carlos, Leonardo, Freddy, Andres, Alberto, Samuel Cruz, Hugo Magallanes, Ricardo Ramos, Victor Algarín, Joshua and Joel Vicente, Wilfredo and Edith Vargas, the Hernandez and Lopez family—Jorge, Eddie, Karaly, and Lourdes, Maurey Bolden, Liz Aguilar, Roslyn Friedman, and Noraida Díaz.

Finally, I want to thank my editor, Henry Carrigan, for believing in this project. "It has truly been a pleasure working with you, HC." Thank you! I also thank all the folks at Trinity Press International for their help in making this book a reality.

Introduction

The sensibility I am worrying about typically expresses itself as an enthusiasm for the local.

—Catherine Keller[*]

I believe that our times call for forms of thought and discourse that dare to be socially broad, integrative, and holistic—in short, "public" in orientation. Increasingly, I see a need for discourse that can attract the attention and support of a large and diverse audience: for colloquies that, although attentive to their specific contexts, can somehow move beyond the space of local knowledge—the space of specific culture and identity—and can project a comprehensive and galvanizing emancipatory sociopolitical vision that could pull persons beyond boundaries of difference to work toward worthy public goals. Given the declining standards of living experienced by millions in our nation and globally, the rampant cynicism and apathy that afflict our public life, the strengthening of global interests and forces, the deterioration of a spirit of solidarity, the fracturing of utopian energies along group lines of difference, and the increase of social antagonism we have witnessed, it is important that those who work for justice put forward overarching visions and broad analyses that seek to grasp and transform the social whole.

The irony of the contemporary intellectual scene is that in a time when the need for comprehensive and integrative thought has increased, liberationists and progressives have generally taken to circumscribing their ambitions and visions, choosing to dedicate themselves principally to the promotion of particular cultural and identity commitments. This tendency is characteristic of a general mood that holds sway in our era, one that predisposes

* Catherine Keller, "Seeking and Sucking: On Relation and Essence in Feminist Theology," in *Horizons in Feminist Theology: Identity, Tradition, and Norms,* ed. Rebecca S. Chopp and Sheila Greeve Davaney (Minneapolis: Fortress Press, 1997), 63.

people to fragmentary and provincial thought rather than to broad visions and analyses, to the sense that "we are all part of one garment of destiny,"[1] to the consideration of the quality of our lives together in and as a society, and to any sense of the whole.

This widespread tendency has affected the discipline of theology. Specifically, and paradoxically, it has influenced liberation theologies in the United States. In spite of the ameliorative and social commitments declared by U.S. liberation theologians, and, therefore, their implicit public aspirations, these theologies have not often exhibited a public perspective and/or public discursive quality, nor have they paid much serious attention to the complexities involved in doing theology as public discourse. In brief, few liberation theologies have looked into the possibility of theology becoming public discourse in ways that may be adequate to the justice demands of our age, connecting the task of theology to some conception of public discourse theory, to a general understanding of the idea of the public of civil society, and to a credible comprehensive sociopolitical project for justice that could harmonize the emancipatory interests of diverse and currently fragmented constituencies.

Although this inadvertency is identifiable in theology overall and in U.S. liberation theologies generally, my concern in this project is mainly with the way in which it manifests itself in and affects Hispanic/Latino theological discourse. Beginning in 1975, with the publication of Virgilio Elizondo's *Christianity and Culture*,[2] and reaching a boom and mature stage in its articulated form during the 1990s, U.S. Hispanic/Latino theology has quickly developed into a formidable theological tradition composed of varied liberationist discourses that speak of and to the confounding reality of Latino/a life in the United States. Although Hispanic/Latino theology in particular, like U.S. liberation theology as a whole, assumes the public character and relevance of theological reflection, it has not yet advanced or espoused this public dimension by way of deliberate reflection on the exigencies and conditions

---

1 I borrow this line from Cornel West, *Race Matters* (New York: Vintage Books, 1994), 11.

2 See Virgilio Elizondo, *Christianity and Culture: An Introduction to Pastoral Theology and Ministry for the Bicultural Community* (Huntington, Ind.: Our Sunday Visitor, 1975). I submit that the move toward a thorough, systematic, book-length theological articulation of Latino/a life and culture, written from a fully intentional and uniquely Hispanic perspective in the United States, begins with this 1975 publication by Virgilio Elizondo, a Mexican American theologian who has been active as a religious leader since the early 1960s and is still one of the most internationally recognized Latino/a religious figures. For more on the overall historical development of Latino/a theology, see my article "Strangers No More: An Introduction to, and Interpretation of, U.S. Hispanic/Latino(a) Theology," in *The Ties That Bind: African American and Hispanic American/Latino(a) Theology in Dialogue*, ed. Anthony B. Pinn and Benjamín Valentín (New York: Continuum, 2001), 38-53.

involved in theology becoming public discourse in our fractious times. A fundamental assumption of this composition is that Latino/a theologians can enhance the theoretical scope of their theology, and might also heighten its sociopolitical relevance in the national context, by directly engaging the question of what tasks and features characterize public discourse and, correspondingly, the role of the "public intellectual."

My aim in this study is to put forth a call and to set an introductory, and mostly descriptive rather than didactic, course for the conceptualization of Latino/a theology as a form of public discourse. I must concede that this exposition is principally motivated by my own disenchantment with what I perceive to be an at times unconscious and unreflective commitment to a discursive cultural politics of identity program in Latino/a liberation theology. To be sure, there is ample reason for this emphasis. We Latino/as have always had to struggle consistently and zealously not only to keep alive our distinctive historical and cultural identities, but also to claim our membership as legitimate citizens and active agents in this nation. Insofar as the Latino/a experience in the United States has been played out within the context of cultural imperialism and racism, and insofar as Latinos and Latinas have had to contend with denigrating images and discriminating forces that frustrate positive self and group identity, it is not surprising that Hispanic/Latino theologians and Latino/a scholars in general have devoted a great part of their attention to the task of cultural, identity, and difference recognition.

Moreover, I grant that any comprehensive political project that is genuinely concerned with the remedy of injustice must make room in its agenda for the consideration of issues related to the defense of group identity, the end of cultural domination, and the requirements of recognition. These concerns and struggles have everything to do with justice and must continue to be part of any emancipatory project, and, therefore, of Latino/a liberation theology.[3]

---

3 Here I want especially to distance myself from facile dismissals of identity politics, and of the importance of cultural issues and recognition claims for the theorizing of justice, recently advanced by some liberals and leftists. My statements throughout this work should make clear, however, that I am also leery of the decoupling of cultural politics from social politics, and the relative eclipse of the latter by the former that has at times appeared in leftist discourses that promote a cultural politics of identity and difference too uncritically. For an eloquent but one-sided critique of cultural and identity politics tendered from a leftist perspective, see Todd Gitlin, *The Twilight of Common Dreams: Why America Is Wracked by Culture Wars* (New York: Metropolitan Books, 1995). For a more nuanced and balanced critical approach to cultural and identity politics, see Nancy Fraser, *Justice Interruptus: Critical Reflections on the "Postsocialist" Condition* (New York: Routledge, 1997), esp. 11-39, 189-205; and from a refreshingly Latina perspective, see Linda Martin Alcoff, "Latina/o Identity Politics," in *The Good Citizen*, ed. David Batstone and Eduardo Mendietta (New York: Routledge, 1999), 93-112.

Nevertheless, I believe that Latino/a theology has tended to focus predominantly on discussions of symbolic culture, identity, and difference, and has, therefore, given too little attention to the critical scrutiny of the multifaceted matrices that impinge upon the realization of a broader emancipatory political project and energy. As important as it is, I believe that the emphasis on specific localization that undergirds much of our liberationist discourse, which lends itself to an insular enchantment with matters of culture, identity, and difference, is too narrow to foster the kinds of overarching and harmonizing emancipatory visions that the goal of social justice requires in our time. Thus, I submit that as critical theorists of justice, Latino/a theologians must engage not only the possibilities but also the ambiguities and even limitations that inhere in the discursive paradigm of identity and cultural recognition that has been so enthusiastically embraced by them. I am particularly concerned with how the enthusiasm for a circumscribed discourse of identity, cultural recognition, and cultural justice can, if not adequately checked and supplemented, distract us from examining other axes of social stratification with equal urgency and appropriate sustained attention; from addressing the social fragmentation, loss of civil bonds, political balkanization, and fracturing of utopian energies that we are witnessing in the realm of civil society; from sufficiently promoting a desire for connection and coalition building across boundaries of group difference; and, thus, from advancing a much broader response to social injustice.

Hispanic/Latino theology is far from a homogeneous and static body of work; this theological tradition is composed of varied discourses, each one offering its own subtlety. Thus, the universal applicability of my hypothesis regarding Latino/a theology's privileging of "local" symbolic culture and identity, and/or specific localization, at the expense of a wider sense of the "public" has limitations; it may apply more to some theologies than to others. Nevertheless, I believe that there is sufficient evidence for my viewpoint. To be clear on this point, my suggestion is simply that Latino/a theology has thus far, whether by design or not, given more sustained attention to matters that pertain to the realm of cultural theorizing, and thus to the space of specific cultural identity, than to matters that pertain to the realm of broad social analysis and theory. That is to say, issues such as the discovery, defense, celebration, and reconstruction of cultures and identities; the achievement of cultural and identity recognition; and the fight against assimilationist tendencies have so far received more detailed examination in Latino/a theology than have issues related to broad-based social analysis. The latter issues would include, for instance, the examination and critique of political economy and classism; the consideration of racial and ethnic social relations; the

engagement with public discourse and policy; the problem of political balkanization and the exploration of social arrangements that could harmonize
the interests of diverse and currently fragmented constituencies in the realm
of civil society; and the consideration of the possibilities and exigencies for
multiracial coalitional politics in our present society. The recurring use of,
and significance attributed to, the concepts of "mestizaje" (Latino/a cultural
and racial hybridity) and "popular religion," and the Latino/a cultural reality
in U.S. Hispanic/Latino theological works clearly reveals a turn toward culture. Such concepts are usually used to examine the space of symbolic culture, identity, and cultural difference, and lend themselves more to forms of
cultural, rather than broad-based social and political, theorizing.

To be sure, my point here is not that Latino/a theology has not in any way
considered the broad social issues I have mentioned above. Issues pertaining,
for instance, to political economy, class, broad-based social mobilization,
political theory, and racial or social relations—in short, matters pertaining to
the broader realm of social analysis—have indeed received consideration in
that theology.[4] My suggestion is simply and more precisely that these latter
broad social issues and concerns have not received as much sustained attention in Latino/a theology as have those that pertain to the realm of cultural
theory. Given that a great number of our theologies devote more energy to
exploring the possibilities of cultural revaluation, to reclaiming positive personal and cultural identity, and to the assertion of specificity and difference
than to scrutinizing the structural nature of society, the conflicts and problems

---

4 See, for example, María Pilar Aquino's engagement with the markets and ideologies of
globalizing neocapitalism in her article "Theological Method in U.S. Latino/a Theology: Toward
an Intercultural Theology for the Third Millennium," in *From the Heart of Our People: Latino/a
Explorations in Catholic Systematic Theology*, ed. Orlando O. Espín and Miguel H. Díaz
(Maryknoll, N.Y.: Orbis Books, 1999), esp. 29-32; Ada María Isasi-Díaz's description of five
modes of oppression and description of the contours of a "mujerista" account of justice, taking
into account matters of political economy and exploitation, in her essay "Un poquito de justi-
cia-A Little Bit of Justice: A Mujerista Account of Justice," in *Hispanic/Latino Theology:
Challenge and Promise*, ed. Ada María Isasi-Díaz and Fernando F. Segovia (Minneapolis:
Fortress Press, 1996), 325-39, and also her dealings with the issue of social solidarity in
"Solidarity: Love of Neighbor in the 1980s," in *Lift Every Voice: Constructing Christian Theologies
from the Underside*, ed. Susan B. Thistlethwaite and Mary Potter Engels (San Francisco: Harper
& Row, 1990), 31-40; Harold Recinos's discussion of the important matter of national identity
in the first chapter of his book *Who Comes in the Name of the Lord? Jesus at the Margins*
(Nashville: Abingdon Press, 1997), 15-36, and his look into the process of globalization in chap-
ters 3 and 4 of his book *Jesus Weeps: Global Encounters on Our Doorstep* (Nashville: Abingdon
Press, 1992), 55-99; and Eldin Villafañe's look into Hispanic/Latino and African American
social relations in chapter 6 of his book *Seek the Peace of the City: Reflections on Urban Ministry*
(Grand Rapids: Eerdmans, 1995), 57-63.

of political and economic privilege, and the prospects for cross-cultural communication and alliance-producing discursive and political enterprises in the wider realm of civil society, it is reasonable to claim that Latino/a theology has been marked by a concern with identity and symbolic culture. It is not entirely misplaced to label as identity politics many of the claims for justice that Hispanic/Latino theologians have made.

To be sure, my point is not that such an emphasis on cultural theorizing, cultural justice, and identity recognition is inherently faulty. These issues must continue to be a part of the reflective agenda particularly for those theologies that arise out of the context of historically subordinated and oppressed groups in the United States, as is the case with Latino/a theology. My point is that a theology that aims to promote social justice, as Latino/a theology unequivocally does, must guard against giving most of its sustained and mature attention to matters of particular culture, identity, and cultural difference. Rather, it must carefully uphold the possibility and desirability of comprehensive, integrative, and programmatic thinking, searching for a critical bivalent approach that can help it to appropriately connect and balance the exigencies of cultural theorizing, politics, and justice with those of social theorizing, politics, and justice; to connect the study of local signification with that of broad social structures and relations; and to connect the interests and concerns of the politics of identity with those of social solidarity and emancipatory coalitional politics.[5] This needed synthesis calls for a public vision and disposition, and for modes of public discourse, for overarching visions and analyses based upon a keen sense of the justice demanded of our historical moment, and upon an integrative perspective that seeks to grasp and transform the social whole. Conversely, the desire for this sort of synthesis and disposition, for these sorts of overarching emancipatory visions and analyses, and for this kind of integrative sociopolitical perspective characterizes public discourse.

The fundamental argument of this book is that Latino/a theologians should be attentive not only to the needs of "local" theologies but also to the possibilities of "public" theologies that can engage the broader context of social and political life, and that may revitalize a populist sentiment and coalitional energy in our society. Accordingly, it seeks both to point to the need for a conception of Latino/a theology as translocal and transcultural "public" discourse and to provide a theoretical description of public discourse that takes into account the justice demands of our age. To put it simply, this

---

5 My general posture and terminology here is inspired by Nancy Fraser's critical social theory, set forth in *Justice Interruptus*.

introductory work calls for Latino/a theology to become public discourse, describing, in the process, the broader sociopolitical realities that make such a discursive perspective necessary and the contours of an emancipatory public discourse that promotes coalition building across racial, cultural, gender, class, and religious lines.

Having outlined what this work sets out to do, I must clarify what it does not attempt to do. This work does not set out to elaborate a detailed, fully developed, Latino/a public theology. Rather, as introduction, this book will simply set a stage by identifying a need for, concerns related to, and elements for a theory generative of, a more public Latino/a liberation theology. The aim of this work is not, therefore, to grasp or to give answer to all of the implications involved in the discussion of its topic, but rather, to initiate it, to make others aware of the need to address it and enter into a dialogue about its possible dimensions.

What this work offers, then, is a preface to a public theology—one that focuses on the exigencies for and the tasks of public discourse. In this book I have worked to provide a description of public discourse, its importance, concern, emphases, and features, in the hopes of tendering a theoretical and descriptive basis that may be useful in the development of future emancipatory public theologies. The contribution I offer in this prefatory and descriptive work is modest; but I believe it is a crucial one. This book perhaps can serve to highlight the urgent need for public visions and discourse in our time; to point out some dynamics that can cut short a public disposition and relevance in our theologies; to describe some of the tasks and characteristics of an emancipatory public discourse; and, thus, to serve as an invitation for others to conceptualize the tasks of theologies that aspire to go public as public discourse.

My outlook in this work is deeply informed by the moral emphasis and ameliorative impulse of liberation theology. My outlook is also informed, however, by other sources, such as constructive theology, critical social theory, American pragmatism, public sphere theory, critical cultural theory, postcolonial thought, and U.S. Latino/a studies.[6] Some of the distinctiveness of

---

6 My discursive framework draws especially, although not exclusively, upon the historicist and pragmatic constructive theology espoused by Gordon Kaufman and Linell Cady; the critical social theory and public sphere theory advanced by Nancy Fraser; the prophetic pragmatism and description of the role of the public intellectual put forward by Cornel West; the critical cultural theory tendered by Susan Friedman; and the suggestions of Linda Martin Alcoff for Latino/a Identity Politics. See, for example, Gordon D. Kaufman, *An Essay on Theological Method* (Atlanta: Scholars Press, 1979), *In Face of Mystery: A Constructive Theology* (Cambridge: Harvard University Press, 1993), and *God-Mystery-Diversity: Christian Theology in a Pluralistic World* (Minneapolis:

this work can be traced to my blending of these various theoretical elements. Its distinctiveness also stems from my hope to create better intersections between two fields of discourse that have not entered into substantive internal dialogue: liberation theology and public theology. The fact is that liberation theologians in general have not directly engaged the question of the public and/or publicness. Conversely, theologians who have examined the query of the public have not often explicitly engaged the question of liberation. Moreover, the emphases I attach to the notion of public discourse in this work have not often been clearly articulated in nor exemplified by U.S. liberation theologies or public theologies. By tackling these issues and concerns, I hope to create new discursive bridges and to hint at new possible directions for Latino/a theology, liberation theology in general, and for public theology in the United States.

Although the description of public discourse set out here is, of course, closely related to my own interests in Latino/a and liberation theology, it is my hope that the ruminations put forth here will be of help to all theologians who are interested in the role of public discourse and the possible relation of prophetic theology to American public life. The interpretations and descriptions offered here outline a call for and a general approach to the construction of theologies that promote an integrative public perspective that seeks to grasp and transform the social whole. A commitment to pursuing the overarching emphases I have laid out for an emancipatory public discourse "can take place in—though usually on the margin of"[7]—a variety of theological traditions. What is necessary is a desire to make a difference in the world, a concern for social justice, a yearning to move, occasionally and/or when necessary, beyond the space of specific cultural knowledge and allegiance in order to make liberatory connections across the boundaries of difference in our society—in short, what is necessary is a desire to go public with our thoughts, discourses, and activisms.

Fortress Press, 1996); Linell Cady, *Religion, Theology, and American Public Life* (New York: State University of New York Press, 1993); Nancy Fraser, *Unruly Practices: Power, Discourse, and Gender in Contemporary Social Theory* (Minneapolis: University of Minnesota Press, 1989) and *Justice Interruptus*; Cornel West, *The American Evasion of Philosophy: A Genealogy of Pragmatism* (Madison: University of Wisconsin Press, 1989), *Prophetic Reflections: Notes on Race and Power in America* (Monroe, Maine: Common Courage Press, 1993), *Race Matters*, and, with Henry Louis Gates Jr., *The Future of the Race* (New York: Alfred A. Knopf, 1996); Susan S. Friedman, *Mappings: Feminism and the Cultural Geographies of Encounter* (Princeton, N.J.: Princeton University Press, 1998); and Linda Martin Alcoff, "Latina/o Identity Politics."

7 I borrow this line from Cornel West, *The American Evasion of Philosophy*, 232.

I begin my discourse in chapter 1, "The Staging Ground of U.S. Hispanic/Latino Theology," with an attempt to delineate some of the historical events and social conditions and dynamics that invoked the centrality of culture and identity in Hispanic/Latino theology. For sure, much more than what has been said in this brief and selective sociohistorical sketch could be said. Yet, my aim here is in no way to provide a full-fledged history of Latino/a cultures or of the various groups' interrelations, but rather, simply first to provide a glimpse of who Latino/as are, and second to suggest some of the issues integral to understanding the staging ground of Hispanic/Latino theology and especially its stress on the categories of identity and symbolic culture. In providing such a brief and selective narrative, I have opted to tell a bit of the histories of the central groups in the United States that are labeled Hispanic or Latino in order to provide at least a general notion of both their diversity and historical relatedness.

Chapter 2, "Traversing the Enchantment with Symbolic Culture and Identity Politics in U.S. Hispanic/Latino Theology," examines two of the central ways in which the emphasis on Latino/a culture and identity has received expression within U.S. Hispanic/Latino theology. It is my belief that the interconnected concern with self-identity and cultural identity is most manifest in the recurring use of, and significance attributed to, the concepts of "mestizaje" and "popular religion" in the writings of most Hispanic/Latino theologians. In this chapter, I consider the writings of two U.S. Hispanic/Latino theologians who have written extensively on and are often quoted in reference to the theorizing of mestizaje (i.e., Latino/a hybridity) and popular religion: Virgilio Elizondo and Orlando Espín. I suggest that in whatever manner the term "mestizaje" is employed, and no matter what secondary meaning may be attributed to the study of popular religion, the main thrust behind the use of these concepts is a concern with the proper remembrance, defense, and celebration of Latino/a cultural identity and difference. Although this emphasis greatly characterizes Hispanic/Latino theology overall, I perceive that the privileging of cultural and identity theorizing and the central focus on matters of cultural injustice are clearly and especially apparent in the Hispanic/Latino theologies of Elizondo and Espín. In my years of reading Hispanic/Latino theology, I had gradually become aware of the tendency of many Latino/a theologians to privilege symbolic culture, identity, and specific positionality at the expense of a wider sense of the public. Accordingly, in this chapter I chose two influential theologians in whose work this tendency is especially discernable.

After offering an analysis of key writings by these two authors—one that seeks to evoke a better appreciation of the commitment to the theorizing of

Latino/a symbolic culture, identity, and difference found in them—I argue that it is now the proper time for Latino/a theologians to engage not only the possibilities but also the ambiguities and limitations that inhere in the discursive paradigm of identity and cultural recognition and more generally in a cultural politics of identity and difference. Accordingly, the remainder of this chapter considers four salient dilemmas that such a discursive paradigm confronts and that point to the need for the conceptualization of Latino/a liberation theology as a form of transcultural *public* discourse. In discussing these complications, I propose that Latino/a theologians must be willing and able to play beyond symbolic culture, identity, and the space of specific knowledge and difference, not by way of a thorough dismissal or obliteration of these matters and concerns, but rather, through a careful supplementation that plays up those interstitial sites of interaction, interconnection, and exchange in our civil society—sites that can allow for comprehensive, coalitional, and broadly benefiting emancipatory public goals and activity. In short, I suggest that what we need and should strive for are theologies that may function as public discourse.

Chapter 3, "Cultivating a Public Perspective in Hispanic/Latino Theological Discourse," delves into the notion of public theology, charting some of the ways in which that concept has been employed and then advancing a distinctive general description of public discourse that may contribute to Latino/a theological construction. What ensues is a definition of public theology as a form of discourse that couples either the language, symbols, or background concepts of a religious tradition with an overarching, integrative, emancipatory sociopolitical vision in such a way that it movingly captures the attention and moral conscience of a broad audience and promotes the cultivation of those modes of love, concern, and courage required both for individual fulfillment and broad-based social activism. With such a definition of public theology in place, I proceed in chapter 3 to suggest that this overall description of public theology involves three overarching discursive tasks: (1) cultivating a public disposition in society and in intellectual work; (2) promoting multiracial social coalitions of struggle for justice; and (3) developing a discourse that can facilitate the engagement of a broad and varied constituency within the realm of civil society. The remainder of the chapter explores the implications of these discursive goals for Latino/a theology, offering, in the process, a brief but penetrating social analysis that at once highlights the way in which the justice demands of our time call for the valuation of the public realm and of a public perspective and also uncovers some of the dynamics and sensibilities that militate against the cultivation of a much needed public disposition in the United States. Beyond suggesting the contours and tasks of a public theology, in this chapter I try to promote a general understanding of the concept of the public and of public discourse.

Chapter 4, "Expanding Visions, Fusing Horizons," seeks to integrate the cultural and the social, the local and the public, in our theory of public discourse, vouching for what might be labeled a locational publicness in Latino/a theology. I submit that the theorizing of public space and discourse does not require that we underplay our particular social and cultural locations or that we disregard matters of culture, identity, and difference, but rather, that we return to them in a newly spatialized way—one that plays up the liberating possibilities that inhere in those interstitial sites of interaction, interconnection, and exchange "in between" differences in our society. After examining two general directions that have been pursued in the theorizing of the public, I call attention to the potential that exists in the concept of "subaltern counter*public*"[8] discourse to fuse the specific concerns of cultural and identity politics so prevalent in the works of the Latino theologians whom we examined in chapter 2 and the aspirations for a broader social politics of liberation. I end in this chapter by suggesting that this concept of public space and discourse offers Latino/a theologians particularly, and liberation theologians generally, a heuristic device at the level of a theory of discourse that can help us to connect the cultural with the social in our theologies; to fuse our specific identity political interests to a broader emancipatory sociopolitical project; to expand both the theoretical and practical relevancy as well as the liberating potential of our theologies; and, thus, better to witness "God's crossing over between and among us" in our current U.S. society.

My guiding aim in this book is simply this: to help Latino/a theology in particular, and liberation theology in general, speak more ably of and to the broader challenges that a comprehensive project for social justice confronts in an increasingly stratified and fragmented U.S. social context, and to *go public* with its discourse.

---

8 In my use of this term, I italicize the segment "public" in order to give emphasis to the public dimension or quality of this discursive form.

Chapter I

The Staging Ground of U.S. Hispanic/Latino Theology

LATINO/A LIFE IN THE UNITED STATES

I have an idea that there is much importance about the Latin race's contributions to the American nationality that will never be put with sympathetic understanding and tact on the record.

—Walt Whitman*

In a country that is conditioned to react more to images than to substance, the persistent task of creating a more profound understanding of the legacy and continuous contributions of U.S. Hispanics and constructing new nonstereotyped images is still confronting us.

—Edna Acosta Belén†

We are beginning to realize that we are not wholly at the mercy of circumstance, nor are our lives completely out of our hands...We are slowly moving past the resistance within, leaving behind the defeated images.

—Gloria Anzaldúa‡

---

* Walt Whitman, "The Spanish Element in Our Nationality," in *The Works of Walt Whitman*, vol. 2, ed. M. Cowley (New York: Funk & Wagnalls, 1948), 402.

† Edna Acosta-Belén, "From Settlers to Newcomers: The Hispanic Legacy in the United States," in *The Hispanic Experience in the United States: Contemporary Issues and Perspectives*, ed. Edna Acosta-Belén and Barbara R. Sjostrom (New York: Praeger, 1988), 103-4.

‡ Gloria Anzaldúa, foreword to *This Bridge Called My Back: Writings by Radical Women of Color*, 2d ed., ed. Gloria Anzaldúa and Cherríe Moraga (New York: Kitchen Table/Women of Color Press, 1983).

INTRODUCTION

One of the distinctive features and important achievements of contemporary theology is its emphasis on the historical character of all theological constructions, what we may call the "earth-bound"[1] nature of theology. This salutary sensibility has led to the understanding that, whether explicitly acknowledged and articulated or not, all theologies are influenced by background conditions as they are shaped by social location and class interests as well as personal experiences and exigencies. The distinguishing mark of liberation theology, in all of its varying manifestations, is its *explicit* attention to and articulation of the contextual specificity that conditions it, as well as its demand that such contingencies not be concealed. That is to say, liberation theologies outwardly acknowledge that theology is always a "secondary moment" of reflection: "Life comes first, theology comes only thereafter, striving to understand and serve life."[2]

As this last description makes clear, liberation theologies attempt both to understand life and to serve it. Particularly, liberation theologies fulfill the striving to serve life by bringing unjust suffering and the delimitation of many people's life choices into the purview of theological reflection. Christian liberation theologies are modes of discourse that rethink human existence, the Christian tradition, and present Christian practice by, as Rebecca Chopp puts it, placing attention on "the nonsubjects of history, those who have been denied any voice or identity in history by their fellow humans."[3] Because there are many who have been made "nonsubjects of history," liberation theology expresses itself in many forms, each particular one coming with its own subtlety.

In the United States, feminist and African American theologies of liberation have received greatly deserved notice for their original contributions to the task of theological construction. However, alongside these liberation theologies, even if with less publicity until now, Latino and Latina theologians have been developing a distinctive form of liberation theology written from the perspective of Latino/a life in the United States. Although influenced by the mode of liberation theology that emerged in

---

1 I borrow this term from Anthony B. Pinn, *Earth Bound: Toward a Theology of Fragile Cultural Memory and Religious Diversity* [working title] (Minneapolis: Fortress Press, forthcoming).

2 Otto Maduro, "Liberation Theology," in *A New Handbook of Christian Theology*, ed. Donald W. Musser and Joseph L. Price (Nashville: Abingdon Press, 1992), 288.

3 Rebecca Chopp, *The Praxis of Suffering: An Interpretation of Liberation and Political Theologies* (Maryknoll, N.Y.: Orbis Books, 1986), 3.

Latin America, Latino/a theologians have had to address the particular and confounding realities endemic to life in the United States, and have, in the process, created an inimitable theological expression that is simultaneously subversive and focused on survival. On the basis of the experiences of large numbers of Latinos and Latinas, as well as the similar experiences of other subordinated groups, these theologians have had to recognize that there may be sources of oppression other than economic—for example, racial, sexual, cultural—causing the sufferings of many people in our society.[4]

---

4 The influence of Latin American liberation theology on U.S. Hispanic/Latino theology is undeniable. Latino/a theologians in the United States have in various published accounts acknowledged this influence, and have noted the continuous relationship that exists between these two theological forms. Nevertheless, seeking to be attentive to their own contextual specificity, and hoping in this way to incorporate liberation theology's methodological stress on particular contextuality, Latino/a theologians have sought from very early on to develop a theology that would respond to the particularities of Hispanic life in the United States. Whether for this reason or others, some perceptible differences can be detected between Latin American liberation theology and U.S. Hispanic/Latino theologies of liberation. Latino/a theologies in the United States, for instance, have given more emphasis to cultural and aesthetic dimensions of experience, as well as to sexist forms of oppression, than has Latin American liberation theology (at least more so than earlier Latin American theologies of liberation emanating from the so-called third world). However, U.S. Latino/a theologies have not analyzed the dimensions of political economy as thoroughly as have liberation theologies deriving from Latin America. Moreover, U.S. Hispanic/Latino theologians have not often borrowed from Marxist analysis when they have dealt with political economy within the United States. As I see it, because Latino/as in the United States, like other disadvantaged groups in our society, suffer injustices that are traceable both to political economy and to culture, it is very important that Hispanic/Latino theologians seek to strike a reflective equilibrium that places equal and equally mature focus on matters of cultural and socioeconomic analysis. Whether by way of borrowing from Marxist analysis or some other critical theoretical framework, U.S. Latino/a theologians should, I suggest, pay more attention to problems of justice that derive from the domain of political economy and that imply the advancement of a social politics of multiracial cooperation. This is not to say that we should abandon the theorizing of "symbolic" culture and identity in our liberatory theologies, but rather, that we must continue to strive to better couple the interests of cultural politics to those of social politics. For some works that note the relationship between Latin American liberation theology and U.S. Hispanic/Latino theology, see Allan Figueroa Deck, *Introduction to Frontiers of Hispanic Theology in the United States*, ed. Allan Figueroa Deck (Maryknoll, N.Y.: Orbis Books, 1992), esp. xiv-xv; Gilbert R. Cadena, "The Social Location of Liberation Theology: From Latin America to the United States," in *Hispanic/Latino Theology: Challenge and Promise*, ed. Fernando Segovia and Ada María Isasi-Díaz (Minneapolis: Fortress Press, 1996), 167-82; and María Pilar Aquino, "Theological Method in U.S. Latino/a Theology: Toward an Intercultural Theology for the Third Millennium," in *From the Heart of Our People: Latino/a Explorations in Catholic Systematic Theology*, ed. Orlando O. Espín and Miguel H. Díaz (Maryknoll, N.Y.: Orbis Books, 1999), esp. 14-20.

Undeniably, some attention has been paid to the peculiar interlocking effect that the fissures of gender and class have upon the quality of life in the United States, but the topics of cultural identity and racism especially have assumed focal importance for Latino/a theologians. We can easily grasp the reasoning behind this emphasis in U.S. Hispanic/Latino theology, and in Latino/a scholarship as a whole, when we examine the history of Latino/as in this nation. To put it bluntly, from the very beginning we Latinos have had to struggle consistently and zealously not only to keep alive our distinctive historical and cultural experiences, but also to claim our membership as legitimate citizens and active agents in this nation. Hence, even as Latino/a theologians have struggled to reveal and oppose the ways in which sexism and unjust socioeconomic policies cause much human misery in the United States, they have laid emphasis upon the legacy of cultural marginalization and racism. Given the atmosphere of overt and covert racism and the depreciation of Hispanic cultures experienced by Latinos and Latinas in the United States, Latino/a theologians have been inclined to enfold their liberatory discourses in cultural terms in order to help counter U.S. efforts at cultural homogenization; to replace denigrating images of Latino/as with self-defined images; and to assist in the incorporation of Latino/as as full, equal, and participating citizens into the society in which we live.

In chapter 2, I will discuss some of the different ways in which the emphasis on Latino/a identity and culture receives expression in U.S. Hispanic/Latino theologies. But before proceeding to such an examination, I must sketch the history of Latino/as in the United States so that we may better understand the social conditions and dynamics that informed the centrality of "identity" and "symbolic culture" in those theologies. Through this overview, I hope to demonstrate that the unrelenting experience of racial discrimination and cultural despotism endured by Latino/as provided important grounds for the evocation of the categories of identity and culture in U.S. Hispanic/Latino theology. Indeed, insofar as the Hispanic experience in the United States has been played out within the context of racism and cultural and ethnic friction, it is not surprising that Hispanic/Latino theologians have devoted a great part of their attention to the task of cultural affirmation and differentiation. Thus, I argue that the focus on matters of cultural identity and difference has been not only legitimate but also necessary.

Nevertheless, Latino/a theologians need to engage not only the possibilities but also the limits of a discourse centered on identity, symbolic culture, and difference. Rather than mostly celebrating specific forms of identities, cultures, and difference, a liberatory theology that aims for ameliorative social action must seek to provide the religious or spiritual basis for the integration of the struggle for equality and justice into broader spheres of everyday life. This task can best be addressed by appealing to a broader public community and a comprehensive sensibility based on the existence of widely shared values and exigencies. Theologically speaking, this suggests the need to be attentive to the possibilities of "public" theologies. On the other hand, however, the struggle to revitalize and assert a local cultural or ethnic identity always arises from the need to purge denigrating images and discriminating forces from the broader public realm. Identity discourses are, after all, based on demands for fuller participation in democratic life. Hence, rather than simply dismissing the paradigm of identity and difference, we must understand the conditions and reasons that led to its existence even as we attempt to move beyond it.

What follows in this chapter is an attempt to delineate some of the historical events and social conditions that have led to the centrality of cultural identity in U.S. Hispanic/Latino theology. My aim here is in no way to provide a full-fledged history of Latino/a[5] cultures or of the various groups' interrelations, but rather, to suggest some of the issues integral to understanding the staging ground of that theology and the cogent reasons that motivate its methodology and agenda, especially its stress on the categories of identity and culture.

HISPANICS OR LATINOS: THEIR RECENT PAST AND PRESENT

Although the popular perception is that Hispanics are foreign newcomers to the United States, Hispanic history in North America predates the history of the United States by more than two centuries. Hispanics, also increasingly known as Latino/as, are "Americans" who were already inhabiting the territory that today constitutes the United States long before the arrival of the first Pilgrims at Plymouth Rock, the founding of the original thirteen British

---

5 Throughout this work I will generally use the signifier "Latino/a" to refer to Latinos and Latinas, except in areas where such a gender-conscious designation may prove cumbersome. Although both terms have limitations and are variously problematic, I prefer to use the panethnic umbrella term "Latino/a" rather than "Hispanic," believing that it better embraces all Latin American nationalities, some of which have no ties to Spain. Hence, although these terms are employed synonymously, I mostly use "Latino" and "Latina." Nevertheless, when referring to the theological production emanating from the different Latino/a communities, I will generally use the term "Hispanic/Latino." I do this because certain Latino/a theologians prefer the term "Latino," while others prefer to use the term "Hispanic," to coalesce the U.S. experiences of peoples with Spanish-speaking ancestry and to refer to their theologies. For a good presentation of the objections that could be raised against both "Hispanic" and "Latino," see Jorge J. E. Gracia, *Hispanic/Latino Identity: A Philosophical Perspective* (Malden, Mass.: Blackwell, 2000), esp. 1-26.

colonies, and the British colonists' declaration of independence from Britain in 1776. The Hispanic legacy in what is now known as the United States begins with the Spanish exploration and colonization of the North and South American continents that began with Christopher Columbus's arrival in the Americas in 1492. Not too long after Columbus disembarked on American soil, these new territories were to be claimed for Spain and opened up to Spanish explorers searching for new sources of wealth. In a bit of historical irony, the vast devastation caused by the violent Spanish conquest of this new territory and the decimation of its indigenous populations were to lead to something new: the formation of new cultures and, if we wish to use such terminology, new races out of the intermingling and fusion of three distinct races and cultures. Historian Edna Acosta-Belén provides a masterful summation of this historical occurrence:

> In areas where the indigenous populations had been larger, their descendants survived and amalgamated to a large extent with the Spanish conquerors; in other areas, such as the Caribbean islands, the Indian populations were almost totally extinct by the end of the first century of colonization. Slaves from Africa were introduced early in the sixteenth century to replace or supplement the decreasing Indian labor force in agriculture, mining, and domestic service. Black slaves also intermingled with the Spanish and Indian groups, creating through the centuries new cultures and a mixed population in the Americas that integrated the three races to varying degrees. The *mestizaje* (race mixture) produced by the fusion of the white, Indian, and black races and cultures is one of the most distinctive features of the Spanish conquest and colonization of the Americas, and hence of Latin American and U.S. Hispanic cultures.[6]

Along with the Spanish, these new Mestizo-Hispanic populations settled in a vast North American territory that was incorporated into and controlled by the Spanish Empire, an empire that by the early nineteenth century had extended from the Mississippi River to the current U.S. Southwest and included Florida. This legacy has since evolved to incorporate the histories, cultures, peculiarities, and contributions of a host of different, yet historically and culturally linked, persons.

In spite of this history, we U.S. Latinos are often viewed as "pseudo-Americans"; as "undeserving Americans"; as perpetual "aliens" in the nation,

---

6 Acosta-Belén, "From Settlers to Newcomers," 85.

regardless of our citizenship status and years of residence; and as an ethnic minority that is simply to be tolerated or, at best, assimilated into the dominant Anglo cultural tradition. The fact that recent U.S. census figures show that 64 percent of the Latino population was born in the United States, and that approximately half of the remaining 36 percent arrived here legally, is also often overlooked in most discourses addressing U.S. national identity.[7] For much of U.S. history, the Latino legacy and presence in the United States generally has been unacknowledged and depreciated. Consideration of that presence has only recently come to the fore, largely because of the wide currency of the panethnic term "Hispanic," which was first officially used during the 1980 census to refer to the different populations of Spanish-speaking cultural descent living in the United States, and because of the new-sprung national xenophobia that has accompanied the startling growth of the U.S. Latino/a population. Certainly, based on population profiles alone, because of their growth in numbers, Latino/as merit attention. But there is much more about the Latino/a populace and its history that at last deserves recognition, evaluation, and respect.

Recent U.S. census estimates report that Latinos, numbering about 35.3 million individuals, are presently the largest so-called minority group in the United States, constituting approximately 13 percent of the total U.S. population.[8] Because Latino/as continue to be a young and fast-growing group with a median age of 26.4 years, census tabulations predict that these population figures will continue to swell in the near future. This growth in numbers carries with it certain economic, social, and political implications. Socioeconomic indices, for instance, reflect that U.S. Latino/as are the fastest growing segment of the labor force in this country. Himilce Novas, known for her recent popular history book on Latinos, also points out that recent market research conducted by *Fortune 500* corporations has identified an estimated purchasing power of $300 billion among U.S. Latinos.[9]

Fortunately, within the realm of public decision making, the number of Latino/a political representatives has risen as a result of the growth in size and visibility of the Latino/a population. Although they are still underrepresented,

---

7 Note also that if we count the Puerto Rican residents living on the island of Puerto Rico, who are U.S. citizens by political decree, as part of the U.S.-born-and-raised Latino/a constituency, then the percentage of U.S.-born Latino/as is even greater.

8 See Eric Schmitt, "Census Figures Show Hispanics Pulling Even with Blacks," *New York Times on the Web*, 8 March 2001; and information from the 2000 census provided by Mike Davis, *Magical Urbanism: Latinos Reinvent the U.S. City* (New York: Verso, 2000), 1-10.

9 Himilce Novas, *Everything You Need to Know about Latino History* (New York: Plume Books, 1994), xi-xii.

in recent years U.S. Latino/as have seen some gains in self-representation, and we now can point to a growing number of public figures who have had a recent impact in the U.S. public administrative sphere. Such figures include, for example, Antonia Novello (U.S. surgeon general under President George Bush); Henry González (Texas congressman and former chair of the Banking Committee); Luis Gutiérrez (Illinois congressman); Loretta Sánchez (California congresswoman); Fernando Ferrer (Bronx borough president in New York City and a recent New York City Democratic mayoral candidate); Rosemary Berkett (chief justice of the Florida Supreme Court); and others who have added their voices to those of such long-standing public representatives as Hermán Badillo, Olga Méndez, Nydia Velázquez, and José Serrano—to mention just those on the New York political scene.

Within the realm of popular culture, in the "*post I Love Lucy decades,*"[10] Latino/a contributions have come to general notice thanks to the influence of, for example, the musical genius of the late Tito Puente, and the exhilarating Latin-jazz riffs of other accomplished performers such as Eddie Palmieri, Dave Valentín, Michel Camilo, and Poncho Sánchez; the recent crossover popularity of singers and/or songwriters such as Gloria Estefan, the late Selena, Ricky Martin, Marc Anthony, Jennifer López, Enrique Iglesias Jr., Christina Aguilera, and Shakira; the popularization of salsa, merengue, and other forms of tropical music through the appeal of performers such as Marc Anthony, India, Tito Nieves, the Barrio Boyz, DLG (Dark Latin Groove), Proyecto Uno, Olga Tañón, Oro Sólido, Rubén Blades, and Chayanne; the athletic prowess of sports stars such as Sammy Sosa, Alex Rodríguez, Bernie Williams, Juan González, Mary Jo Fernández, and Trent Dimas; the acting success of screen artists such as Andy García, Jimmy Smits, John Leguizamo, Jennifer López, Salma Hayek, and Rosie Pérez; the overwhelming success of television networks such as Telemundo and Univisión, which have created popular media attractions such as Paul Rodríguez, Cristina, Don Francisco, and Sábado Gigante; as well as the literary genius of Sandra Cisneros, Esmeralda Santiago, Cristina García, Julia Álvarez, Rudolfo Anaya, Richard Rodríguez, Oscar Hijuelos, Abraham Rodríguez Jr., Oscar "Zeta" Acosta, Ron Arias, Piri Thomas, and so many others.

Even so, there is another reality of Latino/a life that cannot be ignored: the reality of disproportionate poverty and unemployment levels; of labor exploitation; of limited or poor educational, income, housing, and health opportunities; of a deeply rooted and historically verifiable Anglo contempt for anything Latino; of the hurtful experiences of racist attitudes

10 I have borrowed this phrase from Novas, *Latino History*, xii.

and negative stereotypes; of the denial of substantive access to decision-making processes, wealth, and legal forms of entrepreneurial activity; of cultural alienation; of the pervasive limitation of life choices and of hope itself; and of the concomitant spread of existential and collective nihilism that comes as a result of these dehumanizing living conditions. Latino/a scholarship as a whole, and U.S. Hispanic/Latino theology in particular, seeks to keep these confounding realities closely in mind as it examines the place of Latino/as in the U.S. society historically, sifts out and celebrates neglected elements of Latino cultures, and ventures upon the construction of a collective and critical Latino/a social identity.

Up until now I have been speaking mostly in pan-Latino/a terms, referring to Latino/a life in a general and unqualified manner. There is legitimacy and even profit in the use of an all-inclusive term such as "Latino" or "Hispanic" to speak about the experiences of those people in this country who can in some way trace their ancestry to one or more Spanish-speaking countries. Nevertheless, we must acknowledge that these terms are ethnic labels that lump together the histories and racial-cultural idiosyncrasies of different peoples. In point of fact, Latinos are actually, as Juan Flores puts it, "an ethnicity of ethnicities, an 'ethnic group' that does not exist but for the existence of its constituent 'subgroups.' "[11] The umbrella terms "Latino" or "Hispanic" need not be disengaged from the different historical trajectories of the groups they call to mind. Simply put, the problem that may arise with the prolonged and unnuanced use of a term such as "Hispanic" or "Latino" is that it could divert attention away from the varied historical, racial, class, linguistic, and gender experiences of the different nationalities to which it refers: the Mexican-American/Chicano, Puerto Rican, Cuban, Dominican, Central American, South American, and, in some rarer instances, even Spanish and Brazilian peoples living in the United States. And although it is certainly true that to a large extent the stories of each of these groups converge within the national context of the United States (when we either cross the border or, as in most cases, the border crosses us), the Latino/a experience nevertheless is composed of various internal subnarratives. Each one of these narratives deserves particular attention. Hence, before entering into a discussion of the emergence of a critical panethnic identity, I think it appropriate to give a brief accounting of the historical trajectory of each subgroup or nationality.

---

11 Juan Flores, "Pan-Latino/Trans-Latino: Puerto Ricans in the New Nueva York," in *Centro: The Journal of the Center for Puerto Rican Studies* 8, nos. 1/2 (1996): 176.

THE MEXICANS AND MEXICAN AMERICANS/CHICANOS

Sowell Thomas, in his book *Ethnic America,* accurately points out that some of the newest and oldest Americans are from Mexico.[12] This comment hints at the historical and cultural diversity that exists within those peoples known as "Mexicans," "Mexican Americans," or "Chicanos/Chicanas." Among this collective group, constituting the largest percentage of Latinos, at about 64.3 percent of the total U.S. Latino population, we find cultural and historical heterogeneity: it includes recent immigrants from Mexico; not-so-recent immigrants from Mexico who have acquired U.S. citizenship but may still feel close affinity to Mexico; second- and third-generation U.S. citizens who might describe themselves as Chicanos and Chicanas, thus reflecting a biculturality born of and from the U.S. experience and context; as well as many whose ancestry can be traced to the earliest Spanish-speaking settlers of the southwestern territories of the United States, and who may even differentiate their culture from that of more recent Mexican immigrants. This cultural and historical heterogeneity notwithstanding, we can legitimately state that the U.S. history of Mexicans and Mexican Americans or Chicanos is commonly marked by, and actually begins with, events and processes that transpired in the early nineteenth century.

From the late 1490s up until the early 1800s, Spain had been able to maintain control over its North American colonies, but by the 1830s it had lost control over all of these colonies. Of particular importance in this ceding of power, itself the result of numerous movements for independence, is the achievement of self-rule by Mexico and its establishment as a nation in 1821. Upon winning its independence, Mexico became heir to Spain's northern provinces, which included all of the territories that make up what is today known as the U.S. Southwest. But the young Mexican nation's rule over these territories was very brief. Already by 1847 most, and then by 1853 all, of Mexico's northern territories had become the property of the United States.

The insurrection of Texas and, later, Texas's annexation by the United States hold a central place in the events that eventually altered the boundaries between Mexico and the United States. In 1821 the Spanish government had given an Anglo colonist by the name of Moses Austin permission to settle three hundred Anglo families in Texas. Shortly after having been granted permission for his settlement venture, Moses Austin died of tuberculosis. After the death of Moses, his son, Stephen Austin, took the reins of the project and established a large Anglo colony in Texas. Historical evidence suggests that these first Anglo settlers were gracious, compliant, and honorable habitants.

---

12 Sowell Thomas, *Ethnic America* (New York: Basic Books, 1981).

Many of the Anglo settlers brought in by later entrepreneurs, however, were not as considerate. Historian Oscar Martínez describes these later émigrés:

> Unlike Austin, some of the later empresarios [sic] failed to choose settlers carefully, allowing many ruffians, drifters and criminals to be part of the colonies. It appears that most of these undesirable elements arrived after 1830. They displayed feelings of racial superiority, denigrated the Mexican political and judicial systems and ignored laws that did not suit them, especially statutes pertaining to religion, slavery, foreign trade and immigration.[13]

Unfortunately, this Anglo impudence toward Mexicans and Mexican cultures was to become an unremitting problem that would not only shape Anglo stereotypical images of Mexicans but of all Latino/as.

An Anglo and Tejano coalition abetted by the U.S. government led to the declaration of Texas independence in 1836. In 1845 the United States annexed Texas to its territory, and in the process angered Mexicans who interpreted the U.S. fostering of Anglo rebellion in Texas as a clear indication of the expansionist persuasion of the United States—one that came at the expense of Mexico. Chicano historian Rodolfo Acuña clarifies the motivations behind this U.S. incursion into Texas:

> To Anglo-Americans, the Texas War resulted because of a tyrannical or, at best, an incompetent Mexican government that was antithetical to the ideals of democracy and justice. The truth is that the roots of the conflict extended back to as early as 1767 when Benjamin Franklin marked Mexico and Cuba for future expansion.[14]

After a rupture in diplomatic relations, war broke out between Mexico and the United States in 1846 over a dispute involving the territory adjacent to the Rio Grande. In 1847 U.S. troops brutally invaded and captured Mexico City. Shortly thereafter, on February 2, 1848, the United States forced Mexico to sign the Treaty of Guadalupe Hidalgo, which ceded the northern Mexican territories to the United States. Overall, as a result of this forced treaty and

---

13 Oscar J. Martínez, "A History of Chicanos/Mexicanos along the U.S.-Mexico Border," in *Handbook of Hispanic Cultures in the United States*, vol. 2, *History*, ed. Alfredo Jiménez (Houston: Arte Público Press, 1994), 263.

14 Rodolfo Acuña, *Occupied America: A History of Chicanos*, 2d ed. (New York: Harper & Row, 1981), 3.

other later U.S. acquisitions, Mexico was forced to yield almost half of its land, transferring over to the United States all the territory that today comprises the states of California, Arizona, New Mexico, Colorado, Kansas, Nevada, Oklahoma, Utah, and Wyoming.

The U.S. conquest of the Southwest set off a process that would transform U.S.-Mexico borderlands history and affect the lives of many in both Mexico and the United States even until our present day. Rodolfo Acuña poignantly captures the dynamics set in place by the U.S. conquest of the Southwest, and also explains elements of the Mexican experience *within* U.S. society:

> The tragedy of the Mexican cession is that most Anglo-Americans have not accepted the fact that the United States committed an act of violence against the Mexican people when it took Mexico's northwestern territory. Violence was not limited to the taking of the land; Mexico's territory was invaded, her people murdered, her land raped, and her possessions plundered. Memory of this destruction generated a distrust and dislike that is still vivid in the minds of many Mexicans, for the violence of the United States left deep scars. And for Chicanos—Mexicans remaining within the boundaries of the new United States territories—aggression was even more insidious, for the outcome of the Texas and Mexican-American wars made them a conquered people. Anglo-Americans were the conquerors, and they evinced all the arrogance of military victors.[15]

From the very beginning of this forced border realignment, Mexican negotiators displayed sympathetic concern for those Mexicans who were going to be left behind in the territories conquered by the United States. Articles VIII, IX, and X of the Treaty of Guadalupe Hidalgo specifically dealt with the rights that would be granted to those Mexicans who had been living in the newly conquered land. According to these articles, Mexicans in these territories had one year to decide whether to relocate by moving their homes and livelihoods into Mexico or to remain in "occupied Mexico." Acuña chronicles that "about 2000 elected to leave," but "most remained in what they considered *their* land."[16]

Besides establishing a time frame for possible Mexican relocation, the Treaty of Guadalupe Hidalgo was supposed to allocate citizenship, property,

---

15 Ibid., 3.
16 Ibid., 19.

and religious rights to those Mexicans who were unable or unwilling to move after the U.S. conquest. But in spite of these treaty allotments, violations of Mexican rights became commonplace, and many Mexicans lost their land, suffered discrimination, and were exposed to distressing, dehumanizing, and downright dangerous living conditions. The pervasive segregation, cultural oppression, and legalized persecution endured by the *Mejicanos* essentially set in place conditions that were to relegate them to indeterminate underclass status. As Oscar Martínez aptly puts it, "In effect, the Chicanos of the Southwest became a colonized group, having undergone foreign conquest and marginalization within the American system."[17]

The border rearrangement had other immediate effects, which are still being felt today by Mexicans and Chicanos. One effect is economic: it includes the conversion of Mexican frontier settlements into "satellites of the U.S. economy"; the devastation of Mexican business due to unequal competition exerted by Anglo-American industries; and a resulting Mexican economic dislocation that has historically forced many Mexicans to emigrate into the United States. Already by the 1880s there were railroads owned by U.S. corporations that connected northern Mexico to the United States for the purposes of transporting Mexican workers to U.S. worksites that needed cheap labor. Thus began a pattern in which Mexicans have been enthusiastically welcomed into the United States when the need for cheap labor arises, and then have been ostracized and even sent back forcibly and illegally when the need diminishes.

Concerning this tendentious U.S. attitude toward Mexicans, historian Geoffrey Fox notes,

> Mexicans and Mexican-Americans had to cope with two contradictory types of Anglo behavior toward them. One was the attempts to recruit them to work in the mines, fields, and factories, especially in boom times, including luring workers from south of the border. This was because Mexicans were the handiest source of cheap labor in the Southwest…The other contradictory behavior was harassment by Anglos, especially in economically slack times…For Mexicans, therefore, the United States was alternately welcoming and threatening: Anglos needed Mexicans but didn't really want them around.[18]

---

17 Martínez, "History of Chicanos/Mexicanos," 265.

18 Geoffrey Fox, *Hispanic Nation: Culture, Politics, and the Construction of Identity* (Tucson: University of Arizona Press, 1996), 78.

This course of action has been repeated during different historical periods. Enthusiastic U.S. recruitment of Mexican workers took place, for instance, during the construction of the U.S.-Mexico railroad system in the 1880s; when the United States became involved in World War I; when the Bracero Program was created in 1942, during World War II, to provide the U.S. economy with a steady supply of Mexican workers; and still occurs as undocumented workers are lured and subsequently exploited by U.S. employers who find loopholes in immigration and wage laws. Conversely, Mexicans have been targeted as a primary group for deportation and "repatriation" during periods of low U.S. economic activity, such as in 1917 with the passing of a restrictive U.S. immigration law that especially focused on Mexicans; during the Great Depression when large-scale unemployment led to a massive voluntary and involuntary repatriation of Mexicans; again during the economically unstable postwar period of the 1950s; during the deployment of "Operation Wetback" to curtail the flow of undocumented Mexican workers who crossed the border by swimming across the Rio Grande; and more recently with the passing of restrictive immigration bills born from a xenophobic congressional response to the overall growth of the U.S. Mexican population.

The generally contemptuous attitude demonstrated by the dominant U.S. Anglo-American society toward Mexicans has not been limited to migrant or immigrant Mexicans. Rather, it has extended to all Mexicans alike, including those born in the United States, and has, in addition, been expressed not only in economic and legal terms but also racially and culturally. It is necessary to note, for instance, that during the various deportation ploys it was not uncommon for U.S.-born Chicano/as and other Mexican U.S. citizens to be deported on the basis of their being Mexican Americans. This fact certainly points to the existence of a racist, or at least culturally exclusive, sensibility in the U.S. public sphere during these "repatriation" ventures. But Mexicans/Chicanos, and all Latinos in general, have always endured this sort of racialist or culturally exclusivist attitude. As to Mexicans and Chicano/as, we can document the presence of anti-Mexican/Chicano bias in, for example, the passing of laws in the 1920s that sought to deny Mexican migrant workers and immigrants public medical assistance. Concurrently, this was also the period that saw Ku Klux Klan activity begin in the Southwest, with Mexicans and Chicano/as being targets of threatening action. Race-based antagonism against Mexicans and Chicano/as also became dramatically apparent during the sensationalized trial of various Mexican American men in what came to be known as the 1942 Sleepy Lagoon case.

This case revolved around the mysterious death of a young man named José Díaz, who had attended a party on the evening of August 1, 1942, and was found dead the next morning on a dirt road near the party site. Although no wounds were found on Díaz's body, and even though there were many other possible explanations for his death, police blamed it on various members of a Mexican American *pachuco*[19] street gang named the 38th Street Club. The press, exemplifying the anti-Mexican attitudes of the early 1940s, exploited the Sleepy Lagoon case to exaggerate the social threat posed by *pachuco* activity and to further incite anti-Mexican sentiments in the U.S. Southwest. Rodolfo Acuña has pointed out the prejudices evoked by this case:

> Similar gangs existed among Anglo youths, but as the state of war intensified nativistic feelings, Anglos singled out the *pachucos*. Racial xenophobia heightened in what, at the time, was a racially and culturally homogeneous Los Angeles community. Very few Blacks lived in Los Angeles County. Los Angeles did not have the large ghettoes of European immigrants peculiar to eastern cities. Japanese-Americans had just been rounded up and sent to internment camps. Chicanos became obvious scapegoats for nativists and racists. Angelenos read with interest accounts of the activities of the "foreign" gangs, the so-called Chicano hoodlums.[20]

The racist overtones of this case were illustrated not only by alarmist press reports. A police report made by Captain Ed Duran Ayres, then head of the Foreign Relations Bureau of the Los Angeles Police Department, for instance, concluded that all Chicanos, due to their Indian and/or Aztec ancestry, were inherently criminal and violent. So also, it was noted that the Honorable Charles W. Fricke, presiding judge in this case, allowed certain judicial aberrations to occur that were damaging to the Mexican defendants. Assistant District Attorney Clyde C. Shoemaker, for example, was allowed to instruct jailers not to allow the defendants to cut their hair or change their clothes, so that they might make a more menacing impression on the jury. It was also odd that, in a case involving alleged gang activity, unequal sentences were handed out to the twenty-two accused youngsters—charges ranged

---

19 *Pachucos* was the term given to street gangs comprised mostly of Mexican American and, at times, other Hispanic youths who had grown up in U.S. inner-city areas and often wore stylish outfits known as zoot suits. For a dramatized and cinematic portrayal of these zoot-suiters, and of the Sleepy Lagoon case itself, see the film *Zoot Suit* (MCA Universal Home Video, 1981).

20 Acuña, *Occupied America*, 324.

from assault to first-degree murder. More than a year after the case's conclusion, on October 4, 1944, the Second District Court of Appeals unanimously reversed the lower court's decision, noting that the trial had been conducted in a biased manner, that the constitutional rights of the defendants had been violated, and that there was no evidence linking the accused Chicano youths to the death of José Díaz.[21]

The racially motivated antagonism toward Mexicans, however, did not end with the conclusion of the Sleepy Lagoon trial; if anything, it was to gain strength. Following this sensational trial, various violent attacks on young Mexican American men were reported, highlighted by a deplorable rampage led by American soldiers and sailors in 1943 in which several zoot-suiters and other uninvolved Mexican/Chicano youngsters were randomly assaulted. As a result, a number of riots broke out in the California cities of Los Angeles, San Diego, and Oakland, provoked by a corrupt and prejudiced police system that did not interfere with white assailants in such attacks but often arrested innocent Mexican Americans for allegedly instigating riots. Numerous other experiences such as these made it necessary for U.S. Mexicans/Chicanos to organize and initiate measures designed to procure civil and human rights and the promotion of a healthy, assured, and coherent Chicano/a sociocultural identity.

Until the late 1960s, the grievances of the Mexican American/Chicano communities generally went unanswered, as effective self-representation was denied by a gerrymandering political system bent on the curtailment of Mexican political power. It was not until the Chicano movement of the mid-1960s, itself part of the larger movement for civil rights in the United States, that Chicano/a protests began to have an appreciable effect on the state of local and public Chicano life. Many grassroots movements emerged during this time that promoted some tangible communal, electoral, and political gains, and led to broad-based, all-embracing movements for social change. Cesar Chavez's United Farm Workers Union; the establishment of an alternative, though short-lived, third political party called La Raza Unida Party; the emergence of many militant Chicano groups among young people and students; the formation of COPS (Communities Organized for Public Service); and the appearance of numerous activist church-based movements—all are examples of Chicano/a-led popular fronts that arose to seek the amelioration of social ills that disproportionately affected U.S. Mexicans/Chicanos and other Latino/as.

---

21 For a more detailed sketch of the Sleepy Lagoon case, see Acuña, *Occupied America*, esp. 323-29.

As a whole, the critical and seditious politics advocated by these Chicano/a-led movements for change called into question prevailing conceptions of Chicano—and overall Latino—history, identity, and culture. Following the Chicano/a *movimiento* for civil, social, and human rights of the 1960s and 1970s, a critical historicist orientation emerged among Chicano scholars and activists. In their writings, they challenged previous ahistorical accounts of the origins of the Chicano community and reexamined the links between that community and Mexico. As María de los Ángeles Torres notes, "Alternative frameworks like the internal colonial model looked at the connections between the U.S. conquest of Mexico's northern territory in the mid-1800's and labor exploitation to understand the persistence of poverty and racism in the Southwest."[22] The works of Rodolfo Acuña, Juan Gómez-Quiñónez, Carlos Zazueta, Tomás Almaguer, and Mario Barrera particularly offer scholarly witness to this subversive interpretative emphasis in U.S. Mexican/Chicano studies.[23]

The Chicano movements of the 1960s and 1970s also motivated Chicano/a intellectuals to explore issues related to Chicano/Latino identity and culture and the overall place of Latino/as in the broader U.S. society. The more recent literary works of popular Chicana and Chicano writers (such as Patricia Preciado Martín, Gloria Anzaldúa, Cherríe Moraga, and Sandra Cisneros, among the women; and Antonio Villareal, Rudolfo Anaya, and Oscar "Zeta" Acosta, among the men) continue to demonstrate this subversive stress on identity, culture, and social analysis. Along with a multitude of others in the U.S. Mexican/Mexican-American/Chicano communities, these thinkers and activists continue to struggle against anti-Mexican stereotypes and policies; seek to reconstruct an accurate portrayal of U.S. Chicano history; undertake the task of ameliorating those social ills that stifle the ability of many Chicano/as and other U.S. citizens to live truly free and dignified lives; and, in the process, attempt to contribute to the democratic experiment known as the United States.

---

22 María de los Ángeles Torres, "Transnational Political and Cultural Identities: Crossing Theoretical Borders," in *Borderless Borders: U.S. Latinos, Latin Americans, and the Paradox of Interdependence*, ed. Frank Bonilla et al. (Philadelphia: Temple University Press, 1998), 174.

23 See especially Acuña, *Occupied America*; Juan Gómez-Quiñónez, "Notes on the Interpretation of the Relations between the Mexican Community in the United States and Mexico," and Carlos Zazueta, "Mexican Political Actors in the United States and Mexico: Historical and Political Contexts of a Dialogue," in *Mexican/U.S. Relations: Conflict and Convergence*, ed. Carlos Vásquez and Manuel García (Los Angeles: University of California Press, 1983); Tomás Almaguer, "Toward a Study of Chicano Colonialism," in *Aztlan: Chicano Journal of Social Sciences and the Arts* 1 (fall 1970): 7-21; and Mario Barrera, *Race and Class in the Southwest* (Notre Dame, Ind.: University of Notre Dame Press, 1979).

THE PUERTO RICANS

The Puerto Rican presence in the United States, like that of the Mexican American, also extends back to the nineteenth century, especially in New York, where many revolutionary exiles, involved in the struggle for the independence of Puerto Rico and Cuba from Spanish control, had sought refuge. Among the most popular of these Puerto Rican freedom fighters were figures such as Ramón Emeterio Betances, Eugenio María de Hostos, and Bonocio Tío and his poet wife, Lola Rodríguez de Tío. Another prominent Puerto Rican nineteenth-century migrant was Arturo Schomburg, who, as a revolutionary black Puerto Rican, cultivated a kindred alliance with the New York black community and became interested in the study of black culture and history. As Edna Acosta-Belén notes, "Today the Schomburg Center for Research in Black Culture stands as a tribute to the man who served two communities and two cultures."[24]

The Puerto Rican presence in the United States became even more pronounced, however, after the United States wrested control of Puerto Rico from Spain in 1898 and attempted to carry out a large-scale restructuring of the island's administration, involving a wholesale transformation of the existing political, production, and economic systems. These changes set in motion processes that would bring a much larger exile population into the United States. The general motivation for these later migrations was not the search for political refuge, as it had been for earlier revolutionary Puerto Rican exiles, but rather, a retreat from an encumbering economic displacement brought about by U.S. industrial interests on the island. Essentially, the driving force behind U.S. military intervention in the Caribbean and in Central America was always the desire to extend the notion of the "Manifest Destiny" of the United States beyond national borders, through the expansion of U.S. foreign markets in lush agricultural lands. This philosophy, clearly enunciated in the Monroe Doctrine of 1823, the Roosevelt Corollary of 1904, and other foreign policy statements, led to the U.S. occupation of Puerto Rico and the entrenchment of U.S. industries on the island, ostensibly to promote development.

At first, the United States administered the island directly under military rule, but after 1900 it governed Puerto Rico through a civil administration appointed by Washington. In 1917 U.S. control of Puerto Rico was further solidified with the congressional passing of the Jones Act, which made Puerto Ricans on the island citizens of the United States. From the very beginning of the U.S. colonization of Puerto Rico, however, American interests looked to

---

24 Acosta-Belén, "From Settlers to Newcomers," 94.

the island for economic opportunities. The U.S. industrial incursion into Puerto Rico was particularly noticeable in the sugar, tobacco, and coffee industries. The modernization of these industries, carried out by U.S. corporations, led to the displacement of many Puerto Rican farmers and workers. The dislocations in the local economy that ensued from this industrial and economic irruption, along with hardships brought about by a series of natural disasters that crippled the island's agricultural industries, contributed greatly to the mass migrations of Puerto Ricans into the United States, particularly to New York City.

The greatest of these migrations occurred after World War II.[25] Between 1940 and 1950 the numbers of Puerto Ricans inhabiting the United States grew from a reported 69,967 to 301,375. These numbers continued to increase through the 1950s and early 1960s, the years immediately following the official designation of Puerto Rico as a commonwealth.[26] One of the factors that particularly influenced the massive dislocation of Puerto Ricans from the island to the United States during the interwar years was the creation and then implementation of Operation Bootstrap. Virginia Sánchez Korrol outlines the general traits of this policy:

> The surge in the island's exodus bore marked economic underpinnings directly related to Puerto Rican development under Operation Bootstrap. The plan to industrialize Puerto Rico saw the light of day under the island's Commonwealth government. Its main thrust rested on the relocation of American corporate and manufacturing concerns to Puerto Rico in exchange for tax incentives and a cheap pool of labor educated and Americanized under the "Stars and Stripes."[27]

At first, following the first decade or so of its implementation, it seemed as if Operation Bootstrap would be an enormous success in Puerto Rico. But it would soon become apparent that Operation Bootstrap had its uncongenial side, trading off immediate and transitory economic growth

---

25 Those Puerto Ricans who entered the United States in the twentieth century from Puerto Rico should technically be considered migrants rather than immigrants, for they are U.S. citizens by decree even if born on the island. Hence, they are not foreigners entering the country but citizens who have relocated within U.S. controlled territories.

26 For more information on the political process that led to the proclamation of commonwealth status in Puerto Rico, see Arturo Morales Carrión, *Puerto Rico: A Political and Cultural History* (New York: W. W. Norton & Company, 1983), esp. 256-307.

27 Virginia Sánchez Korrol, "In Their Own Right: A History of Puerto Ricans in the U.S.A.," in Jiménez, ed., *Handbook of Hispanic Cultures*, 291.

for long-term Puerto Rican dependency. Again, Virginia Sánchez Korrol contributes to our understanding of the implications of this economic plan for Puerto Rican development:

> By eliminating agrarian production and expanding the importation of American goods, Operation Bootstrap fostered greater dependency on the United States....The combination of rapid population growth in Puerto Rico, chronic underemployment and the limitations wrought by industrialization reinvigorated the propensity to emigrate. Under the Commonwealth government, public policies both facilitated and encouraged emigration as an "escape valve" that would ease the structural pressures of industrialization.[28]

Hence, in short, Puerto Rican migration into the United States, which was to become significant after World War II except for a period of reverse migration back to Puerto Rico in the late 1960s and early 1970s, has been largely induced by U.S. involvement in the island.

For the most part, these dislocated Puerto Ricans settled in urban centers of the United States, establishing themselves in locations where they might find job opportunities. In general, they were unskilled or semiskilled blue-collar workers. Hence, they moved into Chicago, Milwaukee, and other major cities throughout the United States, where they thought that employment opportunities were more favorable. But the largest number of Puerto Ricans, following the trend set by the earliest revolutionary Puerto Ricans who sought safe haven on U.S. shores in the nineteenth century, settled in New York City. Here they would create a strong enclave in the neighborhood of East Harlem that eventually came to be known simply as "el Barrio," a Puerto Rican term for "the neighborhood."

Life in these urban enclaves has not been easy for Puerto Ricans, to say the least. Unfortunately, the great Puerto Rican migrations to the United States coincided with an urban economic shift to a postindustrial and service-based economy. Moreover, this period saw the beginnings of enormous business relocations wherein many corporations were to take their capital and leadership potential to the suburbs. These structural changes, added to the crumbling of urban infrastructures due to growing populations, were to set in place the conditions that led to the urban blight that still engulfs large parts of our major cities. The large numbers of Puerto Ricans who migrated to the United States during this period of urban upheaval, particularly

---

28 Ibid., 291.

between the decades of the 40s and the 70s, found themselves locked into declining sectors of the employment market production and facing harsh living conditions. On top of all this, Puerto Ricans have had to contend with the debilitating effects of an assiduous institutionalized racism and a pervasive pattern of anti-Latino ethnic discrimination that has created an unequal playing field in all areas of life. Historian Adalberto López draws a poignant picture of Puerto Rican life in the inner cities of the United States when he describes theirs "as a world of unsympathetic and bigoted social workers and teachers, brutal policeman, broken families, small children bitten by rats and young men and women driven by their surroundings and hopelessness to crime and drugs."[29]

Faced with these trying conditions, many of these Puerto Ricans held on to the hope that their sojourn in the United States would be temporary and that they would return to Puerto Rico once they had gained some financial security. This hope even led to a rather large return migration of Puerto Ricans back to the island in the 1960s. Virginia Sánchez Korrol lucidly explicates the sensibility that led to this short-lived Puerto Rican repatriation trend, which was quelled by equally harsh living conditions in an increasingly U.S. run Puerto Rico: "American society, in their eyes, was too ethnically and racially divided and the possibility of 'making it' for Puerto Ricans did not seem like a viable option"; furthermore,

> There was no doubt that mounting discrimination and prejudice compounded the migration experience permeating it so assiduously that Puerto Ricans would never replicate the European immigration/assimilation paradigm. As one sociologist stated, "Puerto Ricans entered a heterogeneous society that articulated an assimilationist, melting pot ideology, but that, in fact, had evolved a racial order of dual ethnic queues."[30]

In short, a large population of Puerto Ricans was to become entrapped within a confounding existential reality. On the one hand, the politically sanctioned U.S. corporate encroachment on the economy of Puerto Rico would cause difficult economic conditions in the island that encouraged migration into the United States; on the other hand, most Puerto Ricans were relegated to dismal social and economic conditions in an unwelcoming U.S. society.

---

29 Adalberto López, *The Puerto Ricans: Their History, Culture, and Society* (Cambridge, Mass.: Schenkman Press, 1980), 323.

30 Korrol, "In Their Own Right," 292-93.

Despite these challenges and odds, Puerto Rican communities in the United States have managed to find ways to survive and even to thrive in many respects. As Virginia Sánchez Korrol notes,

> Long-term, stable communities did exist despite poverty, limited education, decay, urban renewal and gentrification. And these communities continued to produce writers, artists, professionals, leaders and ordinary productive citizens, who have since gone on to make positive contributions. Poor, but intact, barrios nurtured a bulwark of hometown clubs, religious associations, athletic teams, social clubs and beauty pageants, along with a more formal, leadership producing structure that dealt head on with the socio-political dimensions of the dominant society.[31]

Clearly, then, not every aspect of life in the Puerto Rican barrios revolved around drugs, crime, and hopelessness.

The dignified survival and success of many in these communities owes much to the tenacity and courage of numerous U.S. Puerto Rican freedom fighters, and the support networks that they created, who sought to ameliorate inequality at all levels of social life. This arduous struggle for survival and dignified living among U.S. Puerto Ricans has occasioned various prominent social movements and advocacy organizations of historical significance in the United States. The critical and ameliorative impetus of socially engaged Puerto Ricans has, for instance, engendered grassroots organisms such as the Puerto Rican Forum, created in the 1950s to advocate for equitable representation in antipoverty legislation, and ASPIRA, which began in 1961 to offer mentoring programs for gifted Puerto Rican and other Latino students whose educational opportunities have been limited. Puerto Rican activism has also effected the formation of the Puerto Rican Family Institute, created in 1963 with the purpose of providing support for new migrant Puerto Rican families, and, in 1972, the well-known Puerto Rican Legal Defense and Education Fund, modeled on the NAACP, to provide educational guidance and legal support to "minority" urban youth.

Puerto Rican activism also gave rise to more militant advocacy movements, especially during the 1960s and early 1970s in the wake of the civil rights movement. Among these were such groups as the Young Lords, the Puerto Rican Socialist Party, and the Puerto Rican Students' Union. These latter groups introduced elements of a more radical politics intended to

---

31 Ibid., 296.

challenge the dominant society as well as established Puerto Rican/Latino leadership, and to take issue with the police brutality, debilitating poverty, oppressive housing and health conditions, constraining educational opportunities, denigrating Puerto Rican stereotypes, and overall discrimination that vexed Puerto Rican life in the United States.

The significance of these Puerto Rican social movements for change, measured by their success in bringing about substantial social improvement, cannot be disputed. Nevertheless, Puerto Ricans continue to be plagued by delimiting social structures in the United States. Their case, in fact, serves to contradict the idea that Latino poverty and general malaise can be attributed solely to immigrant status and, therefore, can and will be eliminated after a process of Latino assimilation into the dominant Anglo culture and society. Puerto Ricans are not immigrants—they are born citizens of the United States—and yet they continue to be among the worst off of "ethnic" or "racial" communities in the United States in just about every social and economic category.[32] Sociologists of religion Ana María Díaz-Stevens and Anthony Stevens-Arroyo point out,

> They live under U.S. law, are familiar with government programs such as food stamps, and are taught English in all the public schools on the island. If citizenship, political prowess, knowledge of U.S. law, familiarity with social programs, and instruction in the English language were conditions for socioeconomic achievement, Puerto Ricans would be the Latin American or Latino group most likely to succeed. Yet instead of ranking first, Puerto Ricans in the United States rank next to last—behind even many new immigrants from Latin America.[33]

---

32 For helpful economic comparisons of Puerto Ricans with other Latino subgroups, and overall economic comparisons between Latinos and other U.S. populations in the recent past, see Frank D. Bean and Marta Tienda, *Hispanic Population of the U.S.* (New York: Russell Sage Foundation, 1987). See also Gregory DeFreitas, *Inequality at Work: Hispanics in the U.S. Labor Force* (New York: Oxford University Press, 1991); Rodney Hero, *Latinos and the U.S. Political System: Two-Tiered Pluralism* (Philadelphia: Temple University Press, 1992), esp. 31-55; Joan Moore and Raquel Pinderhughes, eds., *In the Barrios: Latinos and the Underclass Debate* (New York: Russell Sage Foundation, 1993); and Rebecca Morales and Frank Bonilla, eds., *Latinos in a Changing U.S. Economy: Comparative Perspectives on Growing Inequality* (New York: Russell Sage Foundation, 1993).

33 Ana María Díaz-Stevens and Anthony Stevens-Arroyo, *Recognizing the Latino Resurgence in U.S. Religion: The Emmaus Paradigm* (Boulder, Colo.: Westview Press, 1998), 27.

The Puerto Rican experience, then, serves as evidence that there are certain pervasive social and structural roadblocks that hinder Latino/a success in the United States. Although it is naive and simplistic to place blame for the various indices of Latino distress on a single cause, we cannot ignore the detrimental effect that racial and cultural discrimination has had on the socioeconomic condition of most Puerto Ricans and Latinos as a whole.

The racial, ethnic, and cultural exclusion experienced by U.S. Puerto Ricans gave rise to a critical social consciousness that found expression not only in the political realm, as mentioned above, but also in the cultural productions of first- and second-generation Puerto Rican writers, poets, and artists within the United States. The works of first-generation Puerto Rican writers such as Emilio Díaz Valcarcel, Pedro Juan Soto, and René Marques (particularly in his classic *La Carreta* [1953]), detailed the frustration and alienation experienced by those migrating Puerto Ricans who had been translocated from the green island to the continental urban barrios of the United States. Whereas first-generation Puerto Rican writers focused on the migration experience, second-generation writers directed their thinking to the vicissitudes of "ethnic" life in the United States. The theme of racial and cultural discrimination is pervasive in this body of second-generation U.S. Puerto Rican literature. The creative works of Piri Thomas, Pedro Pietri, Tato Laviera, Nicholasa Mohr, Edward Rivera, and Sandra María Esteves in particular summon "America" to be true to its democratic ideals, attacking the institutionalized racism and class-based discrimination that "ghettoized" Puerto Ricans, Latinos, and other "ethnic" groups.[34]

With the literary works of Tato Laviera, Nicholas Mohr, and Edward Rivera, a new hybrid identity began to receive articulated expression—one that recognized but also transcended the oppressive existential conditions that Puerto Ricans faced in the United States. These sought to balance a nuanced portrayal of the plight of U.S. Puerto Ricans with an appreciative presentation of the strengths, vitality, and self-determinacy of this community. Another important idea expressed in these later works is that of biculturality. This sought to account for the cultural duality of second- and third-generation Puerto Ricans who had been born and raised in the United States, but who, in a sense, felt marginalized from the cultural mainstream both in the United States and in Puerto Rico; the U.S.-born Puerto Rican was portrayed as one who is neither exclusively "American" nor Puerto Rican, but actually a combination of both cultures. These later works also brought

---

34 For more on this subject, see Korrol, "In Their Own Right," esp. 292-94; and Carrión, *Puerto Rico*, esp. 319-52.

attention to the "black" element in the Puerto Rican racial and cultural heritage, highlighting it as a potential point of identification with the U.S. African-American community. In this way, these works contributed to the understanding of the cultural duality of second- and third-generation Puerto Ricans, and to the promotion of an autochthonous, critical, and nuanced U.S. Latino/a identity.[35]

In short, despite the distressing conditions that it has experienced in the United States, it becomes clear, as we enter the twenty-first century, that the Puerto Rican community, through its democratic political mobilization and cultural impact, has contributed much to the formation of a U.S. Latino/a identity and to the reinterpretation and transformation of the idea of U.S. society as a whole.

THE CUBANS

Before the 1959 socialist revolution in Cuba, spearheaded by Fidel Castro, Cuban immigration to the United States had been relatively small. Nevertheless, Cubans had already left an imprint on the United States before the 1959 revolution, having resided in territories that are now part of the United States, such as San Augustin, Florida, as early as the 1560s and having gained a notable presence in the United States by the nineteenth century. The early U.S. Cuban community had particularly grown as political exiles sought temporary safety from proindependence revolutions back in Cuba, just as did their Puerto Rican counterparts. Many of these early Cuban immigrants remained in the United States even after the defeat of Spain, establishing migratory patterns for later arriving Cubans. The Cuban presence in the United States received an even greater boost when Vicente Ybor relocated his cigar manufacturing business from Cuba to nearby Key West in 1869 and then to Tampa in 1886, and in the process attracted Cubans of working-class and multiracial backgrounds to Florida. It is believed that in all, about ten thousand Cubans left the island to settle in the areas of Key West and Tampa, as well as in New Orleans and New York, other locations that saw the growth of the cigar industry between the years of 1868 and 1895.

The numbers of Cubans in the United States grew rapidly after 1961, however, following Fidel Castro's successful overthrow of Fulgencio Batista's regime in January 1959 and his efforts to nationalize the Cuban economy

---

35 For a good sampling of U.S. Puerto Rican writings that demonstrate this bicultural and binational identity, see Joy L. DeJesús, ed., *Growing Up Puerto Rican: An Anthology* (New York: William Morrow & Company, 1997).

along socialist lines. Edna Acosta-Belén rightly notes that two distinct motivations lie behind the massive waves of Cuban immigration into the United
States during the twentieth century, one political and the other economic:

> The U.S. government has defined the influx of Cubans into the
> United States as a political exodus, but it has been argued that indi-
> vidual determinants of immigration were frequently economic, par-
> ticularly in more recent years. The first generation of Cubans who
> arrived in the early years of the revolution expected to return to Cuba
> after the overthrow of the Castro government. This is not the case for
> the more recent arrivals, especially those who came in the 1980
> Mariel boatlift, the second largest wave of Cuban immigrants within
> a single year.[36]

Acosta-Belén's perception is important, for it impels us to take into
account the economic and racial diversity that exists within the U.S.
Cuban communities.

The first immigrants to arrive on U.S. shores after the 1959 Cuban revolution were mostly Cubans who had been associated with Batista's government. These were to be followed by Cuba's socioeconomic elite.
Overwhelmingly, these Cuban exiles, comprising a population of about
215,000 immigrants who departed Cuba for the United States between 1959
and 1962, were members of the ruling or middle classes in Cuba and thus
were professionals and/or businesspeople. Cuban immigration to the United
States was to decrease dramatically after the 1963 missile crisis and the resulting closure of direct travel between Cuba and the United States. Between 1965
and 1973 the doors to Cuban emigration were reopened due to political and
economic turmoil related to Cuba's adjustment to a new socialist government, and approximately 302,000 new Cubans, predominantly of middle-
class status, were to join the earlier elite Cuban émigrés on U.S. shores. This
growth in numbers allowed for the establishment of a strong Cuban presence
in the United States, and for the creation of Cuban enclaves, particularly in
Miami, Florida, and in the Union City–West New York regions of New Jersey.

Sociologists Kenneth Wilson and Alejandro Portes have differentiated
Cuban incorporation into the United States from immigrant experiences that
have followed assimilationist or internal colonialist patterns, as in the case of
Europeans and other Latinos, arguing that the situation of the first post-1959
immigrant Cubans in U.S. society can best be characterized as an "economic

---

36 Acosta-Belén, "From Settlers to Newcomers," 95-96.

enclave"—one that shares similarities with the immigrant experience of Jews, the Japanese, and, more recently, the Chinese and Koreans.[37] Helen Safa, a prominent Latina anthropologist, assists greatly in the understanding of Wilson and Portes's concept of an "economic enclave" when she notes that

> economic enclaves tend to be characterized by a strong entrepre-neurial element, beginning in the first generation... These entrepre-neurs build up small enterprises that tend to employ fellow immi-grants and serve primarily the needs of the ethnic community. This economic advance is followed by consolidation and growing political influence in successive generations.[38]

Various factors aided the development of these Cuban economic enclaves, most noticeably in the Miami, Florida, area. First, the vast majority of Cubans who entered the United States after the socialist revolution back in Cuba were white and of upper- or middle-class status, and they brought cap-ital, entrepreneurial or career skills, and other resources that facilitated their socioeconomic success in the United States. Second, as political refugees seek-ing to escape from Castro's socialist regime, these Cubans enjoyed an enthu-siastic welcome from a U.S. government that was appreciative of any and every opportunity to deride Cuba's administration. This reception was sweet-ened with state assistance, which took the forms of monetary and resettle-ment aid, educational and retraining programs, college tuition loans, and relaxed citizenship requirements. So also, the high concentration of Cubans in specific areas of the United States, most notably in the Miami–Fort Lauderdale area, where approximately half of the Cuban population settled, aided the formation of such Cuban economic enclaves.

Hence, the Cuban communities that formed in the United States imme-diately after Cuba's revolution generally fared well in economic terms. In this sense, the U.S. experience of these mid-twentieth-century Cuban immigrants differs from that of other Latino groups, and even from that of later arriving Cubans, many of whom have faced poverty in the United States. The earlier immigrants' higher economic status engendered a distinct mode of social consciousness in this particular segment of the U.S. Cuban community. For one thing, because they had left Cuba in disagreement with the radical

---

37 See Kenneth L. Wilson and Alejandro Portes, "Immigrant Enclaves: An Analysis of the Labor Market Experiences of Cubans in Miami," *American Journal of Sociology* 86 (September 1980): 295-319.

38 Helen I. Safa, "Migration and Identity: A Comparison of Puerto Rican and Cuban Migrants in the United States," in Acosta-Belén and Sjostrom, eds., *Hispanic Experience*, 144-45.

socializing revolution set in place by Castro's regime, and had benefited from the U.S. government's desire to use their Cuban exodus as a means to discredit Cuba's emerging socialism, this community was, to say the least, averse to the radicalism that was emerging in other Latino sectors during the 1960s and 1970s. Clinging to an exilic identity, these Cubans predominantly saw themselves as temporary U.S. sojourners who were awaiting the imminent collapse of socialist Cuba, and so they concentrated their initial activist efforts on the deposition of Castro's government. This exilic identity endured a transformation, however, as the U.S. Cuban community was to come to the realization that their efforts at defeating the Cuban government militarily were ultimately to prove futile and unprofitable. As Gerald Poyo and Mariano Díaz-Miranda put it, "If the 1960's was primarily the decade of exile politics aimed at returning to Cuba, the next decade was a time of acceptance of their new society, adaptation, the emergence of ethnic communities."[39]

In a short time, three distinct social strategies emerged within the U.S. Cuban community. One segment of the Cuban population, those who held on to the hopes of eventually seeing Castro's regime vanquished back in Cuba, sought alliances with the American political Right. Another group, mostly comprised of younger Cubans who became aware of the discriminatory patterns they would have to contend with as "ethnic Americans" in their adopted country, made ties with the more progressive segments of other Latino communities, particularly the Chicanos and Puerto Ricans. Finally, a third social group avoided political activism and concentrated on the advancement of business careers.[40]

Ethnic awareness among U.S. Cubans increased when hopes for an imminent return to Cuba faded, and it especially gained momentum with the arrival of later Cuban immigrants who shared neither the economic nor racial makeup of earlier arriving Cubans. In 1980 a new wave of 125,000 Cuban refugees entered the United States in the Mariel boatlift. Unlike the Cuban émigrés who had entered the United States in the 1960s and 1970s, this later group tended to be poorer, darker, and younger. And because the Cold War was losing some of its intensity by this time, these later Cuban migrants did not benefit from the federal relief programs that were extended to the so-called golden Cuban exiles of the 1960s and 1970s. Also, these later groups were to feel the sting of U.S. ethnic discrimination and racism more strongly than earlier Cuban migrants because of their darker skins. These

---

39 Gerald E. Poyo and Mariano Díaz-Miranda, "Cubans in the United States," in Jiménez, ed., *Handbook of Hispanic Cultures*, 313.

40 For further details on these three social strategies, see Fox, *Hispanic Nation*, esp. 111-15.

factors contributed to the appearance of higher rates of unemployment, poverty, and social dislocation in the U.S. Cuban community.

The "ethnic awareness" that came with the Cuban population's protracted experience in the United States, especially outside of the relatively homogenous Cuban enclaves, and the emergence of a more pronounced racial and economic diversification within it have led to an activist appreciation in the Cuban community that complements the emergence of a critical sociocultural identity in other Latino sectors. Along with the other U.S. Latino subgroups, Cubans are leaving their mark on the United States in every sphere of life, and in the process are contributing to the Latinization of the United States, the development of a critical panethnic identity among Latino/as, and the redemocratization of U.S. public life.

OTHER LATINOS: CENTRAL AND SOUTH AMERICANS, AND DOMINICANS

The three Latino nationalities that have received the most attention in the United States until now have been the Mexican-American/Chicano, Puerto Rican, and Cuban. But there are other nationalities that are included under the term "Hispanic" or "Latino," some of which have come to gain recent national recognition because of their growing numbers. The loose category commonly referred to as "other Hispanics" presently comprises as much as 22 percent of the total U.S. Hispanic/Latino population. This category most often includes the following populations: (1) several nationalities from Central and South America, primarily from Nicaragua, El Salvador, Guatemala, Colombia, Ecuador, Argentina, Venezuela, Peru, and Chile; and (2) the Dominicans, who derive from the Dominican Republic. Immigration from these two sources of Latino population has especially grown in recent times, and deserves some attention here.

The more recent waves of Latin American immigration to the United States owe much to the political repression and revolutions in Central and South America during the 1970s and 1980s. The numbers of Salvadorans and Guatemalans have especially increased. Movement from these two countries into the United States began to gain momentum in the late 1970s as political violence became severe in Guatemala and El Salvador. It is important to note that U.S. foreign policy has often exacerbated political turmoil in these and other Latin American countries. Once in this country, however, the great majority of these Latin American immigrants face a different sort of hardship, most often in the forms of poverty, the stigma of being labeled "aliens," and the anguishing threat of deportation, especially when xenophobic sensibilities grow strong in the United States. Although in general none of the Central and South American immigrant communities have yet formed their own homogeneous enclaves, but live instead alongside other Latinos in general "Latino/a" neighborhoods, they have managed to make their presence felt in such places as the Pico-Union/Westlake area in Los Angeles, the Mission District in San Francisco, various neighborhoods in New York City, and increasingly in the Washington D.C. area, where Salvadoran habitation is especially strong.[41]

The Dominican community has also grown in the United States due to a steady flow of immigration from the Dominican Republic during the last three decades. The Dominican presence is exceptionally strong in New York City, particularly in the upper West Side of Manhattan. Emigration from the Dominican Republic to the United States intensified after the 1961 assassination of long-time dictator Rafael Trujillo caused political turmoil back on the Caribbean island. As with other such cases, American foreign policy played a subtle but influential role in the pattern of Dominican immigration as it sought to implement its goals of gaining ground in the Dominican government, protecting U.S. political and economic interests in the Caribbean regions, and ensuring an influx of cheap labor into the United States. The flow of Dominican U.S. immigration has increased steadily during the last two decades as economic conditions in the Dominican Republic have worsened.[42]

As with Mexicans/Chicanos, Puerto Ricans, and segments of the Cuban community, these other Latinos have mostly been relegated to the lower tiers of the U.S. labor market, and as a consequence they have suffered from

41 For more on Central Americans in the United States, see Norma Chinchilla, Nora Hamilton, and James Loucky, "Central Americans in Los Angeles: An Immigrant Community in Transition," in Moore and Pinderhughes, eds., *In the Barrios*, 51-78. Theologian Harold Recinos has provided a useful sketch of the Salvadoran communities in the United States in "Politics, Martyrdom, and Life Story: Salvadoran Refugees Speak a Word of Life to the United States," *Journal of Hispanic/Latino Theology* 5, no. 2 (1997): 5-21. On Central and South American U.S. immigrants, see also Cary Davis, Carl Haub, and JoAnne L. Willette, "U.S. Hispanics: Changing the Face of America" in Acosta-Belén and Sjostrom, eds., *Hispanic Experience*, 3-55.

42 For more information on Dominican Latinos and Latinas, see Nancie González, "Peasant Progress: Dominicans in New York," *Caribbean Studies* 10, no. 3 (1971): 154-71; Vivian Garrison and Carol Weiss, "Dominican Family Networks and United States Immigration Policy: A Case Study," *International Migration Review* 13, no. 2 (1979): 264-83; Joan Moore, "The Social Fabric of the Hispanic Community since 1965," in *Hispanic Catholic Culture in the U.S.: Issues and Concerns*, ed. Jay Dolan and Allan Figueroa Deck (Notre Dame, Ind.: University of Notre Dame Press, 1994), 29-32; Jorge Duany, *Quisqueya on the Hudson: The Transnational Identity of Dominicans in Washington Heights* (New York: CUNY Dominican Studies Institute, 1994); and Ramona Hernández, Francisco Rivera-Batiz, and Roberto Agodini, *Dominican New Yorkers: A Socioeconomic Profile* (New York: CUNY Dominican Studies Institute, 1995).

inadequate educational, income, housing, health, social, and personal opportunities. Because of this, and because of the sense of a pervasive pattern of racism and cultural exclusion radiating from the dominant Anglo culture and society, these communities have increasingly joined with the older and more established Latino communities in order to forge a pan-Latino/a social identity and to develop a more unified front against conditions of inequality and injustice in the United States.

FORGING A PANETHNIC LATINO/A IDENTITY

As the group sketches provided above demonstrate, differences abound within the diverse Latino nationalities living in the United States. The various Latino subcultures and populations may be distinguished by their distinct national origins and varying migration or immigration experiences at different periods of U.S. history. Often, these subcultures and populations can even be set apart by disparate racial, class, generational, religious, and regional factors. Without doubt, then, it is true that to a certain extent these different histories translate into divergent experiences within the overall U.S. Latino/a population. To put it plainly, Latino/as do not constitute a homogeneous group. Nevertheless, in spite of such diversity, it is possible to speak of the emergence of a collective group identity among Latino/as and thus to speak of Hispanics/Latinos as forming an ethnic unity in the United States. Latino philosopher Jorge Gracia, in his erudite book *Hispanic/Latino Identity*, convincingly proposes that talk of a group identity among Latino/as can be based on historical relatedness instead of on common properties. In other words, for Gracia, what ties Latinos and Latinas together, and also separates them from others, is history and the particular events of that history rather than the sharing of some genetic essence or the sharing of some essential characteristic that is common to all of them in all times and places.

Employing Wittgenstein's metaphor of family resemblance to explicate his position, Gracia offers that Latino/as are bound by the same sort of relationality that ties members of an extended family. He points out that, to be a member of a family, one does not need to be tied genetically to its other members, nor does one need to exhibit thorough symmetry with its other members. "Indeed," Gracia points out, "the very foundation of a family, marriage, takes place between people who are added to a family through contract, not genesis. And in-laws become members of families indirectly, again not through genesis."[43] Moreover, families are not coherent wholes; rather, "they are made up of related clusters of persons with different, and sometimes incompatible characteristics."[44] Similarly, although there are no common properties to all those people whom we wish to call Hispanics, it is nevertheless possible to speak meaningfully of a Hispanic/Latino collective identity if one does so on the basis of historical relations. And Gracia claims that the point in history when we came together was in 1492, during the encounter of Iberia and America; it makes no sense to speak of Hispanics/Latinos before the encounter in 1492 between Europe and America. Our family came into being, so to say, as a result of the complex web of historical relations that followed this encounter. Thus, Gracia proposes that when we speak of Hispanics, " we mean the community of persons who, since the end of the fifteenth century, has become a kind of family, not always, or necessarily, tied politically, racially, linguistically, culturally, genetically, or by class, but rather historically, by a web of relations that distinguishes it from other communities and explains some of the features which characterize it at various points in history."[45]

Gracia's historical approach to Latino/a identity is well founded and can help to displace problematical myths of homogeneity among Hispanics. The ethnic label "Hispanic" or "Latino" certainly points out a highly differentiated group of persons. Nevertheless, it has become very evident, particularly in the last three decades, that the different segments of this population have often rallied around points of similarity and shared concerns, and in the process they have started to forge a fragile pan-Latino identity. Thus, the unfolding of something like a conscious and willful collective Latino/a identity is based not only on reasons of the past but also on parallel responses to the "problems of 'making sense' of our lives"[46] in the United States. In this sense, widely shared sociopolitical conditions have played a role in the forming of a Hispanic/Latino panethnic identity. As the social histories of these different communities merged and interacted within the context of the United States, a certain collective identity began to be felt among the different peoples of Hispanic/Latino descent. Increasingly, Latino/as are interacting with one another and are creating a new form of panethnic identity to the extent that they search for common social, economic, and political agendas as one group.

The increasing appeal of the idea of a collective identity among Latino/as arises from comparable social realities shared by most, although not all, U.S.

---

43 Gracia, *Hispanic/Latino Identity*, 50.
44 Ibid.
45 Ibid., 88.
46 I borrow this line from Enrique T. Trueba, *Latinos Unidos: From Cultural Diversity to the Politics of Solidarity* (Lanham, Md.: Rowman & Littlefield, 1999), 32.

Latinos regardless of their original nationalities, and from the existence of several widespread cultural similarities. These convergences include, for instance, the sharing of certain widespread cultural traits, varyingly manifested in the use of the Spanish language by many, though not all, Latino/as, and many other customs, rituals, and life sensibilities; an ubiquitous exilic sensibility that arises from the fact that the countries of origin of most Latino/as have at some point or another been annexed or colonized by the United States, and the fact that even those born in the United States (64 percent of all Latinos) often feel marginalized in their own country of origin; a prevalent sense of being a hyphenated people, at once part of two or more countries, cultures, and/or nationalities; the commonplace encounters with racial discrimination; the widespread sense of cultural alienation that stems from living within a dominant society that seeks the total victory of its own excluding Anglo culture; and the fact that Latino/as have mostly found themselves at the bottom of the economic ladder with a very limited degree of freedom to improve on their socioeconomic condition. In light of these and other similarities, we can legitimately conclude that although the Latino/a population is diverse within itself, it is, nevertheless, increasingly identifiable as a whole within the context of the United States. Since the 1960s, the U.S. Latino/a communities have more and more accepted this idea of wholeness and have rallied around a sense of collectivity and panethnicity, manifest in their growing identification with the umbrella terms "Hispanic" and "Latino." As Edna Acosta-Belén notes, "The shorthand label is turning into a symbol of cultural affirmation and identity in an alienating society that traditionally has been hostile and prejudicial to cultural and racial differences, and unresponsive to the socioeconomic and educational needs of a large segment of the Hispanic population."[47]

In fact, U.S. Latino/as have been using similar coalescing terms and have been finding common rallying points to work together under a panethnic identity since early on in their U.S. history. There are numerous examples of early organizations, periodicals, and movements that employed such panethnic terms as "Latino," "Hispano," "Latin," or simply "Spanish-speaking" to express the parallel experiences of people of Spanish-speaking ancestry in the United States and to create solidarity among them. "The sense and practice of a 'Latino/Hispanic' unity across national lines," the eminent Juan Flores notes, " goes way back, as does the recognized need for names to designate such tactical or enduring common ground."[48] In this sense, then, what is new

---

47 Acosta-Belén, "From Settlers to Newcomers," 84.
48 Flores, "Pan-Latino/Trans-Latino," 175.

in the use of umbrella signifiers is the popularization and promulgation of a collective mood among the different Latino subgroups, which correspondingly is evinced in their increased acceptance of the self-identifying terms "Hispanic" and "Latino."[49]

Certainly, the official use of the term "Hispanic" in the 1980 census has a lot to do with the wide currency of such generic designations among Latino/as. But several other factors have also greatly contributed to this process of panethnic self-naming. Five factors, in particular, led to the advancement of a collective social consciousness in the U.S. Latino/a community: (1) a steady growth in the U.S. Latino/a population, due to various large migration and immigration waves that brought newer Spanish-speaking peoples into the United States, especially between the decades of the 1940s and late 1970s, and also the prodigious growth of the older resident U.S. Latino/a communities; (2) a vast Latino/a urban migration, which was spurred on by the desperate need for cheap labor in city factories, particularly during and right after the entry of the United States into World War II in 1941, an occurrence that brought about greater concentration and visibility of Latino/as in the growing urban regions of the United States; (3) a greater recognition of the structural forms of racism that often stood in the way of Latino/a fulfillment; (4) the awareness, through numerous lived experiences, of a growing U.S. xenophobia that targeted Latino/as as a result of their growing numbers; and (5) a greater acknowledgment of the economic, political, and even cultural hurdles that the great majority of Latino/as faced in the United States. As a whole, the pronounced concentrations of Latino/as in U.S. urban settings would lead to a heightened recognition among Latino/as of the need for a protean struggle to ameliorate those dismal conditions in U.S.

---

49 Félix Padilla has observed that this recognition of the need for a panethnic identity among Latinos—what he terms an expression of "Latinismo"—tends to be situational: "The Latino-conscious person sees himself as a Latino sometimes and as a Puerto Rican, Mexican American, Cuban and the like at other times." The distinct populations of Latin American descent living in the United States tend to come together under an umbrella term such as "Latino" when they feel that there may be social and political gain achieved from panethnic unity. During other times, Latinos may refer back to their national identities. Nevertheless, it is clear that the sense of "Latinismo," of a panethnic identity, has increasingly grown among Latinos and Latinas. For more on this subject see Félix Padilla's influential book *Latino Ethnic Consciousness: The Case of Mexican Americans and Puerto Ricans in Chicago* (Notre Dame, Ind.: University of Notre Dame Press, 1985); and his article "On Hispanic Identity," in Jiménez, ed., *Handbook of Hispanic Cultures*, 292-303. See also B. E. Aguirre and Rogelio Sáenz, "A Futuristic Assessment of Latino Ethnic Identity," in *Latino Studies Journal* 2, no. 3 (1991): 19-32; and Suzanne Oboler, *Ethnic Labels, Latino Lives: Identity and the Politics of (Re)Presentation in the United States* (Minneapolis: University of Minnesota Press, 1995), esp. 1-16.

life that disproportionately affected certain groups of people. This sensibility, in turn, engendered a new identity among U.S. Latinos and Latinas.

In short, already by the mid 1960s, the myth of the United States as a land of equal opportunity, and as a place that ensured liberty, justice, and a good life for all, had lost much of its credibility in the U.S. Latino/a community. The continued experience of poverty and discrimination led to the emergence of a new, keener, collective identity. No longer would Latino identity concern itself chiefly with the cultural and political issues transpiring outside of the United States, in the countries of origins or ancestry for many. Rather, that identity would now focus primarily on the dynamics of life in the United States. Sociologist and historian Anthony Stevens-Arroyo concisely captures this shift in collective identity when he observes that increasingly from the 1960s onward, "no longer was the burden of change and adaptation laid exclusively on Latinos seeking to be Americanized: now, America itself was expected to change."[50]

This emerging Latino critical social consciousness fermented during the decade of the 1960s, giving rise to a flurry of first secular, and then religious, theological, and ecclesiastical, movements for social change. Manifesting the growing sense of collectivity among Latino/as, these movements tended to be pan-Latino in orientation. Alliances such as La Raza Unida Party, the Young Lords, the Brown Berets, Crusade for Justice, the Puerto Rican Socialist Party and Student Union, MECHA, MALDEF, and others contained tangible pan-Latino elements and worked for the overall self-determination of U.S. Latino/as. Although these movements focused on the particular conditions of Latino/as in the United States, they also displayed a salutary wider humanistic vision that sought to enter into solidarity with other oppressed groups, especially African Americans, and contributed to the larger countercultural movements of the time—the civil rights movement, labor movements, war protests, and educational reform movements.

Even as many of these organizations have either ceased to exist or have declined in power, the sensibility and the hope that brought to fruition these movements for social change have managed to live on in the community. This critical consciousness has found strong expression in the epistemological framework of Latino/a scholarship; specifically, U.S. Hispanic/Latino theologians have written and done theology under the sway of this social consciousness. In short, much of Latino/a theology bears witness to the influence of this search for and advancement of an availing and distinctive

50 Anthony Stevens-Arroyo, "The Emergence of a Social Identity among Latino Catholics: An Appraisal," in Dolan and Deck, eds., *Hispanic Catholic Culture*, 110.

Latino identity. I suggest that a suitable appraisal of U.S. Hispanic/Latino theology should take into account the centrality of this emphasis, as well as the
lived conditions that have occasioned it.

I have tried to provide a brief overview of the history of Latino/as in the
United States in order to suggest something of the overall plight that has
evoked the emphasis on identity and culture in U.S. Hispanic/Latino theological scholarship. I suggest that the concern with selfhood and cultural particularity in Latino theology, and in Latino scholarship as a whole, arises in
large part from a history of struggle against cultural exclusion and racial discrimination in the United States. To put it bluntly, Latino/as have long struggled both to claim their full citizenship as legitimate U.S. citizens and to pro-
tect their cultural identity; they have arduously and proudly defended their
"freedom to be American citizens and still be what we are—Puerto Ricans, or
Chicanos, or Latinos."[51] In spite of the differences that exist among the different Latino nationalities, whether of national origins, time of arrival in the
United States, racial composition, or class, linguistic, and gender experiences,
the twofold and interconnected struggle for full citizenship and the preservation of identity and heritage is in some manner common to all.

As an expression of liberation theology, the mission of U.S.
Hispanic/Latino theology has been to understand and serve Latino/a life,
with the general hope of promoting comprehensive democratic participation
in the United States. Of necessity, although they have not entirely disregarded the possibilities of a broad emancipatory humanistic vision,
Hispanic/Latino theologians have made unjust Latino suffering and delimitation the entry point for their liberatory Christian discourses. Particularly,
from very early on, they have placed great emphasis on contesting the ongoing pressure for cultural homogenization and the incessant practice of racial
discrimination in the United States, impulses that usually promote and
require the depreciation and exclusion of all but the dominant Anglo culture.
These particular concerns provided ground for the evocation of the categories of identity and culture in U.S. Hispanic/ Latino theologies.

This emphasis on identity and culture receives expression in various
ways. I devote a significant portion of the next chapter to an exploration of
two central ways in which this concern is demonstrated and theologically
articulated in the emerging tradition of U.S. Hispanic/Latino theology. I also
point to some of the challenges and limitations that this overall paradigm of

---

51 Blanca G. Silvestrini, "The World We Enter When Claiming Rights: Latinos and Their
Quest for Culture," in *Latino Cultural Citizenship: Claiming Identity, Space, and Rights*, ed.
William V. Flores and Rina Benmayor (Boston: Beacon Press, 1997).

identity and difference faces in our contemporary milieu, as I continue to make a case for the present need of a conception of U.S. Latino/a theology as a form of public discourse.

Chapter 2
Traversing the Enchantment with Symbolic Culture and Identity Politics in U.S. Hispanic/Latino Theology

There is no way, it seems to me, in which people of the world can act, can speak, can create, can come in from the margins and talk, can begin to reflect on their own experience unless they come from some place, they come from some history, they inherit certain cultural traditions... There's no enunciation without positionality... And in that sense, the past is not only a position from which to speak, but it is also an absolutely necessary resource in what one has to say.

—Stuart Hall[*]

Our survival as a species depends on our ability to recognize the borders *between* difference as fertile spaces of desire and fluid sites of syncretism, interaction, and mutual change.

—Susan Friedman[†]

But we have no patterns for relating *across* human difference as *equals*. As a result, those differences have been misnamed and misused in the service of separation and confusion.

—Audre Lorde[‡]

---

[*] Stuart Hall, "Ethnicity: Identity and Difference," *Radical America* 23, no. 4 (1990): 19.

[†] Susan S. Friedman, *Mappings: Feminism and the Cultural Geographies of Encounter* (Princeton, N.J.: Princeton University Press, 1998), 66.

[‡] Audre Lorde, "Age, Race, Class, and Sex: Women Redefining Difference," in *Out There: Marginalization and Contemporary Culture*, ed. R. Ferguson et al. (New York: The New York Museum of Contemporary Art, 1992), 282.

The most authentic Latina women and Latino men who are creating
a new Latino story and culture in this country are those who live and
practice life in the service of transformation by caring deeply about
others, about Latinos, as well as members of all other groups.

—David Abalos.[§]

INTRODUCTION

The longing to remember who we are, as ethnically and culturally situat-
ed persons, has rarely commanded high regard in theological scholarship. Yet,
this is precisely the aspiration that lies at the heart of U.S. Hispanic/Latino
theology. I dare say that much of the uniqueness of that theology derives
from the centrality that it gives to matters of self-identity and cultural identity. Latino/a theology has been at the fore of the movement within U.S. liberation theologies to add the categories of culture and identity to the liberationist paradigm in Christian theological discourse; to the reflexive spheres of
race, class, and gender it has added cultural identity.

From its beginning, U.S. Hispanic/Latino theology has emphasized
issues such as identity, the maintenance of Latino/a cultural traditions, and,
therefore, the use of cultural resources in theological reflection. This stress
on identity and culture arises from a legitimate concern with the survival of
Hispanic/Latino people as a people in the United States. Latinos have
shared the historical experiences of conquest, colonization, and political
infringement; a general sense of the depreciation of their cultures; and
common encounters with overt ethnic and racial prejudice as well as persistent assimilationist assumptions that threaten their identities. Hence,
Hispanic/Latino theologians have become convinced that the defense and
maintenance of a salutary sense of cultural identity must be made part of a
liberating theological discourse.

The emphasis on identity and culture in U.S. Hispanic/Latino theology is
expressed in a number of ways. The interconnected concern with self-identity and cultural identity is most manifest in the recurring use of, and significance attributed to, the concepts of "mestizaje" and "popular religion" in the
writings of most Hispanic/Latino theologians. Even a cursory reading of

---

§ David Abalos, "The Personal, Historical, and Sacred Grounding of Culture: Some
Reflections on the Creation of Latino Culture in the U.S. from the Perspective of the Theory of
Transformation," in *Old Masks, New Faces: Religion and Latino Identities*, ed. Anthony Stevens-
Arroyo and Gilbert Cadena (New York: The Bildner Center for Western Hemisphere Studies,
1995), 169.

these works shows clearly that these two motifs hold a special significance for Latino/a theologians. Indeed, it is difficult, if not impossible, to find a work in Hispanic/Latino theology that does not refer to one or both of these concepts. In whatever manner the term "mestizaje" is employed, and no matter what secondary meaning may be attributed to the study of popular religion, the main thrust behind the use of these concepts is a concern with the proper remembrance, defense, and celebration of Latino/a cultural identity and difference. In this sense, the terms "mestizaje" and "popular religion" are employed as explanatory categories that synchronously depict the cultural and even racial hybridity that characterizes Latino/a identity; help point to what is different and new about that identity in the United States; and provide fertile space for new formations and celebrations of cultural identity to take hold. The underlying quest in the theological interpretation of mestizaje and popular religion is, then, the remembrance of who we are as Latino/as, the disclosure of *lo que es nuestro* (what is uniquely ours), and the move from a shame-filled self-image to a shame-less identity that celebrates Latino/a culture and difference in spite of the depreciating pressures often exerted by the dominant Euro-Anglo culture in the United States.

In this chapter I pore over the writings of two noteworthy U.S. Hispanic/Latino theologians in order to delineate their use of the concepts of mestizaje and popular religion, and to demonstrate how the prominence of matters of ethnic and cultural identity reveals itself in the employment of these categories. Two clarifications are necessary here. First, in order to limit the scope of this chapter, I restrict my synopsis of the use of mestizaje and popular religion in Latino/a theology to the work of a theorist who has made considerable use of, and has either been noted as a pioneer in, or is often quoted in reference to, these two categories. Hence, I explore the way in which the concept of mestizaje is featured in the work of Virgilio Elizondo, and on popular religion I take a look at Orlando Espín's published works.[1] Second, I state at the outset that my aim in this chapter is not to pursue a full-fledged

---

1 I am aware that my selection of Virgilio Elizondo and Orlando Espín, two male Latino theologians, as representatives of U.S. Hispanic/Latino theology may be problematic to some. I am in no way being dismissive of the gender issue implicated here, or of the great and corrective contributions that Latinas have made to theology. The rationale for my choice of these two particular Latino theologians as case studies in my survey on the centrality of identity and culture matters within U.S. Hispanic/Latino theology is as follows. First, it is important to note that, although the contributions of Latina theologians to Hispanic theology are palpable from very early on, the published offerings of Latina theologians so far have tended to be concentrated in the writings of only a precious few Latinas. Although, fortunately, the number of Latina theologians is increasing, most of the published works on Latino/a theology are still authored by a

study of the history of scholarship on mestizaje and popular religion, nor is it my intention to attend to the full range of possible criticisms that can be made of the use of these terms. Rather, my synopsis of Elizondo's and Espín's use of these categories simply seeks to demonstrate how a concern with ethnic and cultural identity and difference is central to U.S. Hispanic/Latino theology.[2]

---

small number of Latina women. This exiguity can at times confine one's alternatives, especially as it concerns certain particular topics. Second, in respect to the concept of mestizaje, Virgilio Elizondo was in fact the first theologian to employ Latino/a mestizaje, specifically Mexican American mestizaje, as a starting point for Hispanic theological reflection in the United States. As pioneer of the theological translation of lived mestizaje, his texts have come to be influential and are frequently cited by Hispanic theologians writing on the subject. Moreover, while other Latino and Latina theologians have mentioned the concept of mestizaje in their writings, Elizondo still remains the theologian who has employed this concept most extensively and creatively. Other Latina and Latino theologians have assumed the importance of mestizaje as a locus for Hispanic theological reflection and have devoted segments of their writings to the concept of mestizaje that have given it a refined theoretical status, but in Elizondo's writings the conceptualization of mestizaje receives a primary focus that is at yet unparalleled. Hence, because Elizondo is considered the pioneer of the theological interpretation of Hispanic mestizaje, because he has made extensive and expansive use of the concept of mestizaje, because he is the Hispanic theologian most commonly cited in reference to the theological theorizing of mestizaje, and because he is the theologian who most pronouncedly and repeatedly connects the theorizing of mestizaje to the generalized goal of cultural and identity affirmation, it is intellectually sensible that Elizondo be the reviewed theorist when it comes to a study of the use of this concept in Latino/a theology. Third, on the topic of popular religion, Orlando Espín's writings offer the most clear-cut and generalized theorizations of Latino/a popular religious expression as a form of subaltern resistance to Euro-Anglo cultural imperialism in the United States. In sum, for the purposes of this chapter, in which I seek to demonstrate the prominence of identity and cultural issues in Hispanic theology, Virgilio Elizondo and Orlando Espín are simply the most useful subjects to pursue. I suggest that the strong emphasis placed on matters of identity and culture displayed in the works of these two theologians can also be grasped most generally throughout the annals of U.S. Hispanic/Latino theology. Although I believe that this emphasis greatly characterizes Hispanic/Latino theology overall, I contend that the privileging of cultural and identity theorizing, and the central focus on matters of cultural injustice, are clearly and especially apparent in the Hispanic/Latino theologies of Virgilio Elizondo and Orlando Espín.

2 Although the two thinkers whom I focus on here are Catholic, it is important to note that the interest in mestizaje/mulatez, or hybrid cultural identity, and popular religion also extends to Protestant Latino/a theologians and religious scholars. Examples of Protestant Hispanic/Latino theological writings that have considered the theme of mestizaje/mulatez are Justo González, *Santa Biblia: The Bible through Hispanic Eyes* (Nashville: Abingdon Press, 1996), 77-90; and several of the articles found in José David Rodríguez and Loida I. Martell-Otero, eds., *Teología en Conjunto: A Collaborative Hispanic Protestant Theology* (Louisville: Westminster John Knox Press, 1997). For a look at the treatment of popular religion within the writings of Protestant Latino/a thinkers, see Tito Paredes, "Popular Religiosity: A Protestant Perspective," *Missiology* 20, no. 2 (1992): 205-20; Edwin D. Aponte, "*Coritos* as Active Symbol in

Furthermore, in this chapter I argue that it is important that Hispanic/Latino theologians come to terms not only with the possibilities but also the limitations of a theology centered on matters of local identity, symbolic culture, and difference. The axes of identity and culture are, in fact, always embedded in a larger web of shifting social and political relations that must be equally kept in mind when theorizing on matters of identity, culture, or difference. Hence, these matters must be understood in relation to broader societal constituents, stratifications, and crises that transcend the space of the self and the local but nevertheless influence everyday personal and local realities. Because of this, I want ultimately to suggest that a theology that aims to promote social justice cannot be limited to discussions of symbolic culture, local identity, subjectivity, and difference. Matters of self-identity and cultural identity are of vital importance, and therefore they must continue to be a part of the reflective agenda particularly for those theologies that emanate from the context of subordinated and oppressed groups in the United States. Yet, marginalized theological voices in particular should be attentive not only to the needs of "local" theologies but also to the possibilities of "public" theologies that can engage the broader context of social and political life and may revitalize a populist sentiment and coalitional energy in U.S. society. The predilection toward, and/or the provisional privileging of, matters of ethnic and cultural identity and difference in our theologies should not detract us from examining the possibilities of a theology that adequately and movingly speaks of and to the broader matrices of social life, and that inspires the energy and moral vision necessary for coalitional activism and alliance building across racial, cultural, gender, class, and religious differences in our increasingly fragmented public and civic realm. Taking into account certain recent challenges posed to Hispanic theology's foundational paradigm of cultural identity and difference, I point to the need for a conception of that theology as translocal and transcultural "public" discourse.

CULTURE, IDENTITY, AND DIFFERENCE: MESTIZAJE AND POPULAR RELIGION

Latino Protestant Popular Religion," *Journal of Hispanic/Latino Theology* 2, no.3 (1995): 57-66; Carlos F. Cardoza-Orlandi, "Drum Beats of Resistance and Liberation: Afro-Caribbean Religions, the Struggle for Life, and the Christian Theologian," *Journal of Hispanic/Latino Theology* 3, no.1 (1995): 50-61; and Harold Recinos, "Popular Religion, Political Identity, and Life-Story Testimony in an Hispanic Community," in *The Ties that Bind: African American and Hispanic American/Latino(a) Theologies in Dialogue,* eds. Anthony B. Pinn and Benjamín Valentín (New York: Continuum, 2001), 116-28.

LATINO/A CULTURE AND IDENTITY MATTERS

Hispanic/Latino theology in the United States is manifestly a culturally contextualized theology of liberation; in fact, some have labeled it a cultural theology. It is indeed a cultural theology, not only by virtue of the fact that as theology it is always necessarily a product of culture, but also because, as Latina theologians Ada María Isasi-Díaz and Yolanda Tarango rightly point out, it purposely gives witness to our struggle to "maintain the values of our culture as an intrinsic element of our self-identity and of our struggle"[3] for liberation in the United States.

Culture is a recurrent theme in Hispanic/Latino theology, and in Latino/a discourse overall, both as a basis to counteract the ethnic prejudice and cultural subjugation with which Latinos have often had to contend, and as a way of fostering self-affirming identities. Given the histories of social marginalization, exploitation, powerlessness, cultural devaluation, and hurtful negative stereotypes that may lead to crises of identity, this turn to culture is an important and necessary strategy. It is often taken for granted in this country that the fragile *American* experiment in democracy actually began with the plight of the early Hispanic peoples who inhabited this land. Hispanic U.S. history was marked very early on with the violent conquest of Mexicans, Hispanic mestizos, and their lands. And even after professing and demonstrating our love for and allegiance to this country, we Latinos continue to endure questions regarding our legitimacy not only as citizens but also as persons. Latinos have at times been deemed inadequate, as people who do not belong, and inherently as a problem people. On top of this, the assimilationist dogma that frequently creeps into our national discourse has often held that Latinos must erase their past in order to become "authentic" U.S. Americans. This process of cultural subjugation has materialized in different forms throughout U.S. history. Recently, it is seen in the English-only initiatives that have sought to undercut the advancement of bilingualism in U.S. public life, and in the inflammatory politics of immigration control that led to the passage of Proposition 187 in California. At other times, the obstacles to cultural knowledge, positive self-identity, and collective identity take on more covert and personal configurations. Yet, whether overtly or covertly, and whether of public or personal impact, the dynamics of the depreciation of culture, and the preoccupations with a viable self identity that arise as a result, continue to influence Latino/a life. In light of these historical realities, many have come to the conclusion that identity and culture are salient topics: Latino/a identity and culture do matter.

---

3 Ada María Isasi-Díaz and Yolanda Tarango, *Hispanic Women: Prophetic Voice in the Church* (Minneapolis: Fortress Press, 1992), xii.

The vitriolic attacks on identity that accompany the general depreciation of Latino/a cultures in the United States have motivated a turn to culture in Latino scholarship, and indeed among Latinos as a whole. For good reason, U.S. Latinos have given culture a central place in their search for and reconstruction of a denied positive identity. In the words of Blanca Silvestrini, culture has provided Latinos "a sense of belonging to a community, a feeling of entitlement, the energy to face everyday adversities, and a rationale for resistance to a larger world in which members of minority groups feel like aliens in spite of being citizens."[4] Overall, the turn to culture and cultural consciousness has allowed Latino/as the opportunity to examine neglected elements of their cultures and histories and to highlight those features that make Latinos unique, and it has offered them a fertile space in which to reconstruct, revitalize, or reassert their ethnic and cultural identities.

Deeming the search for positive self-identity and collective cultural identity a crucial component of liberation in the United States, and wanting to contribute to this aspiration among Latinos, Hispanic/Latino theologians have made cultural activism an integral part of their theologies. In light of the continued existence of strategies of cultural oppression in our so-called postcolonial era within the United States, and the corrosive effects that these have on the cultivation of self-affirming identities, Hispanic theologians have devoted a great part of their reflective energies to questions of identity and cultural consciousness, in the hopes of both resisting the assimilatory pressures and prejudices that exist in U.S. life and promoting cultural affirmation among Latinos.

THE CULTURAL CONFIGURATIONS OF LATINO/A MESTIZAJE

The task of self-cultural affirmation in the case of Latinos in the United States, however, is a rather intricate endeavor, for besides having to contend with the threats of an often hostile dominant Euro-Anglo culture bent on the assimilation of other cultures, Latinos must come to terms with an ambiguity that lies at the heart of their cultures and, therefore, their identities. Latino/a cultures and identities are always, in fact, at the very least the result of a syncretic, eccentric, and disjointed fusion of Iberian, Amerindian, African, and Euro-American cultures.[5] The term most commonly used in literature to speak of this ambiguity and multilayered hybridity that lies at the

---

4 Blanca G. Silvestrini, "The World We Enter When Claiming Rights: Latinos and Their Quest for Culture," in *Latino Cultural Citizenship: Claiming Identity, Space, and Rights*, ed. William V. Flores and Rina Benmayor (Boston: Beacon Press, 1997), 43.

5 See Coco Fusco, *English Is Broken Here: Notes on Cultural Fusion in the Americas* (New York: The New Press, 1995), 33.

heart of Latino cultural history and identity is "mestizaje." The term "mestizaje" generally refers to "the process of biological and cultural mixing that
occurs after the violent and unequal encounter between cultures."[6]

The particulars of the multidimensional biological and cultural fusion—
the mestizaje—that marks Latino/a history began to emerge in the sixteenth
century with the arrival of Spanish conquistadores in the Americas, and are
related to the rather rapid Spanish conquest and colonization of most of
Central and South America, Mexico, large segments of the Caribbean, and
much of what is now the southern and western United States. Historians of
the Spanish colonial period have established that much of the early Spanish
interest in these territories centered on mining.[7] The development of these
mines, however, required a larger supply of labor than the Spanish colonizers
were willing or able to provide on their own. The result was that the conquered indigenous populations were soon forced into mining labor. But the
oppressive labor conditions, scant nourishment, broken family life, and dis-
ease that were part of this harsh life of indenture under Spanish rule combined to bring about a swift and dramatic decline in the native populations.
As Alex García-Rivera aptly notes, this mass extermination affected not only
the native Amerindian population but also "had tragic consequences for the
people of Africa."[8]

What García-Rivera is alluding to in this statement is the fact that in
order to augment a rapidly declining indigenous labor force, the Spaniards
took to introducing large numbers of African slaves from the western coast of
Africa to the Americas.[9] The proximity of these three groups of people in the
Americas occasioned the emergence of a new biological and cultural context
as the Spanish/Portuguese, Native American, and African populations
increasingly intermingled, creating large populations of mestizo/a and
mulatto/a peoples, (i.e., peoples of mixed ancestry). Moreover, crosses
between these hybrid, bicultural populations and other peoples commonly

---

6 Alex García-Rivera, *St. Martin de Porres: The "Little Stories" and the Semiotics of Culture*
(Maryknoll, N.Y.: Orbis Books, 1995), 40.

7 See Charles Gibson, *Spain in America* (New York: Harper & Row, 1966), esp. 1-47, 112-
35; Leslie Bethell, ed., *The Cambridge History of Latin America*, 11 vols. (Cambridge:
Cambridge University Press, 1984-95), esp. 1:149-388, 2:67-149; and Alfredo Jiménez, ed.,
Handbook of Hispanic Cultures in the United States, vol. 2, *History* (Houston: Arte Público
Press, 1994), esp. 23-183.

8 García-Rivera, *St. Martin de Porres*, 42.

9 See also Herbert S. Klein, *African Slavery in Latin America and the Caribbean* (Oxford:
Oxford University Press, 1986); Frederick P. Bowser, "Colonial Spanish America," in *Neither
Slave nor Free: The Freedman of African Descent in the Slave Societies of the New World*, ed. David
W. Cohen and Jack P. Greene (Baltimore: Johns Hopkins University Press, 1972), 19-58.

took place so that almost innumerable racial, ethnic, and cultural mixtures came into being in the Americas. Present-day Latin American and U.S. Latino populations have been especially marked by this history, and are in some way the biological and cultural result of the "violent and unequal encounter of these cultures" during the Spanish colonial period.

But in the case of U.S. Latinos, mestizaje (i.e., cultural hybridity) takes on an added element, for in this instance, we also need to take into account the influence of cultural traditions and life experiences in the United States. Latino identity and culture is actually, therefore, the result of a confluence of contexts and cultural heritages that at the very least includes Iberian, Native American, African, and also Euro-Anglo influences. Hence, the search for and reconstruction of a denied positive cultural identity must eventually come to terms with the hybrid experiences that shape so much of Latino life. It must also negotiate the ambivalences and transgressive possibilities that mark Hispanic mestizo/a consciousness, one that always emerges from "the dynamics of moving between worlds, and feeling at home and not at home in more than one."[10]

At first glance, one can come to the erroneous conclusion that the complex hybridity that lies at the center of this cultural history necessarily leads to an existential incoherence, one that limits the capacity to produce positive identity. Recent cultural activism and, indeed, the daily lives of many Latinos, however, confirm that fortunately this is not so. Latino/as have managed to develop new cultures and identities that juggle, blur, and blend the historic and cultural genealogies that make up their heritage into a meaningful existence. Latinos in the United States have lent living credence to Homi Bhabha's assertion that hybridity could give rise to "something different, something new and unrecognizable, a new area of negotiation of meaning and representation."[11] Affirmation of the lived transcultural experience of Latino/a mestizaje has involved relentless inner and outer struggle, and has always required a strong resolution to transcend menacing existential, political, cultural, and even geographic borders in order to survive sanely and wholly in the United States. When affirmation of mestizaje in the United States succeeds, it does so in the face of national assimilationist pressures, overt or subtle racism, external and internalized stereotypes of inferiority, and long-entrenched biases about miscegenation or mixed-race identity. In short, this affirmation is not something that can be assumed; it must

---

10 Fusco, *English Is Broken Here*, 33.

11 Homi Bhabha, "The Third Space," in *Identity, Community, Culture Difference*, ed. J. Rutherford (London: Lawrence and Wishart, 1990), 211.

be worked on and achieved through "struggle, consciousness raising, and the reconstruction of identities."[12]

The emphasis on mestizaje in Hispanic theology exemplifies one specific attempt, within a larger critical discursive movement among Latino/a writers, activists, and scholars, to generalize and support an affirming cultural identity within a hostile context wherein cultural diversity is often deemed as threatening to national integrity. It also attests to an emerging Latino consciousness that is willing to explore anew the significance of cultural hybridity both within the community and in the broader national context.

The Theorizing of Mestizaje in U.S. Hispanic/Latino Theology: Virgilio Elizondo's *The Future Is Mestizo* and *Galilean Journey*

"The process of translating lived *mestizaje* into written discourse"[13] can be traced back to the late-nineteenth-century and early-twentieth-century writings of the Latin American intellectual José Vasconcelos.[14] In more recent years, however, it has crossed the U.S. border and found a home in the writings of Latino/a scholars and activists such as Daniel Cooper Alarcón, Guillermo Gómez-Peña, Cherríe Moraga, and, especially, Gloria Anzaldúa— writers who have given *mestizo/a discourse* newfound recognition and refined theoretical status.[15]

Even before discourse on hybridity and mestizaje became popular in U.S. cultural scholarship during the late 1980s, a Mexican American theologian by the name of Virgilio Elizondo had already been working on the interpretation of U.S. Latino mestizaje. Indeed, Elizondo, a Roman Catholic diocesan priest widely considered to be the father of U.S. Hispanic theology, is a pioneer of the more recent discourse on mestizaje among Latino scholars. Without doubt, he was the first theologian to employ the concept of mestizaje as a theological starting point from which to interpret the historical experience of U.S. Hispanics. Following his influential lead, most Hispanic/Latino theologians

---

12 Cornel West, *Race Matters* (Boston: Beacon Press, 1993), 15.

13 I have borrowed this choice of words from Víctor Valle and Rodolfo Torres, "The Idea of *Mestizaje* and the 'Race' Problematic: Racialized Media Discourse in a Post-Fordist Landscape," in *Culture and Difference: Critical Perspectives on the Bicultural Experience in the United States*, ed. Antonia Darder (Westport, Conn.: Bergin & Garvey, 1995), 148.

14 See especially Vasconcelos's influential 1925 essay *La Raza Cósmica*, republished in a bilingual edition as *The Cosmic Race/La Raza Cósmica* (Baltimore: Johns Hopkins University Press, 1997).

15 See especially Daniel Cooper Alarcón, *The Aztec Palimpsest: Mexico in the Modern Imagination* (Tucson: University of Arizona Press, 1997); Guillermo Gómez-Peña, *Warrior for Gringostroika* (Saint Paul, Minn.: Graywolf Press, 1993); Cherríe Moraga, *The Last Generation: Prose and Poetry* (Boston: South End Press, 1993); and Gloria Anzaldúa, *Borderlands/La Frontera: The New Mestiza* (San Francisco: Aunt Lute Books, 1987).

have come to see mestizaje, and the realm of culture and identity as a whole, as an important and fertile locus for Hispanic theological reflection.

Like the writings of the theorists mentioned above, Elizondo's work is marked by an autobiographical narrative style that pieces together fragments of personal memories and takes readers through a labyrinthlike journey of self-search and discovery. Elizondo, however, comes to the subject of mestizaje as a Christian theologian. Unlike the texts of the aforementioned Latino theorists of mestizaje, therefore, his reflections on mestizaje also include intricate ruminations on religion and theology. Hence, Elizondo's work contains two reflective poles that he attempts to keep in a sort of Tillichian dialectic or correlation:[16] on the one hand, he puts forward his autobiographical travels; on the other hand, he advances creative theological reflections in light of these. Elizondo's theological pole is particularly grounded in, first, his musings over Latino/a popular religious expression as a medium for the exhibition and defense of cultural traditions and difference, and, second, his analogical study of the historical Jesus' mestizo identity and present-day Mexican American mestizaje. The importance of popular religion for Hispanic/Latino(a) theology will be treated later in this chapter. I will concentrate here on the second of Elizondo's theological themes, especially as it is presented to us in his *The Future Is Mestizo* and *Galilean Journey.*[17]

In the introduction to *The Future Is Mestizo,* a theological autobiography that takes the form of a quest narrative, Elizondo discloses that the turn to culture and matters of identity in his theology finds its beginnings in a gripping identity crisis that had been simmering inside of him since early in his life. "All my life," Elizondo recalls, "I had been pulled in two opposing directions—the U.S. way of life and the Mexican way of life. Sometimes I felt the pull would be so great that it would rip me apart."[18] He elucidates the roots and contours of his Mexican-American identity:

---

16 The reference is to Paul Tillich's famous theological method of correlation, as presented in *Systematic Theology,* vol. 1 (Chicago: University of Chicago Press, 1951).

17 Virgilio Elizondo, *The Future Is Mestizo: Life Where Cultures Meet* (Bloomington, Ind.: Meyer Stone Books, 1988), and *Galilean Journey: The Mexican-American Promise* (Maryknoll, N.Y.: Orbis Books, 1983). It was in Galilean Journey that Elizondo first made extensive use of the concept of mestizaje in his theology. Nevertheless, his usage of this notion can be appreciated already in a 1975 publication, *Christianity and Culture: An Introduction to Pastoral Theology and Ministry for the Bicultural Community* (Huntington, Ind.: Our Sunday Visitor, 1975), esp. 113-28. In either case, Elizondo's theorizing of mestizaje in these two publications precedes the popularity granted to this concept in cultural studies circles following the 1987 publication of Anzaldúa's *Borderlands/La Frontera.* We should acknowledge, however, that mestizo/a discourse has in fact been granted more recognition, refinement, and theoretical sophistication in, and thanks to, the more recent texts written on the subject, whether by secular cultural theorists or theological theorists.

18 Elizondo, *The Future Is Mestizo,* x.

I lived on the border between two nationalities. I was an inside-outsider to both. I was "Mexican" in the U.S. and *gringo/pocho* in
Mexico.... I gradually became more and more aware of the many
things I was not: I was not and would never be, even if I wanted to, a
regular U.S.-American. Yet neither would I be a *puro Mexicano*. There
were identities that I knew that I was and was not at the same time:
U.S.-American, Mexican, Spanish, Indian. Yet I was![19]

These declarations are immensely helpful for the understanding of
Elizondo's work because they reveal, among other things, that his theology
emanates from the space of the self, of identity. Particularly, they disclose
that the starting point of Elizondo's theology is a preoccupation with the
Mexican American's struggle for positive self identity amidst the contradictions that abound in the physical, emotional, and spiritual borderlands of
the U.S. Southwest.[20]

The struggle against cultural oppression and identity suppression has
had a long legacy in Mexican American history, and it is no wonder that
Mexican Americans have had to grapple long and hard with such matters.
The foundational narrative of "Mexicanness" intrinsically involves a dual
story of conquest, colonization, and miscegenation. The first conquest
involved the Spanish subjugation of the indigenous peoples of what is now
Mexico and the Southwest of the United States during the sixteenth century,
and included the imposition not only of Spanish rule but also of Spanish culture. The second consisted of the U.S. invasion and subsequent colonization

---

19 Ibid., 21, 26.

20 Although Elizondo's focus is particularly on the Mexican American situation, his work has
bearing for other groups in the United States. Because the cultural history of every Latino subgroup has been influenced by the dynamics of Hispanic mestizaje either during the Spanish colonial period or in the United States, Elizondo's theorizing of mestizaje is adaptable to every U.S.
Latino subculture. In fact, one might say that Elizondo's work can be useful to all persons of
mixed cultural and racial heritage, whether Latino or not. For a glimpse of a more universal mestizaje, or a hinting toward a wider meaning of mestizaje, within Elizondo's own work, see *The
Future Is Mestizo*, esp. 87-111. We should note, however, that the term "mestizaje," or "mestizo/a,"
technically refers to someone who is an offspring of Iberian and Amerindian/indigenous race
and culture. Hence, it is in every way an appropriate signifier for Mexican Americans and other
Latinos who trace their ancestry directly to Iberian and Amerindian lineage. But Caribbean
Latinos, and others, who are especially or more directly marked by African roots, may find more
resonant the term "mulatez" in emphasizing the African element in their racial and cultural
descent. Thus, the universalistic use of "mestizaje" as a catchall to signify racial and cultural
hybridity may be problematic. Being aware of this fact, and in an attempt to balance the usage of
the terms "mestizaje" and "mulatez," Latina theologian Ada María Isasi-Díaz and Latino biblical

of the great northern regions of Mexico, from California to Texas. The after-effects of these conquests continue to reverberate within the Mexican American psyche. Mexican American culture and consciousness continue to rest firmly upon the dynamics that unfolded during these two conquests. And what unfolds from this history of conquest is in every sense an ambiguity, for it at once grants the resources for the creation of a new being, a new race or mestizo/a people, and also "a site for wounding, a space for the exercise of power over others."[21] Indeed, to this very day, Mexican Americans/Chicanos continue to grapple with this site for wounding at the U.S. borderlands. As Gloria Anzaldúa puts it, in many respects this site continues to be a *"herida abierta* [open wound] where the third world grates against the first and bleeds."[22]

Quite possibly, Elizondo reflects, this wound has most afflicted Mexican Americans at the inner level of the self, and in the realm of signification, of symbolic culture. As he sees it, the worst aspect of these conquests was not the military defeat, not the natural and economic exploitation they effected, and not even the rape and enslavement of the people that followed. Manifesting his strong focus on the realm of symbolic culture and identity, Elizondo suggests that the most poisonous aspect of these conquests entailed the attempt to destroy the worldview, rituals, symbols, and the very means by which the conquered peoples sustained meaning in their existence: "Beneath the violence of physical conquest," he states, "there is the deeper violence of the disruption that destroys the conquereds' worldview, which gave cohesion and meaning to their existence."[23] And surely, wherever there occurs a disruption

---

scholar Fernando Segovia have taken to the use of both terms side by side ("mestizaje/mulatez"). This bifold signifier appears for the first time in Ada María Isasi-Díaz, *Mujerista Theology: A Theology for the Twenty-First Century* (Maryknoll, N.Y.: Orbis Books, 1996). To the best of my knowledge, Fernando Segovia was the first Latino theologian to make use of this more nuanced signifying designation. See his article, "Two Places and No Place on Which to Stand: Mixture and Otherness in Hispanic American Theology," *Listening: Journal of Religion and Culture* 27, no. 1 (winter 1992): 26-40. I regard this as a helpful and noble attempt on their part toward a more inclusive refinement. The predominant inclination, not only in Latino/a theology but also in Latino/a scholarship overall, however, continues to be that of using "mestizaje" in an all-encompassing manner in order to represent hybridity. Although my own preference is for the use of "mestizaje" and "mulatez" side by side, as Isasi-Díaz and Segovia employ them, I use "mestizaje" in the singular throughout this chapter because it is the term that Elizondo employs. Because Elizondo is the focus of my analysis here, I deem it necessary, for the sake of consistency in my presentation and interpretation of his work, to employ the terminology that he uses in his writings.

21 Friedman, *Mappings*, 97.

22 Anzaldúa, *Borderlands/La Frontera*, 4 (my translation).

23 Elizondo, *Galilean Journey*, 10.

in the realm of culture, in the region of symbolic action, one will also necessarily witness obstruction and perplexity in the province of existential identity. In the case of Mexican American history, this twofold disruption actually has taken place twice. As Elizondo acknowledges, this conquest narrative is
not a thing of the past, something merely to be read in our colonial history
books, because even in our so-called postcolonial era pressure continues to be
placed on Mexican Americans to assimilate, to abandon the Mexican way for
the "American" (WASP) way.[24]

Complicating matters further, Mexican Americans have also long confronted the hurtful biases that often accompany a mixed-race and culturally
hybrid identity, prejudices that have not yet completely disappeared. In light
of the widespread influence of Western racialism, and the hold that purist
ways of thinking about race have had in the Western world, the tendency in
our societies has been to speak of interracial and intercultural mixing mostly in derogatory terms. Human biological and cultural hybridity has varyingly been denigrated as the mongrelization of humanity; as the degeneration of
pure race or pure culture; and as a source of inferior beings and ghettoized
cultures. "Mestizaje seems to be one of the universal taboos," and those who
are mestizos have often been "looked down upon as half-breeds, as not fully
belonging."[25] To be sure, although there has been some change in both the law
and the culture of our nation, the concept of a multifaceted identity is still
not easily accepted in the dominant discourse of the United States. Our
national census forms, for instance, continue to equate multiple identity with
nonbeing, as they still do not allow people the opportunity to claim their
multiethnic or multiracial heritages. To claim and affirm an identity marked
by hybridity, therefore, one must still go against the grain. In view of all of
these pressures, Elizondo opts to place his attention firmly on the critical area
of culture and self-definition. Moreover, in the process of his own inner quest
and struggle he comes to the conclusion that the achievement of both an adequate resistance against cultural oppression and an affirming self-identity
inheres in the ability of the Mexican American/Latino to reclaim and live out
the radical potential that exists in a mestizo/a existence. Additionally, by
accepting their hybrid identities, Elizondo suggests, Mexican Americans may
actually "usher in new life" not only for themselves but also "for the betterment of everyone."[26] Briefly put, Elizondo's answer to the cultural hybridity

24 See especially Virgilio Elizondo, "A Bicultural Approach to Religious Education," *Religious Education* 76, no. 3 (1981): 258-70.

25 Elizondo, *The Future Is Mestizo*, 82.

26 Ibid., 84.

of his own Mexican American identity, and the physical, sociopolitical, and psychic pressures that have come with it, is a full embrace of the vulnerable yet transcendent and utopic "in-betweenness" that a mestizo/a existence offers; he fully undertakes in his theology a revaluing of mestizaje and an elucidation of the power embedded within it. Mestizo/a identity, as Elizondo conceives it, admits for much more than pain and dislocation; it is also a liminal space filled with potentiality, and is a prospective site of grace.

At this point, Elizondo's introspective journey takes a rather interesting turn toward Galilee, where he finds Jesus, the historical Jesus as presented by the Christian Scriptures. Specifically, what Elizondo discovers is Jesus' Galilean sociocultural identity, which provides him a powerful metaphor that could shed light not only on the ambiguity but also on the redemptive potential embedded in hybrid identities and, therefore, in Latino/a mestizaje. Yearning to uncover the transcendent potential that exists in the "third space" created by a mestizo/a existence—the positive synergy that lies waiting to be discovered within the dual or multiple identity of culturally hybrid persons—Elizondo draws an analogy between the mestizaje of Mexican Americans and that of the historical Jesus. The basic intention of his analogy is to elucidate both the abstruse evocations of rejection, pain, and spiritual searching that mestizaje evokes in a racially stratified social context, as well as the healing, indeed redemptive, transcendence that it holds for self and society.

Elizondo admits that the connection he came to find between the sociohistorical process of the twofold mestizaje of Mexican Americans and the sociohistorical identity and mission of Jesus came as a surprise to him. He never imagined, even as a long devout Catholic and seminary-trained theologian, that Jesus could have so much to offer to the Mexican American quest for positive identity. And he surmises that the reason he had not done so was that in all his years of Christian living and study he had never been introduced to Jesus' earthly identity, either in the church or in the seminary:

> His socio-cultural identity was simply passed by or idealized into a heavenly existence. The fullness of the Incarnation was not appreciated, and in many ways we Christians are still scandalized by just how human our God became. Through some kind of unidentified fear, the Western world and its theologians seem to have been afraid of dealing with the real earthly identity of Jesus. It is almost as if the West would like to say, "Confess Christ but forget Jesus," the real Jesus who walked our earth, ate our food, and suffered the injustices of our world.[27]

---

27 Ibid., 75.

Yet, Elizondo contends that the Christian gospels, and all of the teachings of our Christian tradition, take on a richer signification when Jesus' socio-cultural identity is taken into consideration and appreciated.

So who was this Jesus? And what was his earthly sociocultural identity? Elizondo points out that he was a Galilean Jew, a descendant of a town of Nazareth in the region known as Galilee. For Elizondo, what is noteworthy about the Galilee of Jesus' time is that it was a great border region between the Greeks and the Jews of Judea that also served as a natural crossing place for international travel routes. Galilee did not command much attention as a religious or intellectual center during Jesus' time, nor did it wield political power, but it was a cosmopolitan place that served as a crossroads for many diverse cultures. "It was," therefore, "a land of great mixture and of an ongoing *mestizaje*,"[28] where different cultures were continuously clashing, interweaving, and fusing to create new syncretic or hybrid cultural traditions. Elizondo points out that, whereas subsequent generations of Christians have glossed over Jesus' earthly identity, the early Christian communities highlighted Jesus' Galilean origin and gave it special significance, as evidenced by the fact that "it is mentioned sixty-one times in the New Testament."[29] He surmises that the significance attributed to Galilee and Jesus' Galilean provenance lies with the notoriety and stigma that came with its border status, with its reputation as a place where various forms of mestizaje were taking place.

Elizondo throws light on that Galilean mestizaje and then proceeds to point out its implications for Jesus' cultural identity and personal social status:

> At the time of Jesus, Galilee was peopled by Phoenicians, Syrians, Arabs, Greeks, Orientals, and Jews. In this mixed, commerce-oriented society, some Jews had allowed their Jewish exclusivism to weaken, but others became more militantly exclusivist. Some of the *goyim* (non-Jews) converted to Judaism and intermarried with Jews.... Religious ideas of other groups were also assimilated, as is evident in the case of the Essenes. A natural, ongoing biological and cultural *mestizaje* was taking place.[30]

This mestizaje, however, was not regarded favorably by the dominant social, cultural, and religious hierarchies of Jesus' time, Elizondo asserts. Galilean Jews were often doubly rejected as hybrid, and as border, persons.

---

28 Ibid., 77.
29 Elizondo, *Galilean Journey*, 49.
30 Ibid., 51.

They were, on the one hand, scorned by those Gentiles who despised Jews, and, on the other hand, "regarded with patronizing contempt by the 'pure-minded' Jews of Jerusalem":

> The natural *mestizaje* of Galilee was a sign of impurity and a cause for rejection. The Pharisees looked down upon "the people of the land" because they were ignorant of the law. The Sadducees looked down upon them because they were somewhat lax in matters of religious attendance and familiarity with the rules of temple worship[31]

Moreover, says Elizondo,

> The Galilean Jews spoke with a very marked accent and most likely mixed their language quite readily with the Greek of the dominant culture and the Latin of the Roman Empire. Peter could deny Jesus, but there was no way he could deny he was a Galilean. The moment he opened his mouth he revealed his Galilean identity.[32]

The point of Elizondo's excursion into the particulars of the historical Jesus is to describe the kind of racial and cultural hybridity that characterized Jesus' sociocultural identity and the pathologies of oppression that it faced. A biological and cultural mestizo identity was a source of ridicule and rejection in Jesus' time, just as it is today. As a child of doubtful birth origins, according to human standards, Jesus possibly was disparagingly considered to be a "halfbreed;"[33] and as a cultural mestizo who was born in Galilee, a hotbed for cultural fusion, he likely was culturally vilified as a deviant. It was no wonder, then, that the pure-minded Jews despised him and became indignant when Pilate proclaimed him king of the Jews. "A scandal to all the pious and the

---

31 Ibid.

32 Elizondo, *The Future Is Mestizo*, 77.

33 The reference here is to Elizondo's intimation that the idea of the miraculous conception of Jesus likely was doubted by many during Jesus' time. Because supposedly Mary and Joseph had not yet entered into marriage; because Jesus was conceived in Galilee, a land inhabited by many soldiers, during a time of Roman military control; and because rape has often gone hand in hand with military conquest historically, Elizondo suggests that many may have suspected that Jesus' biological father could have been a Roman soldier—assuming that Joseph's fatherhood was placed in question. Given the likelihood of such rumors, Jesus very likely had to deal with the hurtful stigma of being considered not only an illegitimate child but quite possibly also with the stigma of being a biologically mestizo child—a child of mixed race (i.e., Jewish and Gentile/Roman). For a non-Latino(a) source that speaks to this particular topic, see Bruce Chilton's *Rabbi Jesus: An Intimate Biography* (New York: Doubleday, 2000).

pure of society. How could such a one be their savior and king?"[34] Yet, as a Galilean Jew, he also was marginalized from the Roman political establishment and considered an outsider within the dominant "Gentile" cultural and intellectual mainstreams of his time. In short, as a mestizo, Jesus experienced firsthand the vulnerability that comes with a borderlands existence, the uneasy feeling of never being quite at home in any of the dominant cultural geographies of his time and, perhaps, on occasion not even in his own body. Elizondo puts it this way:

> When the Epistle to the Philippians says that Jesus became nothing, it is no mere figure of speech. In a very existential way, he became the nothing of all human groups—the *mestizo* whose existence is the nonexistence of permanent exclusion. No matter where you go or where you are, you are never fully accepted because you are the other.[35]

Although Jesus' mestizo identity undoubtedly was regarded with disfavor by most during his time, Elizondo emphasizes that it nevertheless was also a source of healing, indeed redemptive, transcendence. Jesus' beginnings in the highly mesticized environment of Galilee, Elizondo suggests, allowed him the opportunity to learn not just from his Jewish faith but also from the many other traditions that enriched his home territory. This provided fertile ground for the cultivation of an inner capacity in Jesus to move beyond the social and cultural borders of his time, and to break the barriers of separation that these engendered. Being at once an inside-outsider and an outside-insider to the cultural geographies of his time, Jesus inhabited an "in-between" space that uniquely privileged him to see and appreciate the best and worst of the cultures that prevailed in ancient Judea. It was in Galilee, Elizondo intimates, that Jesus first learned to juggle cultures, to develop a plural personality, in order to survive sanely; and it was through the process of this learning that he came to offer something new to his milieu: a mode of being that demonstrated a tolerance for contradictions and challenged the fixity of the delimiting human borders and categories of his time.

Moreover, Elizondo intimates that Jesus' identification with the most rejected of society, and the affinity that he demonstrated toward these people during his ministry, were at least in part the result of his mestizo origins and his own experience of rejection as a borderlands dweller. Having learned of

---

34 Ibid., 77.
35 Ibid., 80.

the virulent side of society's absolutes through his own marginalization and suffering as a mestizo, Jesus, Elizondo suggests, was better able to understand the virtue and indispensability of an inclusive sensibility and ministry. Encapsulating his intimations on Jesus' mestizo identity in the language of a traditional soteriology, Elizondo surmises,

> The apparent nonimportance and rejection of Galilee are the very bases for its all-important role in the historic eruption of God's saving plan for humanity. The human scandal of God's way does not begin with the cross, but with the historico-cultural incarnation of his Son in Galilee.... What the world rejects, God chooses as his very own.[36]

For Elizondo's purposes, then, it is of great consequence that in the Christian narrative of Jesus' life, ultimate redemption is shown to spring forth from the margins, and, more precisely, from the interstitial site that a mestizo/a experience generates. The core of the Christian *evangelium,* as Elizondo sees it, announces that "one of the marginated ones became the source of solidarity and messianic hope among the masses of hopeless people."[37]

The ultimate intention of Elizondo's tracing of Jesus' sociocultural identity is to draw an analogy between it and the Mexican American mestizo/a experience. Accordingly, therefore, his reflections in *Galilean Journey* and *The Future Is Mestizo* end with a comparison of Jesus' mestizo identity and the condition of Mexican American cultural identity today. "Being a Jew in Galilee," Elizondo writes, "was very much like being a Mexican-American in Texas." Just as the Jews of Galilee were "considered too Jewish to be accepted by the gentile population" and yet "too contaminated with pagan ways to be accepted by the pure-minded Jews of Jerusalem, so have the Mexican-Americans been rejected by two groups": the Anglos in America and the Mexicans in Mexico.[38] Yet, just as Jesus was divinely destined to generate new life from the margins, and just as he was able to come to terms with his status as an inside-outsider, Elizondo believes that similarly, Mexican Americans now find themselves in a unique position to advance a liberating mission not only for their own well-being but also for that of others. Reflecting on Mexican American mestizaje as a force for social good, Elizondo points out,

---

36 Elizondo, *Galilean Journey,* 53.
37 Elizondo, *The Future Is Mestizo,* 74.
38 Ibid., 77.

In the light of the Judeo-Christian tradition, the Mexican-American
experience of rejection and margination is converted from human
curse to the very sign of divine predilection.... It is in their margination from the centers of the various establishments that Mexican-
Americans live the Galilean identity today. Because they are inside-
outsiders, they appreciate more clearly the best of the traditions of
both groups, while also appreciating the worst of the situation of
both. It is precisely in this double identity that they have something
of unique value to offer both... As *mestizos* of the borderland
between Anglo America and Latin America, Mexican-Americans can
be instrumental in bringing greater appreciation and unity between
the peoples of the two Americas... The Mexican-American stands in
the midst of both worlds and what in effect appears an unfinished
identity can be the basis for personal understanding and appreciation
of two identities.[39]

The issue taken up by Elizondo is the struggle for positive identity among
Mexican Americans/Latinos and the creative defense of their cultures. The
goal is fully to help Mexican Americans, and Latino/as as a whole, to come to
terms with the racial and cultural hybridity that marks their identities; to
enable them to maintain their marginalized cultural traditions in the United
States; and to elucidate the uniqueness of that culture and identity.[40] Hence,
while Elizondo cursorily deals with issues related to geopolitics, race, national identity, and social analysis in his theological writings, he is chiefly concerned with the realm of self-identity and local culture, and particularly with
the preservation of a salutary self cultural identity among Mexican American
and Latino communities. Toward this end, he theorizes and employs the
notion of mestizaje as a construct that synchronously allows for the accentu-
ation of Mexican American/Latino cultural indistinction and syncretism, the
celebration of the racial and cultural hybridity found within Mexican
American/Latino identities, and the promotion of resistance against conceptions of self and culture that prejudicially privilege the colonizing West and
"white" Anglo-Saxonism. In sum, Elizondo's theological affinity to the concept of mestizaje demonstrates a fundamental privileging of matters of
Latino/a identity, culture, and cultural difference; thus, the area of struggle

---

39 Elizondo, *Galilean Journey*, 100.

40 Again, I must note that Elizondo's focus is particularly on the Mexican American situation. I am here alluding to Latino/as in general, however, because I believe that Elizondo's work
clearly has bearing for other Latino subcultures. Elizondo himself implies and/or allows for this
broader applicability in *The Future Is Mestizo*, esp. 87-111.

for Elizondo's Latino theology is principally the realm of self-identity and symbolic culture.

POPULAR RELIGION IN U.S. HISPANIC/LATINO THEOLOGY: ORLANDO ESPÍN'S *THE FAITH OF THE PEOPLE*

The concentrated concern with cultural affirmation and identity in Latino/a theology is revealed not only in the special role granted to the theorization of mestizaje in the writings of most Latino theologians, but also in the prominent status accorded to the study of U.S. Hispanic popular religion. This theological fascination with popular religion proceeds from the perception that it gives witness to a site of ongoing, albeit covert form of, Latino self-definition and communal resistance against assimilatory pressures in the United States. To put it plainly, Latino/a theologians perceive that the study of Hispanic popular religious expression may provide a window on one of the central ways that Latinos have attempted to maintain their marginalized cultural traditions and, thus, to take their identity back in the United States.

Scholars of "popular religion" are not of one mind about what this term stands for; it has several different and subtle definitions. The term "popular," however, has as its base the Latin word *populus*, a term that refers to people. Therefore, however it may be defined, popular religion always has something to do with "what ordinary people believe and practice and how they incorporate such into their own lives."[41] I propose that the term most generally denotes those sets of religious beliefs and practices that are either distinct from or, rather, not fully the product of religious specialists or of an elaborate "official" ecclesiastical organizational framework. What emerges from this particular definition is the sense that popular religions may in some instances exist alongside formal religious traditions, as in the case of popular forms of Christian Catholicism and Protestant Pentecostalism, whereas in others they can be very distinct from "officially" or "institutionally" sanctioned forms of religions, as it is with certain Afro-Caribbean, Native American, and other nativist based religions. Popular religion, then, as Charles Lippy observes, can be "related to organized religion as we usually think of it, but not equated with it." In sum, this widely encompassing term suggests "the ways in which individuals take religious belief, interpret it in practical terms, and put it to work to do something that will give order and meaning to their lives"[42] independently of the consent of theologians, priests, religious professionals, or ecclesiastical offices.

---

41 Charles Lippy, *Being Religious, American Style: A History of Popular Religiosity in the United States* (Westport, Conn.: Greenwood Press, 1994), 2.
42 Ibid., 2.

For the most part, students of popular religion have tended to view popular religious expression in individualistic and privatistic terms, emphasizing the way it manifests itself among isolated individuals without taking into account how popular religion may also represent a form of communal self-expression. One of the great contributions that Latino/a theologians have made to the study of popular religion is precisely their emphasis on the fact that popular religiosity can indeed be analyzed as a collective cultural entity. That is, these theologians have given prominence to the idea that popular religions can be common to a collective group of people and, therefore, may function to provide a base for the construction both of self-identities and the collective identity of a people. From this vantage point, Hispanic/Latino theologians see popular religion as a source that can contribute to and promote a salutary remembrance, defense, and celebration of cultural identity and difference—an undertaking that is deemed critical to the attainment of positive self-identity among Latinos.

The name of Virgilio Elizondo again looms large in the study of popular religion within the annals of U.S. Hispanic/Latino theology. In the felicitous words of Alex García-Rivera, who is in his own right an important interpreter of Latino/a popular religion, Elizondo was one of the first theologians "who found the possibility of a 'big story' in popular religion."[43] Unquestionably, it was Elizondo who first emphasized the importance of Hispanic popular religious expressions, and then elucidated a method by which to read them as signs of an ongoing cultural and identity struggle among U.S. Latinos. Yet, although Elizondo was the first Hispanic theologian to turn to popular religion as a potential source of self-definition and cultural resistance, other theologians also have come to gain notice for their exceptional work in the interpretation of popular religion. One of these theologians is Orlando Espín, a Cuban Catholic theologian. His work on Hispanic/Latino popular religion, and especially on Latino/a popular Catholicism,[44] has come to attain a sort of

---

43 García-Rivera, *St. Martin de Porres*, 11.

44 The term "Latino/a popular Catholicism" refers to an exhaustive series of nativist, populist-based, yet Catholic-suffused, devotions that are pervasive among U.S. Latino/as and have emerged specifically from the Latino/a people. The term basically denotes the specific form that Catholic Christianity assumes among Latinos and Latinas. One of the distinguishing marks of this Catholicism—herein referred to as "Latino popular Catholicism"—is its syncretic mestizo/a character. Among Latino/as, Catholicism is often fused with other Amerindian (i.e., Aztec, Maya, Inca, Taino, Siboney, Caribe, etc.) and African cultural and religious traditions. The mingling of Spanish Catholicism with religious understandings and practices of Amerindian and African roots among Latino/as is what is generally referred to as Latino popular Catholicism. The designation signifies a wide array of Latino Catholic devotions, rites, practices, and celebrations. These are too numerous to name here, but some prominent examples

paradigmatic status among Latino/a theologians, in large part because of its systematic quality, polemical style, and willingness to propose clear theoretical positions on the interpretation of U.S. popular religion. Espín's enthusiastic projections of popular religion as a site of cultural resistance and identity struggle make him an especially ideal subject for the specific examination I have undertaken here. Hence, to explore the significance of popular religion for the goal of Hispanic identity and cultural affirmation in Latino/a theology, I turn now to Espín's *The Faith of the People*.[45]

---

include (1) devotions to a host of *vírgenes*, such as *La Virgen de Guadalupe* (Our Lady of Guadalupe) and *La Virgen de la Caridad* (Our Lady of Charity); (2) devotions to patron saints such as *San Martín de Porres* and *Santa Bárbara*; (3) a series of festivities and practices that include *Las Posadas* (festivities in honor of the nine months that Mary carried Jesus in her womb), *Nochebuena* (which is part of the wider Advent cycle), *Miércoles de Ceniza* (Ash Wednesday), *El Día de los Muertos* (the Day of the Dead), the *Quinceañeras* ceremonies celebrated during the fifteenth birthday of Latinas, *Los Rosarios* (the rosaries practiced during funerals), *Las Fiestas Patronales* (patron saints celebrations), and a host of *Procesiones* (processions practiced throughout the year); and (4) common expressions of faith such as *Si Dios Quiere* ("If God wills"), *Que Diosito te acompañe y te ayude* ("May God accompany and help you"), and *El hombre pone pero Dios es el que dispone* ("Man proposes, but it is God who disposes"). The majority of Espín's reflections are focused on this particular expression of popular religiosity, particularly because he believes (and I agree) that popular Catholicism remains the most pervasive form of religion among Latinos. Nevertheless, his theorizations clearly are meant to extend to Latino/a popular religion in general. Besides popular expressions of Catholicism, Latino popular religion also includes Protestant variables that take on certain specificity among Latinos such as Latino Pentecostalism, and what may be called *La Iglesia Electrónica* (the electronic church). Other forms of non-Christian, or at least less explicitly Christian, Latino popular religion include *Santería, Palo, Espiritismo* (types of spiritism), and *Curanderismo* (types of native healing practices and rituals).

45 Orlando O. Espín, *The Faith of the People: Theological Reflections on Popular Catholicism* (Maryknoll, N.Y.: Orbis Books, 1997). This book gathers most, or at least the most important, of Espín's writings on Latino/a popular religion and popular Catholicism and is, therefore, the best source for an exploration of his theories on the subject. For other studies of Hispanic popular religion within Latino/a theology, see especially Aponte, "*Coritos* as Active Symbol"; Ada María Isasi-Díaz, *En La Lucha/In the Struggle: Elaborating a Mujerista Theology* (Minneapolis: Fortress Press, 1993), esp. 45-52; Virgilio Elizondo, *La Morenita: Evangelizer of the Americas* (San Antonio, Tex.: The Mexican American Cultural Center, 1980); idem, "Popular Religion as the Core of Cultural Identity in the Mexican American Experience," in *An Enduring Flame: Studies on Latino Popular Religiosity*, ed. Anthony Stevens-Arroyo and Ana María Díaz-Stevens (New York: PARAL, 1994), 113-32; idem, *Guadalupe: Mother of the New Creation* (Maryknoll, N.Y.: Orbis Books, 1997); Orlando Espín, "Popular Catholicism among Latinos," in *Hispanic Catholic Culture in the U.S.: Issues and Concerns*, ed. Jay Dolan and Allan Figueroa Deck (Notre Dame, Ind.: Notre Dame University Press, 1994), 308-59; Roberto Goizueta, *Caminemos con Jesus: Toward a Hispanic/Latino Theology of Accompaniment* (Maryknoll, N.Y.: Orbis Books, 1995), esp. chs. 2 and 5; Paredes, "Popular Religiosity"; García-Rivera, *St. Martin de Porres*; Jeannette Rodríguez, *Our Lady of Guadalupe: Faith and Empowerment among Mexican-American Women*

Espín's interpretations of popular religion are fundamentally grounded in one orienting conviction. According to Espín, regardless of their cultural differences, one common experience binds all Latinos: they are all here, Espín maintains, "as the result of vanquishment." To explain this assertion he writes,

> Some Latino groups are the result of the rape of their ancestors by the conquering Spaniards, while others are the outcome of willing *mestizaje*. There are communities that trace their roots back to the violence of the *encomienda* and others to the violence of the African slave trade. Many were here when the United States militarily conquered and illegally expropriated their land in the nineteenth century. Still others came because they had become the losing victims of political and economic struggles in other lands. But in *all* cases, the Latino cultural communities are here as the result of vanquishment, of having become the losing victim's of someone else's victory. All of the communities (Mexican-American, Puerto Rican, Cuban-American, etc.) are distinct, with their own histories and cultures, as well as with the shared elements of language, religious symbols, and worldview. Yet, behind all the distinctions, and even divisions, there lies this common experience of vanquishment that—however they might explain it—does bind them together.... Latinos are in the United States as the vanquished. And the dominant Euro-American culture treats them as such.[46]

It is from this vantage point that Espín claims popular religion as a means for opposition to cultural oppression and as a device for the establishment of positive self-identity and social identity among Latinos. "Popular religion," Espín submits, "allows its practitioners to discover power there where hegemonic ideology had veiled the possibilities for self-determination. Instead of utter powerlessness, through popular religion's symbols, the people can

---

(Austin: University of Texas Press, 1994); idem, *Stories We Live/Cuentos Que Vivimos: Hispanic Women's Spirituality* (New York: Paulist Press, 1996); and finally, although from more of a sociological than theological perspective, see also the articles in Stevens-Arroyo and Díaz-Stevens, eds., *An Enduring Flame*. Although each of these studies demonstrates its own subtleties, the assumption that popular religion becomes for Latino/as in the lower social strata a means of establishing a positive cultural and social identity is common to all. In my view, however, Espín is the author who most clearly articulates a generalized theory for this position.
    46 *The Faith of the People*, 21.

define themselves as empowered."[47] Popular religion, then, as Espín argues, provides oppressed Latino/as a clandestine yet subversive vehicle by which they can attain meaning and hope. Undergirding Espín's thought here is the sense that in an oppressive context, rarely will the resistance of a disenfranchised people take on direct or overt forms. Rather, oppressed peoples have often taken to the domain of symbolic activity to oppose marginalization and to defend their dignity. Whether through the use of semantic reversals, the fusion of different forms of belief and practices, or the preservation of autochthonous icons and symbols, disempowered groups have frequently turned to culture and spirituality as an insidious conveyor of counteraction and communal self-expression.[48] Espín has creatively integrated this insight into his reading of Latino/a popular Catholicism, viewing it as a prominent, though covert, site both of cultural resistance and self-affirmation for Latino/as in the United States. Espín writes,

> Popular Catholicism is the "shape" that Latino Christianity, doubly vanquished in history, found most meaningful for the affirmation and survival of its cultural identity and of its faith heritage and life... Latino Popular Catholicism can be characterized as an effort by the subaltern to explain, justify, and somehow control a social reality that appears too dangerous to confront in terms and through means other than the mainly symbolic. However, this popular religion is founded on the claim that the divine (identified by the people as the Christian divine) has been and is encountered by them in and through the symbols (ritual, ethical, and doctrinal) of popular Catholicism.[49]

Two interconnected goals lie at the heart of Espín's work on popular religion. On the one hand, as a theologian, he endeavors to defend popular religious expression, and in particular Latino/a popular Catholicism, as a legitimate site of faith and authentic religious form that mediates the triune Christian God and can, therefore, be deemed a principal resource for Christian theology. On the other hand, his desire is to demonstrate how Latino popular Catholicism operates as a province for the protection and

---

47 Ibid., 169.

48 Henry Louis Gates Jr. provides an excellent analysis of this mode of resistance among African Americans in *The Signifying Monkey: A Theory of Afro-American Literary Criticism* (New York: Oxford University Press, 1988). For a first-rate sampling of cultural forms of struggle among Latinos in the United States, see Fusco, *English Is Broken Here*.

49 Espín, *The Faith of the People*, 58, 92.

affirmation of culture and identity. In regard to the first of these symbiotic, yet distinct, aims, Espín comments that popular religion has too frequently been considered as a source of shame or as a blemish to Catholicism. "It has," Espín remarks, "been derided as the superstitious result of religious ignorance, a product of syncretism, a vestige of the rural past, and an ideologically manipulated tool in the hands of those who would abuse simple folk."[50] While he does not dismiss the fact that some of these charges do provide reason for concern in certain situations, Espín contends that there is much more to popular religion than what these simplistic dismissals convey.

Popular Catholicism, Espín argues, can actually be theologically understood as "a cultural expression of the *sensus fidelium*"[51] Here, Espín's reference is to a rather underexplored and undisclosed tradition within Catholicism that places attention on the living witness and faith of the Christian people; his basic intention in excavating and assigning great consequence to this tradition is to infuse the "faith-full" intuition of the common Christian practitioner with as much credence as the written texts of institutional Catholicism. He puts it this way:

> The whole Church has received the revelation of God and accepted it in faith. And, as a consequence, the whole Church is charged with proclaiming, living, and transmitting the fullness of revelation. Therefore, the necessary task of expressing the contents of scripture and Tradition are not and cannot be limited to the ordained ministers of the Church. The whole Church has this mission, and the Spirit was promised to the whole Church for this task. Members of the Christian laity, consequently, are indispensable witnesses and bearers of the gospel—as indispensable as the magisterium of the Church.[52]

In short, according to Espín, the living intuition, witness, and faith of the people, in this case mediated through their culturally infused popular religious expressions, are as inspired and valid as are the written documents and texts of the church's magisterium. And, in view of this premise, Espín proposes that Latino/a popular Catholicism may be regarded as "the culturally possible expression of some fundamental intuitions of the Christian faith."[53]

This theorem brings us to the second of Espín's goals: his attempt to interpret popular Catholicism as a site of cultural resistance and identity

---

50 Ibid., 63.
51 Ibid., 64.
52 Ibid., 66.
53 Ibid., 68.

affirmation. Here again, Espín's theorizations are sufficiently nuanced to incorporate some of the possible oppositions or skepticisms toward popular religiosity. He acknowledges, for instance, that popular religion has frequently appeared to function as a compassionate sedative to injustice among oppressed peoples. He also points out, however, that for Latinos, as with other subordinated groups, it has acted as an important preserver of dignity, positive identity, and hope. With respect to this conviction, Espín writes,

> Today's Latino popular Catholicism still bears the marks of its history, of its Iberian roots, and of the traumatic conquest of Amerindians and African slaves by Christians. It still displays, often through powerful symbols, the expressions of the despair of the vanquished and of their hope for justice.... Religious in expression, content, and experience, this language has long been the code through which hope and courage have been shared and maintained as plausible by generations of Latinos. Fundamental cultural values have found their place in and their medium of dissemination through popular religion. Lastly, and perhaps ultimately more importantly, popular Catholicism embodies a rebellious hope by its very existence as religion. If ... religion is the socialization of the experience of the divine, and if in Latino Catholicism the divine is identified with the Christian divine, then this religion of the subaltern claims that the *Christian* God is to be found in and through the culture and experiences of those considered insignificant by American society and Church.[54]

Espín fleshes out and substantiates his claim for the culture and identity-preserving properties of Latino/a popular Catholicism by pointing to various historical examples. He contends that during independence movements in the Spanish colonial period, it was the popular version of Catholicism that served as the religion of the Hispanic proponents of independence. "It became commonplace," Espín writes, "to find the symbols of popular Catholicism used as gathering banners for the people against Spain."[55] He also correctly points out that the symbols of popular Catholicism have prominently appeared and been associated with some of the most recent and important social and political movements among U.S. Hispanics. "The *Vírgenes* of Hispanic popular Catholicism," Espín reminds us, "have appeared prominently in gatherings, publications, and even on neighborhood walls,

---

54 Ibid., 103.
55 Ibid., 134.

where cultural identity and pride are consciously emphasized." Furthermore, "The United Farm Workers have proudly and frequently displayed images of the Virgin of Guadalupe and of the Virgin of San Juan de los Lagos," and Cuban Americans "have been emphasizing the Virgin of Charity as a unifying cultural (and political) symbol since the 1960s."[56] These "Virgin" symbols, along with the plethora of *Santos* and other popular religious practices and devotions that are so much a part of Latino/a life, seemingly point to the importance of popular Catholicism and other forms of autochthonous spiritualities as a means to safeguard and affirm the distinctiveness of Latino/a cultures and identities in the United States.

All of these religiously imbued forms of communal cultural expressions have continued to live on among the different U.S. Latino/a communities in spite of their ancient heritages, and despite both the availability of many other "official" or "mainstream" religious persuasions and of many efforts to suppress these expressions. Espín posits that one of the reasons for their longevity and continued relevance can be found in their functioning as a form of "epistemology of suffering." That is to say, Espín believes that popular Catholicism is one of the most fundamental ways through which Latinos have attempted to understand, deal with, and make sense of their sufferings, particularly those that stem from human moral evil. To support this position, Espín draws attention to the ubiquity of the "suffering Jesus" portraits among Latino communities, and he suggests that for Latinos, this portraiture conveys the idea that "just as Jesus has endured victimization but not been ultimately conquered, so will their suffering not lead them to be *only* victims at the end." Espín also points out that the symbols of popular Catholicism mostly tend to portray God as provident not in a conquering way, but rather, in a radically caring one. "The God sensed through these symbols," he offers, "is not the powerful, conquering divinity of the victorious and successful, but a parental (maternal!), familial, communal God whose providence is encouragement and support, shared suffering and quiet determination, and final justice-building." Espín reads Latino/a popular Catholicism, as a whole, as "an active creation of symbols and means to foster hope, to sustain communal solidarity, and to prepare for the alternative"[57]

In sum, Espín believes that Latino/a popular Catholicism, and Latino/a popular religious expression as a whole, serves as a conveyor of a history suppressed by the dominant Anglo culture and as a surreptitious medium for cultural resistance and hope. That is to say, Espín believes that the insistence

---

56 Ibid., 155.
57 Ibid., 26.

on preserving these particular, culturally embedded forms of Catholicism points to one of the ways that U.S. Hispanics have attempted both to maintain their marginalized cultural traditions and to defend, affirm, or reconstruct their unique identities in a hopeful manner. In these popular religious practices and devotions, he surmises, we find, "echoes of the creative defense of"[58] Latino/a cultures and identities among U.S. Hispanics.

PLAYING "BEYOND" SYMBOLIC CULTURE, IDENTITY POLITICS, AND DIFFERENCE: THE NEED FOR A PUBLIC THEOLOGY

Where, then, have these interpretive excursions taken us in regard to the understanding of U.S. Hispanic/Latino theology? They have brought us, I hope, to a better appreciation and recognition of the commitment to the theorization of symbolic culture, identity, and cultural difference found in that theology. The underlying pursuit of the enthusiastic theorizations of mestizaje, popular religion, and popular Catholicism found in the work of Virgilio Elizondo and Orlando Espín, and more broadly throughout Latino/a theology, is a defense, celebration, and reconstruction of cultural traditions and identities. Latino theological scholarship as a whole is driven by this fervor to promote cultural affirmation and the achievement of positive self-identity and group identity among Latino/as in the United States. The recurrent references to mestizaje and popular religion in the annals of Hispanic/Latino theology provide ubiquitous examples of this strong, overarching focus.

The overall enchantment with matters of self-identity and cultural identity in Latino/a theology transpires within a social ambiance in the United States wherein Latino cultures and identities have been barraged and threatened by racist stereotypes and a prevailing nationalist dogma bent on the assimilation of all non-Anglo cultures. Thus, the gravitation in that theological scholarship toward a paradigm of cultural and identity recognition, and what Henrietta Moore calls "a passion for difference,"[59] has been not only legitimate but also necessary. Indeed, for Latino/as, just as with other subordinated U.S. groups that have been largely deprived of recognition, respect, and meaningful power, it has been important to devote attention to the defense and celebration of local cultures and identities for the attainment of some measure of community-based political empowerment.

---

58 I borrow these choice words from Fusco, *English Is Broken Here*, 35.

59 See Henrietta L. Moore, *A Passion for Difference: Essays in Anthropology and Gender* (Bloomington: Indiana University Press, 1994).

Latino/a theologians have made enormous contributions to this important endeavor of cultural theorizing, as well as to the overall identification of
cultural difference, the assertion of self-identity and group identity, and the
promotion of a politics of recognition among Latinos. It is greatly unfortunate that these efforts remain largely underappreciated and unrecognized in
the wider academia, society, and church. I hold that Latino/a theology should
be lauded for its fine contributions not only to theological scholarship but
also to the cause of cultural justice in the United States. Yet, precisely because
I feel personally responsible to contribute to the maturation of Latino/a theology, and because I note that its ultimate longing is to discursively contribute to nothing less than the liberation of Latino/a life and the overall
cause of social justice in the United States, I declare my sentiment that now is
the proper time for Latino/a theologians to engage not only the possibilities
but also the ambiguities, contradictions, and even limitations that inhere in
the discursive paradigm of identity and cultural recognition that has so
enthusiastically been embraced by them. Latino/a theology has tended to
focus predominantly on discussions of symbolic culture, identity, and subjectivity, and has, therefore, given too little attention to the critical scrutiny of
the multifaceted matrices that impinge upon the realization of a broader, dis-
tinctively progressive, political project and energy. And I suspect that this
inadvertency stems from the lack of a "public perspective"—a discursive outlook that critically reflects on the social whole and the conditions for comprehensive and equitable human interconnectedness in a given society.

To be sure, there is a sense in which the wider cultural project of theorizing hybridity and syncretism that subsumes, yet extends beyond, Elizondo's
and Espín's work has hinted at a broader sociopolitical significance. In the
postcolonial rendering of Homi Bhabha, for instance, hybridity and/or
hybrid identity is ideally envisioned as a possible "third space" of communication and negotiation that could form a bridge for broader connectivity and,
thus, for coalitional activity in politics and society.[60] Similarly, Mary Louise
Pratt integrates the notion of "in-between-ness" conjured up by the terms
hybridity and syncretism with the goal of cross-communication between
speakers of different ideological and cultural languages.[61] In the work of these
authors, then, the interpretation of what is variously called syncretism,
hybridity, creolization, mestizaje, mulatez, and even the popular points to an
integral yearning for cross-cultural interaction and for the cultivation of anti-
colonial and liberating coalitions.

---

60 See Homi Bhabha, "The Third Space," and *The Location of Culture* (London: Routledge, 1994).
    61 See Mary Louise Pratt, *Imperial Eyes: Travel Writing and Transculturation* (London: Routledge,
1992).

These widely embracing and coalitional emphases, though implied, are not as salient or central in Elizondo's theological rendering of Latino/a mestizaje and Espín's decipherment of Latino/a popular religion. Despite the fact that Elizondo alludes to the hope that the proliferation of mestizo/a identities may lead to new human unity,[62] and despite the fact that Espín's implied hope is that "by rooting himself in the particularity of the lived faith of his own U.S. Latino community he will be able to speak to the larger community,"[63] neither Elizondo nor Espín proffers an explicit relational narrative that could help us to navigate across the boundaries of gender, race, cultural, ethnic, sexual, class, and religious lines of difference that abound in our sociopolitical milieu and that occasionally complicate the possibilities for real social change. This lack stems from their inability to break out of a specifically Hispanic/Latino localism. To put it plainly, although Elizondo's theology of mestizaje and Espín's hermeneutics of popular religion help us to specify and even to complicate the internal space of Latino/a culture, identity, and difference, they do not offer much help in preparing us to journey beyond this circumscribed space in order to cultivate the sort of narratives and social arrangements that could form the basis for a coalitional politics based on parallel experience, shared uncertainty, and common need—the kind of journey that is essential for real change in society.[64]

Fundamentally, the discourse of Elizondo and Espín, like that of hybridity and identity politics generally, is centered on symbolic culture and identity. Elizondo's preoccupation, for instance, is mostly with the inner life of the Mexican American self and community, and with the struggle of that self and community to cultivate positive identity amidst adversity and experiences of oppression based on difference. Espín's preoccupation is mostly to demonstrate how Latinos and Latinas in the United States have taken to symbolic activity to oppose cultural marginalization and to defend their identities and dignity, deploying Latino popular Catholicism in particular as a province for the protection and affirmation of culture and identity. In both cases, the aim is to describe and counter injustices that are rooted in social

---

62 See especially Elizondo, *The Future Is Mestizo*, 100-102.

63 See Roberto Goizueta's foreword to Espín, *The Faith of the People*, xiv.

64 For a thoughtful discussion of the suggestion I make on the importance of genuine connection between different kinds of people for real social change, and the possibilities of alliances based on parallel experience and need, see June Jordan, "Report from the Bahamas," in *On Call: Political Essays* (Boston, Mass.: South End Press, 1985), 39-54. In order to provide a basis for cross-cultural connectivity and a coalitional politics across difference, Jordan suggests, "The ultimate connection must be the need that we find between us. It is not only who you are, in other words, but what we can do for each other that will determine the connection" (p. 47).

patterns of representation, interpretation, and communication, and that have been experienced by Latino/as. The area of struggle for both Elizondo and Espín is, in other words, the interior space of the self, of identity, of culture—in short, the realm of symbolic order. For all of their emancipatory inklings, then, the theological projects of both authors are mostly limited to the destabilizing of colonized culture and the achievement of cultural and identity recognition, reconstruction, and affirmation. Neither project engages in broad-based sociopolitical theorizing, and neither tenders comprehensive analyses that deal with challenges and injustices rooted in the political and economic structuring of society—in the realm of "material culture." Moreover, neither author proffers a discursive framework that brings into consideration the exigency, possibility, and desirability of a galvanizing public perspective that seeks to grasp and transform the social whole. Yet, given the multiple and intersecting injustices experienced by Latino/as and other persons and groups in our society, the multiplication of social antagonisms, and the fissuring of emancipatory social movements in the United States, our theologies must seek to cultivate a more holistic and public disposition and perspective.

Certainly, Hispanic/Latino theology is not a homogeneous and static body of work. Hence, there are limitations to the applicability of my critique here. That is to say, the tendency to focus one-sidedly on culture, identity, and local or specific positionality at the expense of a wider sense of the public, and to the neglect of an equally mature scrutiny of the multifaceted matrices that impinge upon the realization of a broader emancipatory political project, is more tangible in some Latino/a theologies than it is in others.

However, there are currents and developments within Hispanic/Latino theology that evidence movements toward what I consider to be a wider public disposition and vision. The mujerista theology of Ada María Isasi-Díaz, for instance, recognized from very early on the importance of alliance with feminists across the spectrum and especially with womanists. Because of the many dangers faced by Latinas, women of color, and/or poor and working-class women—sexism, racism, classism, and so on—Latina theologians such as Isasi-Díaz have acknowledged the importance of an interstitial perspective all along.[65] This multivalent approach to social justice and this desire for alliance building point toward a wider sense of the public that emerges from, yet also reaches beyond, a particular cultural location.

---

65 See Ada María Isasi-Díaz, "Round Table Discussion: Mujeristas, Who We Are and What We Are About," *Journal of Feminist Studies in Religion* 8, no.1 (spring 1992): 105-25, and *Mujerista Theology*, esp. 86-127.

Additionally, the project of theorizing Latino/a mestizaje and popular religion, which is so central to Virgilio Elizondo's and Orlando Espín's theology in particular and to Hispanic/Latino theology in general, itself offers a premise for the wider construction of the public. In its focus upon hybridity and syncretism, it draws the notion of culture into a wider purview and discourse that could aid in the apprehension of the broader social public. By viewing Latino/a mestizaje and popular religion as a hybrid and heterogeneous cultural construction characterized by problems specific to postcolonial societies, these theologians offer interpretations of cultural identity that are expansive, interactive, integrative, and, therefore, potentially conducive to a sense of the wider public. Thus, inasmuch as it is genuinely understood as a dynamic and border-transgressive concept, the very notion of culture can function to burst the boundaries of a more restrictive analysis of context and to anticipate the possibility of a broader public entity.

The project of theorizing culture and cultural particularity need not be viewed, then, as an impediment to the conceptualization of the public or to the realization of publicness—that is, as long as the idea of culture is not construed in a constrictive manner and centered on a foundationalist identity politics that surrenders the possibility of a wider public voice and vision to a bounded notion of community. At the same time, it is important that the construct of culture not be isolated from the ongoing social processes that produce it, nor that it be construed as a preconstituted force that is either passively internalized or always freely generated by persons. Rather, culture should be viewed as "something created and recreated in the 'material' social interactions of which it is an integral part."[66] Along these lines, projects of the exploration and expression of cultural meaning should be more clearly connected to an emancipatory political program that engages with broader problems of economic, social, and political ordering. Such a move would further the aim of social change. Finally, the theorizing of cultural and ethnic identity need not be concerned only with understanding the characteristics shared by members of a particular group, but also with the dialectical relationship between those within that group and those outside of it. What this requires is the development of relational accounts that focus on the interaction between identities of different groups in society and help to capture "the way in which any efforts to define the others defines oneself and vice versa."[67] These sorts

66 Kathryn Tanner, *Theories of Culture: A New Agenda for Theology* (Minneapolis: Fortress Press, 1997), 50-51.

67 Jorge J. E. Gracia and Pablo De Greiff, "Hispanic/Latino Ethnicity, Race, and Rights: An Introduction," in *Hispanic/Latinos in the United States: Ethnicity, Race, and Rights*, ed. Jorge J. E. Gracia and Pablo De Greiff (New York: Routledge, 2000), 18.

of accounts of identity would help us to steer away from the definition of cultural difference in terms of boundaries separating self-contained cultures and, thus, to allow for possible overlap, interspersal, and interdependence among distinct culturally defined social groups and their members—an allowance that could foster greatly needed pluralistic collaboration. When construed in relational terms, the distinctiveness of cultural identity "is not a matter of 'us' vs. 'them.' Cultural identity becomes, instead, something that lives between as much as within cultures."[68]

The point is, however, first, that there are tendencies already evident within Hispanic/Latino theology that hint at a wider public entity and meaning, and second, that the very theorizing of culture demands—if not yet in ways evident to many Latino/a theologians—the development of a conception of public space. The theorizing of the wider concept of the public can actually be seen as a natural and necessary next development of the theorizing of cultural identity in Latino/a theology. That is, the notion of culture as a dynamic, hybrid, border-transgressive, and even relational concept necessarily calls for serious engagements in theory and in practice with the concept and reality of the public. The contribution of the concept of publicness and/or public space to the theorization of culture and identity would be at once to heighten awareness of the zone in which social, political, economic, and even cultural issues intersect; to promote recognition of the impact that both the presence of and the low regard for the struggles of particular culturally defined constituencies can have on the life of the social whole; to encourage a concern for the quality of our lives together by helping individuals and groups to understand themselves as part of a potentially wider public; and to nurture coalitional energies in civil society.

Given my postulation of the possible intersection of the theorizing of cultural identity and the concept of the public, it should be clear that nowhere is this project motivated by the desire to invalidate Latino/a theological scholarship's commitment to a general cultural politics of recognition that depends on identity-based claims in its call for justice. My desire is simply and more precisely this: that Latino/a theology diversify and amplify its mode of address and recognize the exigency in our contemporary "postsocialist"[69] moment for liberatory discourses that can adequately integrate

---

68 Tanner, *Theories of Culture*, 57.

69 For the use of this term and a full explanation of the notions it conveys, see Nancy Fraser, *Justice Interruptus: Critical Reflections on the "Postsocialist" Condition* (New York: Routledge, 1997), esp. 1-8, 11-39, 173-88. I should clarify here, however, that Fraser uses this term to reflect critically on the general parameters within which leftist political thought and activism has moved, especially in the wake of 1989 (i.e., following the alleged delegitimization of socialism

cultural and identity projects into a wider publicist perspective and move-ment. And, in turn, it is my hope that this humble and prolegomenic invita-tion may help Latino/a theology, first, to more ably speak of and to the broad-er challenges that a comprehensive project for social justice confronts in an increasingly stratified and fragmentalized U.S. social context, and second, to gain a "public" voice.

There are four salient challenges that the present theological enchant-ment with a discursive paradigm of symbolic culture, identity, and cultural recognition confronts, and that point to the need for the conceptualization of Latino/a theology as a form of translocal and transcultural "public" dis-course. In discussing these four, I wish to suggest that the time has come for Latino/a theologians to play "beyond" symbolic culture, identity, and cultur-al difference, not by a thorough dismissal or obliteration of these matters, but rather, through a careful supplementation that plays up those interstitial sites of interaction, interconnection, and exchange in our society and keeps alive the utopic hope of comprehensive and equitable public goals.[70]

---

after the collapse of the Berlin Wall). Three constitutive features, according to her, have marked recent leftist and/or liberationist critical, social, and political thought: (1) there is no credible overarching emancipatory project despite the proliferation of fronts of struggle; (2) the cultur-al politics of recognition has been divorced from the social politics of redistribution; and (3) claims for equality have been de-centered in the face of aggressive market forces and sharply ris-ing material inequality. Overall, we have seen that the struggle for local cultural recognition has fast become the paradigmatic form of political conflict, at times eclipsing a more general, inte-grative, comprehensive socialist project of liberation. I note that the discursive and practical end result of these tendentious practices has been an at-times unperceived restriction of the mean-ing of injustice/justice and oppression/liberation to the cultural or symbolic realm. I believe that Fraser's critical diagnosis of contemporary left-wing social and political thought is accu-rate, and, therefore, that it appropriately serves as a framework for questioning the political imagination that has lately prevailed.

70 For a long time I have been struggling on my own to find an appropriately nuanced the-ological and political grammar that would permit me to criticize the current decoupling of the cultural from the social that is prevalent in identity-based discourses without engaging in a facile dismissal of these. It has only been recently that I have found writings, other than Cornel West's, that are especially akin to my concerns and interests. Specifically, the works of Nancy Fraser and Susan Friedman have proven extremely valuable, particularly Fraser's *Justice Interruptus* and Friedman's *Mappings*. I believe that I am attempting to accomplish in theology what Nancy Fraser, in political philosophy and critical theory, and Susan Friedman, in feminist and cultural studies, are undertaking in their respective fields. Thus, I feel a certain kinship for the works of these authors. Cornel West's "prophetic pragmatism" has also been propitious for my thought process. See especially his description of this perspective in *The American Evasion of Philosophy: A Genealogy of Pragmatism* (Madison: University of Wisconsin Press, 1989). I am greatly indebted to Catherine Keller for introducing me to Susan Friedman's work; I have also benefited from discussions with her and indeed from her own work. See Catherine Keller, *From

The first challenge that Latino/a theologians must acknowledge and appropriately deal with involves the emergence, in the late 1980s and 1990s, of public conversations that highlight the fragmentation, and even balkanization, of the U.S. social context and, therefore, cast a negative light on local identity-based discourses. These recent discussions have again brought the debate on national and civic identity to the fore by warning of a dangerous erosion of civil society in the United States. Besides taking issue with the spread of corrosive forms of individualism, an apparent absence of public goals, a seemingly growing apathy toward civic and political participation, and the fraying of communities and moral traditions, these public discourses have particularly targeted the "multiculturalization" of the United States and the rise of culture- and identity-based politics. Hence, as we stand some thirty years from the great ethnic enlightenment movements of the 1960s, and just into a new century and new millennium, we are now being forced to reconsider the proliferation of multiple constituencies and the place for a politics of recognition in our society. And, even as our nation continues to grapple with the comprehension of its rich inner cultural diversity, some have recently argued that to our detriment we have become a profoundly fragmented society. Exploiting this concern with social fragmentation, certain conservatives have taken to the attack on liberal and leftist causes that historically have been aligned with the defense and celebration of cultural diversity in our nation. The result, in some circles, has once again been the promulgation of an ill-founded and hurtful xenophobia that has at times blossomed into reactionary movements that aim to strip away some of the gains achieved by earlier social movements for civil rights and recognition.

The issue has been raised in a less antagonistic, certainly more well-intentioned, but not completely satisfactory manner by various liberal scholars and sociopolitical commentators. Whether in the form of jeremiads over the rise of *Habits of the Heart* that corrode the sustainment of notions of communal commitment and citizenship in our society, warnings of the dangers inherent in the *Twilight of Common Dreams,* or calls for the renewal of a *Spirit of Community* to offset a "severe case of deficient we-ness in America," liberal commentators have often implied that the achievement of common aspirations, effective political alliances, and any notion of a mass

---

a Broken Web: Separation, Sexism, and Self (Boston: Beacon Press, 1986), and "Seeking and Sucking: On Relation and Essence in Feminist Theology," in *Horizons in Feminist Theology: Identity, Tradition, and Norms,* ed. Rebecca Chopp and Sheila Greeve Davaney (Minneapolis: Fortress Press, 1997), 54-78.

egalitarian movement requires the confinement, if not the outright dismissal, of particularistic group self-assertions.[71]

These recent discussions point to legitimate concerns that must be critically examined. Nevertheless, whether proclaimed by conservatives or liberals, they have generally failed adequately to take into account the experiences of those people who have been excluded from earlier representations of civic polity and who have had to struggle against the burden of structured inequality in the cultural and symbolic, as well as the political and economic, realm. They are, therefore, not sufficiently attentive to the fact that social movements based on commitments to cultural and identity politics arose in the first place to protest "the disguised particularisms—the masculinism, the white-Anglo ethnocentrism, the heterosexism—lurking behind what parades as universal."[72] Identity discourses are, after all, based on demands for greater participation in democratic life. And as such, they should not be regarded as the cause for the apparent current disappearance of noble public goals and grand egalitarian aspirations, but rather, as partial, and therefore incomplete and ultimately insufficient, attempts at a more equitable polity. Hence, rather than simply dismissing those movements associated with a paradigm of the recognition of identity and difference, we need to understand the conditions and reasons that led to their existence even as we attempt to move beyond their linguistic and political frameworks.

Whether it is to agree with, to argue with, or, more appropriately, to nuance these discussions on U.S. public life, it is important that theologians who work from within suffering communities, and who aspire to meaningful liberatory praxis in society, engage with these emerging conversations on civil society in the United States. First, such engagement is necessary, because it is vital that we learn how adequately to respond to and influence public discourse, particularly if we hold any hopes for the transformative relevance of theology. Second, Latino/a theologians should pay attention to the recent discussions on civil society that have emerged in the United States, because they have shifted the discursive context for our theologies. In the decades of the 60s, 70s, and 80s, following the evolution in the grammar of political claims-making from civil rights to identity recognition, the task of contextually and ethnically based thought was to articulate and

---

71 The references are to Robert Bellah et al. *Habits of the Heart: Individualism and Commitment in American Life* (Berkeley: University of California Press, 1985); Todd Gitlin, *The Twilight of Common Dreams: Why America Is Wracked by Culture Wars* (New York: Metropolitan Books, 1995); and Amitai Etzioni, *The Spirit of Community: The Reinvention of American Society* (New York: Simon & Schuster, 1993).

72 Fraser, *Justice Interruptus*, 5.

elaborate the difference of each constitutive cultural and ethnic community. At present, even in light of postmodernist and poststructuralist influences, the assignment seems to be that of speaking about particularity, specificity, and difference in a time when greater emphasis is being placed on forms of balkanization, fragmentation, and the loss of social and civil bonds in our society. To put it bluntly, the intellectual challenge in the present U.S. sociopolitical milieu, especially for those who wish to operate as "organic" and "public" intellectuals, is no longer merely that of developing autochthonous localized cultural discourses and identities; rather, the challenge is more fully that of finding ways to construct discourses that can simultaneously help excluded groups to establish themselves as distinctive communities with distinct social claims, while also situating these claims and concerns in the broader context of the continental "American" society. In short, the task is that of linking issues of race, cultural specificity, and overall individual and communal difference to some notion of a "common or public good."

Indeed, the very concept of the "common" legitimately arouses postmodern suspicion. Hence, it is necessary to keep in mind that notions of a "common or public good" need to be adequately examined and placed in historical perspective. What should be desired, after all, is not a return to a fallacious theory of universality devoid of specificity. Nevertheless, the realization of socially binding activities premised on the aspiration to greater social justice always requires some sense of the "whole," the "common," the "public," or of "shared values." The greatest and most successful social movements for justice generally have recognized that demands for rightfulness and equitableness are best asserted and achieved within a discursive framework based on common experience, rights, and needs in a nation-state and/or global context. As such, the challenge for contemporary liberationist theologies, such as Hispanic/Latino theology, is that of searching for a public rhetoric that may help us to bridge the fissures of race, class, gender/sex, and cultural-identity difference; to negotiate our basic humanness and differences; and to acknowledge the interlocking dimension of the local and global—all this while affirming the importance of historical specificity. Briefly put, the need is for the development of nuanced forms of public thought and public discourse.

Encouragingly, some thinkers are working precisely on the development and advancement of this sort of public thought. Anthony Appiah, Seyla Benhabib, Nancy Fraser, Susan Friedman, Edward Said, Cornel West, and Ellen Meiksins Wood are among those who have engaged the prospects and the limits of the cultural politics of identity, recognition, and difference.[73] In doing so, they present a refreshing and adequately probed cosmopolitanism that is acutely attuned to meaningful markers of situatedness yet transcends the parochial confines of nativist thinking. These cosmopolitanist thinkers are not reactionary conservatives opposed to local cultural consciousness or to the overturning of those deep structures of symbolic and material inequality that continue to exist in our nation and across the globe. On the contrary, they are leftists who have clearly shown themselves to be aligned with progressive causes and genuinely concerned with the contemporary prospects of a credible emancipatory vision. Hence, their pronouncements should not, indeed cannot, be dismissed as the vacillations of persons who are apathetic toward the plight of marginalized and oppressed peoples. Their critical reflections on identity politics, and the chastened universalism they promote, can be esteemed by Hispanic/Latino theologians as exemplary and allied discursive models that point a way to the merging of cultural politics with an integral idea of the public.

The second challenge that should draw Latino/a theology's attention involves its own tendency, as a predominantly cultural theorizing discourse, to de-center class issues and social politics in favor of cultural and identity politics. Issues related to local culture, identity, and the symbolic realm have become so paramount that they apparently have displaced other axes of social stratification from the reflection chart. The result has been an unfortunate "decoupling of cultural politics from social politics, and the relative eclipse of the latter by the former."[74] In a sense, our strong focus on matters of symbolic culture and identity, whether for the defense or celebration of cultural diversity, has unintentionally served to disguise

---

73 See, especially, K. Anthony Appiah, "The Multiculturalist Misunderstanding," *The New York Review of Books* 44, no. 15 (9 October 1997): 30-36; idem, "The Uncompleted Argument: DuBois and the Illusion of Race," in *"Race," Writing, and Difference*, ed. Henry Louis Gates Jr. (Chicago: University of Chicago Press, 1986), 21-37; Seyla Benhabib, *Situating the Self: Gender, Community and Postmodernism in Contemporary Ethics* (New York: Routledge 1992); Fraser, *Justice Interruptus*; Friedman, *Mappings*; Edward Said, *Culture and Imperialism* (New York: Viking, 1993); idem, *Representations of the Intellectual* (New York: Pantheon Books, 1994); West, *The American Evasion of Philosophy and Race Matters*; and Ellen M. Wood, "Identity Crisis," *These Times*, 13 June 1994, 28-29; idem, *Democracy Against Capitalism: Renewing Historical Materialism* (Cambridge: Cambridge University Press, 1995). For other works that explore the topic of public thought, see John Michael, *Anxious Intellects: Academic Professionals, Public Intellectuals, and Enlightenment Values* (Durham, N.C.: Duke University Press, 2000); Richard Posner, *Public Intellectuals: A Study of Decline* (Cambridge: Harvard University Press, 2002); and Richard Rorty, *Achieving Our Country: Leftist Thought in Twentieth-Century America* (Cambridge: Harvard University Press, 1998).

74 Fraser, *Justice Interruptus*, 2.

other serious economic and political disparities that exist in our society. Not surprisingly, Hispanic/Latino theology has lagged behind in its scrutiny of distributive justice issues, (i.e., class analysis) and the development of an adequately comprehensive social theory that connects the local to the public and global and the study of signification to institutions and social structures. Yet, if we truly mean for our discourses to be germane to the fruition of a comprehensive project invested with emancipatory commitments, we must pay adequate attention to the broader material structures in society that generate disadvantage at various levels of social life. This means that our liberatory theological discourses must adequately address not only how cultural identities may be defended and constructed differently, but also how they are produced and sustained within a deeply hierarchical and exploitative society wherein culture is only one among many other axes of stratification.

In this vein, Hispanic theologians must bear in mind that U.S. Latino/as suffer injustices that are traceable not only to the denigration of their culture, but also to socioeconomic exploitation and inequity. It is vital, therefore, that we extend sustained and mature attention to matters of economic justice in our theologies. If our theological discourses are ultimately to be useful in the promotion of a reinvigorated social justice movement that aids impoverished and marginalized Latinos, as well as disadvantaged persons from other ethnic communities in our society, they will have to search for ways of reconnecting cultural and identity politics with broader class and social issues. Moreover, we must remember that culture and the construction of identity always transpires within, and is influenced by, a larger web of shifting social, economic, and political relations. Matters of symbolic culture and identity, and issues regarding how we construct and negotiate culture, identity, and differences, must consistently be addressed in reference to broader societal constituents that affect life as a whole—in short, to a broader national and even global context.

The third challenge is that Latino/a theologians should also explore the possibilities, difficulties, and exigencies for sustained, integrative, and holistic coalitional energies in our society. Latino/a theology thus far has generally failed to develop and support a socially binding discourse that can connect the sociopolitical struggles of Hispanic communities both to the similar struggles of other marginalized groups and to the progressive sensibilities of other constituencies in the United States.[75] My suspicion is that this inadvertency stems from the relative eclipse of social theorizing by the myopic study of signification, identity, and cultural difference in our theologies. Frankly, I

---

75 See Benjamín Valentín, "Nuevos Odres Para el Vino: A Critical Contribution to Latino/a Theological Construction," *Journal of Hispanic/Latino Theology* 5, no.4 (1998): 30-47, esp. 43-46.

perceive that the proclivity toward the theorizing of symbolic culture, local identity, and cultural difference has diverted our attention away from the longing and need in society for wide-embracing connectivity and affiliation. Aimed primarily at valorizing cultural specificity and the reclamation of positive self-identity and group identity, Latino/a theological discourses have not reflected enough on the possible harmonizing of diverse interests in society and the importance of pluralistic alliances of struggle. Yet, the task of alliance building and the need for coalitional energies are particularly pressing today, due to the increase of social antagonism, the fracturing of social movements, the deterioration of a spirit of solidarity, and the increasing chasm between the haves and the have-nots in our society.

I am not naive about the enormous challenges and potential perils that come with the building of coalitions. Indeed, at present we even lack the integrative and holistic visions that can abet progressive coalitions, and we also have to contend with diverse interests and the reality of fragmented constituencies in our society. But, as Susan Friedman points out, "we cannot afford to give up the utopian dream of coalition and connection."[76] This utopic vision is especially pertinent for those historically subordinated persons and groups in society that by themselves lack the power to single-handedly transform present institutional structures. Social change, especially in the United States today, requires the building and nourishment of wider communal bonds among different communities of struggle. Hence, the prospect for progressive institutional transformation in our society ultimately hinges on our abilities to facilitate and sustain holistic social arrangements that can engender broad-based political coalitions across racial, gender, class, and religious lines.

Toward this goal, our theologians need to reflect critically on their emphases and rhetorical models. We must ask ourselves openly whether our discourses facilitate or hinder the vision and energy necessary for affiliation and coalition. For the task of alliance building, we need discourses that highlight those spaces of common experience and need in society, and that bring attention to the basic and full humanity that connects us all. We are in need of discourses that move "beyond theorizing difference to theorizing the spaces in between difference" and seek resolutely to facilitate "a solidarity of difference."[77]

---

76 Friedman, *Mappings*, 66.

77 I borrow the first line in this sentence from Friedman, *Mappings*, 68; and the second from Antonia Darder, "The Politics of Biculturalism: Culture and Difference in the Formation of *Warriors for Gringostroika* and *The New Mestizas*," in Darder, ed., *Culture and Difference*, 15.

Finally, the fourth challenge is that Latino/a theologians must attempt to respond to all these other challenges all while also striving to overcome the marginalization of theology in the broader public sphere. The reality is that theology rarely manages to have an impact or even be heard beyond its disciplinary, professional boundaries. And even within those boundaries, some theological discourses are confined to peripheral niches and limited audiences, as they are treated as appendices to the "mainstream" curriculum. A theology that is inspired by an ameliorative impulse and longs to make a social difference cannot be content with this arrangement.

In sum, what we need and should strive for is a mode of address that can simultaneously (1) engage with and influence public discourse; (2) integrate the cultural and the social through reflection on the social whole and the development of an appropriate theory of the public; (3) facilitate the building of progressive social coalitions of struggle; and (4) gain its own recognition as "public" discourse. I suggest that the concept of "public theology" is a potentially useful tool for this multifaceted discursive enterprise. It may function as a heuristic device at the level of a theory of discourse that can help us to connect the cultural to the social, and our local discursive practices to an effective idea of the public. It is therefore an idea that Latino/a theologians should readily consider.

In the next chapter, I explore the meaning and connotations of the designation "public theology," as well as the insights and blind spots of selected existing public theological models. In doing so, I hope to elucidate the importance of a public disposition in society and discourse; to highlight and complicate some of the components of the notion of the public; to point to some obstacles that can interrupt the cultivation of a sense of the public in contemporary society and discourse; and, thus, to sketch out some of the tasks of, and possible methodological directions for, public theological discourse. My ultimate hope is that this groundwork will be beneficial for the promotion and future development of emancipatory public theologies.

Chapter 3
Cultivating a Public
Perspective in Hispanic/Latino
Theological Discourse

The outstanding problem of the public is discovery and identification of itself.

—John Dewey[*]

Indeed, a narrowed sense of public purpose and political possibility is central to contemporary public life and thought.

—John Ehrenberg[†]

We need to cultivate a sense of the public realm that is based upon the thoroughly relational character of the web of life whose nurturing and transformation holds the key to our own survival and well-being. The task of a public theology is to elicit a recognition of and commitment to the common life within which we exist.

—Linell E. Cady[‡]

MAPPING PUBLIC THEOLOGY

We live in a time when millions of families in our nation are seeing their standards of living decline; when broad economic shifts have resulted in job insecurity for many and in an overall acceleration of social inequality both within our country and across the globe; when historically oppressed and disadvantaged groups are clearly in need of an overarching political imagination that could embrace the varied aspects of their struggles; when our public life is so imbued with cynicism and apathy; when globalizing interests and forces

---

[*] John Dewey, *The Public and Its Problems* (New York: Henry Holt & Company, 1927), 185.

[†] John Ehrenberg, *Civil Society: The Critical History of an Idea* (New York: New York University Press, 1999), 233.

[‡] Linell Elizabeth Cady, *Religion, Theology, and American Public Life* (New York: State University of New York Press, 1993), 92.

are strengthening; and when the threat of ecological devastation and/or nuclear holocaust is felt by many. It is somewhat bewildering that in such a time, many supposedly progressive and/or liberationist intellectuals have chosen to dedicate themselves principally to the promotion of local cultural commitments and to a general logic of localism. It is ironic that in a time when the need for comprehensive and integrative thought has increased, progressive thinkers have taken to circumscribe their ambitions, choosing to focus almost exclusively on the microlevel of specific culture, identity, and difference. This tendency is characteristic of a general mood that holds sway in our historical epoch, one that predisposes people toward fragmentary and localized thought rather than to overarching visions, broad analysis, and any sense of the whole. Given this permeating logic of localism, it is no surprise that the notion of publicness—the sense that "we are all part of one garment of destiny;"[1] that the quality of our lives together in society truly matters; and that integrative perspectives that seek to grasp, and transform, the social whole are possible and necessary—is so rarely prioritized in our times.

Although this logic of localism has marked much of our thought and discourse in the United States, across disciplinary lines, my concern in this project is mainly with the way in which contemporary theological discourse, particularly as it is generated by progressive or liberationist thinkers such as Latino/a theologians, has been gripped and sapped of broader relevance by this general penchant. It is both understandable and paradoxical that those theologies of liberation emanating from the context of oppressed groups, as is the case with U.S. Hispanic/Latino theology, would be so captivated by the discourse of symbolic culture, identity, and recognition and its concomitant logic of localism. It is understandable because for theologies that are organically linked to those subordinate groups that have been deprived of recognition, respect, and equal treatment in the wider society, it has indeed been necessary to construct distinctive ethnic, cultural, and group identities in order to counter forms of either gender, sexual, cultural, or racial-ethnic injustice. It is paradoxical, however, because the kinds of institutional and structural social changes that these theologies seek to foster, for the sake of their oppressed communities and others, cannot be achieved merely through local commitments; social transformation requires broad-based analysis and activism that transcends local confines.

Surely, any comprehensive political project that is genuinely concerned with the remedying of injustices must make room in its agenda for the consideration of issues related to the defense of group identity, the end of

---

1 I borrow this line from Cornel West, *Race Matters* (New York: Vintage Books, 1994), 11.

cultural domination, and the requirements of recognition. Cultural and ethnic prejudice is real. The theological projects of Virgilio Elizondo and Orlando Espín, analyzed in the previous chapter, perceptibly capture, manifest, and contend with this fact. The varied movements aligned with the paradigm of cultural-identity politics in the United States arose in the first place to counter actual, existing forms of inequalities that have been caused by the presence of the many and various prejudices in our society. The struggles of these movements, then, have everything to do with justice. The facile wholesale dismissals of any form of cultural and identity politics that have been proposed in some conservative and even in some liberal and progressive quarters need to be challenged. As important and inevitable as it is, however, the fact is that the general logic of localism that undergirds much of our present progressive and liberationist discourse, which lends itself to an insular enchantment with matters of symbolic culture, identity, and difference, is much too narrow to foster the kinds of overarching and harmonizing emancipatory visions that the goal of justice requires in our time.

First, issues of culture and identity take place within a larger web of social, political, and global dynamics that influence these local provinces and that deserve our equal attention. Second, the reality is that if any sort of social transformation is to be gained in our fragmented public realm, it will be necessary to connect our locational claims for cultural justice and identity recognition to a broader social politic and rhetoric that facilitates the building of alliances across racial, cultural, gender, class, and religious lines. Discursively speaking, this task calls for modes of address that can "travel transculturally while engaging in the local habitus' of one's immediate concern."[2] That is to say, the present challenge facing those who seek justice, particularly those who operate from within the context either of a disadvantaged ethnic or cultural group, is that of constructing discourses that link their local community issues, concerns, and activity to the larger sociocultural and political matrices transpiring in the broader realm of civil society. Toward this goal, our theologies need to be guided by broad sociopolitical imagery and analysis.

Our times call for forms of thought that dare to be socially broad, integrative, holistic—in short, "public" in orientation. Without a broader public disposition and perspective that transcends the realm of local signification and micropolitics, our theologies will become merely "wheels that turn which do not affect the mechanism."[3] It is in light of this suspicion

---

2 I borrow these words from Trinh T. Minha, "An Acoustic Journey," in *Rethinking Borders*, ed. John C. Welchman (Minneapolis: University of Minnesota Press, 1996), 12.

3 Quoted by Cornel West, *Prophetic Reflections: Notes on Race and Power in America* (Monroe, Maine: Common Courage Press, 1993), 180.

and concern that I invoke the concept of a "public theology" as one that may be useful for theologies, such as Hispanic/Latino theology, that are concerned with integral emancipation.

In recent years, some theologians have indeed called for the development of public theologies. And to be sure, theologies and religious discourses that can be characterized as having a "public" quality have existed prior to these appeals. In the twentieth century, we in the United States can point to figures such as Reinhold Niebuhr, John Courtney Murray, Martin Luther King Jr., and, more recently, Jean Bethke Elshtain, Michael Dyson, and Cornel West as prime examples of Christian public intellectuals who have successfully captured the attention of a wide constituency in our society and offered progressive forms of public theological/religious discourse. But these sorts of figures have been rare indeed, as contemporary circumstances, both within the religious and the secular realms, have made it difficult for such theologians and philosophers to emerge. The paucity of such Christian public intellectuals, and the present challenges to religion and theology in the public realms of society, have drawn the attention of various theologians and religious scholars who have, as a result, devoted themselves to the study of the role of religion and theological discourse in public life. Among these we can include David Hollenbach, Robin Lovin, Martin Marty, David Tracy, Richard John Neuhaus, Max Stackhouse, Robert McElroy, Ronald Thiemann, Michael and Kenneth Himes, Linell Cady, Rebecca Chopp, Robert Benne, and Victor Anderson.[4] The term "public theology" does not mean the same thing to each

---

4 See especially David Hollenbach, "Public Theology in America: Some Questions for Catholicism after John Courtney Murray," *Theological Studies* 37 (1976): 290-303; idem, "Theology and Philosophy in Public: A Symposium on John Courtney Murray's Unfinished Agenda," *Theological Studies* 40 (1979): 700-706; Robin Lovin, "Resources for a Public Theology," *Theological Studies* 40 (1979): 706-10; idem, "Social Contract or a Public Covenant?" in *Religion and American Public Life: Interpretations and Explorations*, ed. Robin Lovin (Mahwah, N.J.: Paulist Press, 1986): 132-145; Martin Marty, *The Public Church* (New York: Crossroad, 1981); idem, *Religion and Republic: The American Circumstance* (Boston: Beacon Press, 1987); David Tracy, "Defending the Public Character of Theology," *The Christian Century*, 1 April 1981, 350-56; idem, *The Analogical Imagination: Christian Theology and the Culture of Pluralism* (New York: Crossroad, 1981), esp. 3-98; Richard J. Neuhaus, *The Naked Public Square: Religion and Democracy in America* (Grand Rapids: Eerdmans, 1984); Max Stackhouse, *Public Theology and Political Economy: Christian Stewardship in Modern Society* (Grand Rapids: Eerdmans, 1987); Robert McElroy, *The Search for an American Public Theology: The Contribution of John Courtney Murray* (Mahwah, N.J.: Paulist Press, 1989); Ronald F. Thiemann, *Constructing a Public Theology: The Church in a Pluralistic Culture* (Louisville: Westminster John Knox Press, 1991); idem, *Religion in Public Life: A Dilemma for Democracy* (Washington, D.C.: Georgetown University Press, 1996); Michael Himes and Kenneth Himes, *Fullness of Faith: The Public Significance of Theology* (Mahwah, N.J.: Paulist Press, 1993); Linell E. Cady, "A Model for a Public Theology,"

of these scholars, nor do they align the concept with the same overall theological or political project. "Public theology" has, therefore, become an elastic and somewhat nebulous conception that requires some mapping.

When reading the works of authors who have employed the term "public theology," one notes the prevalence of three projects that are related yet very distinct. First, there are attempts to decipher the role of the institutional churches in the public sphere, and/or to describe the characteristics of a public-oriented church. Second, one meets with efforts to demonstrate the public character of theological discourse—the common criteria of truth that theology might share with other disciplines or modes of discourse. Third, one encounters a broader project still that includes the attempt to devise a theological mode of address that can respond to some of the most pertinent issues facing our nation and that can engage a wide public that transcends ecclesiastical boundaries and also the boundaries between religious and secular orders—all this while also promoting a sense of our common life in our nation and our world.[5] This diversity becomes greater still when we account for the fact that these projects may be attached to distinct sociopolitical ideologies, from conservative to moderate to liberal or leftist outlooks, and to theological orientations or methods that also vary immensely, from neoorthodox to liberal-constructivist and many points between. In view of this, when we use the term "public theology," we must provide some sense of what we have in mind.

Each of the projects that I have mentioned is important to the overall development of public theologies. However, the first two ventures can prove somewhat limiting. The first project, which attempts to interpret the public relevance of the teachings of the institutional churches, may prove limiting if it serves to restrict theology to the language and internal concerns of the

---

Harvard Theological Review 80, no.2 (1987): 193-212, idem, *American Public Life*; Rebecca S. Chopp, "A Feminist Perspective: Christianity, Democracy, and Feminist Theology," in *Christianity and Democracy in Global Context*, ed. John Witte Jr. (Boulder, Colo.: Westview Press, 1993), 111-29, idem, "Reimagining Public Discourse," in *Black Faith and Public Talk: Critical Essays on James H. Cone's Black Theology and Black Power*, ed. Dwight N. Hopkins (Maryknoll, N.Y.: Orbis Books, 1999), 150-64; Robert Benne, *The Paradoxical Vision: A Public Theology for the Twenty-First Century* (Minneapolis: Fortress Press, 1995); and Victor Anderson, *Pragmatic Theology: Negotiating the Intersections of an American Philosophy of Religion and Public Theology* (New York: State University of New York Press, 1998).

5 For some examples of works that exemplify the first type of project, see Marty, *The Public Church*; Thiemann, *Constructing a Public Theology*; and Himes and Himes, *Fullness of Faith*. The classic exemplar of the second type of project is David Tracy; see "Public Character of Theology" and *The Analogical Imagination*. For a clear example that illustrates the third type of project, see Cady, *American Public Life*.

church. Theologians often operate under and lend credence to the misguid-
ed assumption that theology is solely and entirely a work of the church and
for the church. Certainly, the church historically has been one of the central
settings for theology, but it is important to bear in mind that the meaning of
theological language is always tied to the life of a broader culture and that
theological reflection attempts to deal with a wide matrix of human experiences that transcends church life. Theology is foundationally human imaginative work that attempts to make sense of human historical events and experiences, and at its best seeks to orient human activity toward personal fulfillment and greater social justice, through the construction, reconstruction, and
promotion of enabling religious narratives, symbols, notions of God, of the
sacred, of spirituality, or of self-transcendence. Because theology inevitably is
rooted in the self's wider experiences of life and cultures, including but ultimately transcending the boundaries of the church, it should never be regarded as the private property of the church or understood merely as a reflection
on the internal life, concerns, and interpretations of a given religious group.
Hence, although the Christian churches have contributed to its purpose, the
meaning of theology cannot be established solely by reference to the life of
the church; theological reflection and discourse should stand for more than
just the discourse of a church. Theology most generally, and particularly that
theology that aspires to be of service in the wider public realm as public discourse, should not restrict itself to the restatement of church belief or to the
internal concerns of a church.[6]

The second project, which features attempts to highlight the common
criteria of truth that theological discourse might share with other disciplines,
proves limiting in two senses. First, it does not go far enough in describing
what the substantive aim of a public theology should be; second, it tends to
imbue every form of theological discourse with an essential public quality,
thus obscuring what might be distinctive about a theology that consciously
aspires to publicness. In light of these limitations, I use the term "public theology" to describe the attempt to address the pressing issues in a given social

---

6 My understanding of the nature of theological reflection and discourse draws on Gordon
Kaufman's conception of "constructive theology." See Gordon D. Kaufman, *An Essay on Theological
Method* (Atlanta: Scholars Press, 1979); *In Face of Mystery: A Constructive Theology* (Cambridge:
Harvard University Press, 1993); and *God-Mystery-Diversity: Christian Theology in a Pluralistic
World* (Minneapolis: Fortress Press, 1996). For other similar examples and explanations of theology
as a constructive endeavor, see Sallie McFague, *Models of God: Theology for an Ecological, Nuclear Age*
(Philadelphia: Fortress Press, 1987); Peter C. Hodgson, *Winds of the Spirit: A Constructive Christian
Theology* (Louisville: Westminster John Knox Press, 1994); and the articles in Rebecca S. Chopp and
Mark Lewis Taylor, eds. *Reconstructing Christian Theology* (Minneapolis: Fortress Press, 1994).

context and to cultivate a care for the quality of our lives together from within theology.

Specifically, the call for a public theology is the establishment of a theological mode of discourse that must address the following four concerns. First, it must take explicit account of the broad national sociopolitical circumstances within which it takes place. Second, it must nurture a sense of our common life and a concern for the quality of our lives together as a social whole. Third, such a theology should visualize the possibilities and conditions for an overarching emancipatory project that could account for the diverse processes that produce social injustices and could prompt fellow citizens to take public action on behalf of justice. Fourth, it should try to capture the attention of a wide and diverse audience, including many who have ceased to take either religion or theology seriously, with a moving and harmonizing message that would facilitate alliances of struggle across racial, cultural, gender, class, and religious lines.[7] A *public theology*, then, is a form of discourse that couples either the language, symbols, or background concepts of a religious tradition with an overarching, integrative, emancipatory sociopolitical perspective in such a way that it movingly captures the attention and moral conscience of a broad audience and promotes the cultivation of those modes of love, care, concern, and courage required both for individual fulfillment and for broad-based social activism.

This overall description of public theology complies with the four appeals that I made to Hispanic/Latino theology in the previous chapter, and involves, I suggest, three overarching discursive tasks: (1) fostering a public disposition in society and, therefore, in intellectual work; (2) promoting social coalitions of struggle for justice; and (3) developing a discourse that can engage a broad and varied constituency within the realm of civil society. In the remainder of this chapter, I explore the implications of these three objectives a bit further.

---

7 The adjective "public," as I am employing it here, then, denotes four reflective and discursive traits: (1) the disposition to enter into, highlight the potentiality of, and influence the public arenas of citizen discourse and association in the broader social public; (2) the demonstration of an overarching and integrative analytical perspective that seeks to grasp and transform the social whole; (3) the desire to identify and link the many different progressive activisms currently in evidence, through the facilitation of coalitions of struggle; and (4) the ability to attract and energize a wide and diverse populace willing and able to take principled public action on behalf of greater social justice. Whenever I use "public" as a noun, I am referring to the people as a whole in our society and/or, particularly, that arena of citizen discourse and association in society that often is labeled either as "the realm of civil society" or "the public sphere."

THE VALUE OF THE PUBLIC REALM AND A PUBLICIST OUTLOOK

In 1927, John Dewey, one of our best-known philosophers and socio-cultural critics, asserted that "the outstanding problem of the public is dis-covery and identification of itself."[8] These words encapsulate Dewey's lamentations about the lack of a publicist orientation in his time, and also serve to demonstrate that the search for what may be called a public dispo-sition—the inclination of individuals to consider themselves as part of a broader social whole and body politic—is not particularly new. To be sure, the quality of publicness, both in social practice and in thought and dis-course, was as elusive in Dewey's time as it is now. In certain respects, how-ever, the quest for a public sensibility has become more daunting and impor-tant in our time. For good reason, then, Dewey's jeremiad has received renewed consideration within a growing body of literature that reports with alarm of the decline of notions of the public in contemporary life.[9] Most of these recent writings, especially those generated from a leftist outlook, aim to promote an appreciation for the rich diversity that marks our nation; to help us to build bridges across our differences; and to encourage us to dream "common dreams"[10] in spite of our differences.

These writings do well to point both to the decline and to the importance of overarching social goals, and of a sense of "other interest" in society, that may include but should transcend the intimate boundaries of family, friends, and one's own ethnic or cultural group. But their tendency has often been to present a nostalgic reading of history that lacks proper nuance. "Publicness," we are told again and again, "is a quality that we once had but have now lost, and that we must somehow retrieve."[11] Yet, as scholars such as Joan Landes,

---

8 Dewey, *The Public and Its Problems*, 185.

9 Some of the most eloquent examples (written in the United States) are Richard Sennett, *The Fall of Public Man* (New York: Vintage Books, 1978); Robert Bellah et al., *Habits of the Heart: Individualism and Commitment in American Life* (San Francisco: Harper & Row, 1985); and Todd Gitlin, *The Twilight of Common Dreams: Why America is Wracked by Culture Wars* (New York: Metropolitan Books, 1995). Perhaps the most renowned and influential work in this sphere, how-ever, is Jurgen Habermas, *The Structural Transformation of the Public Sphere: An Inquiry into a Category of Bourgeois Society*, trans. Thomas Burger and Frederick Lawrence (Cambridge, Mass.: MIT Press, 1989). Habermas's important work was not written from an American standpoint, nor was it influenced by Dewey's thought. Nevertheless, like Dewey's *The Public and Its Problems* and the other writings mentioned above, Habermas's *Structural Transformation* also calls attention to the loss of a public sensibility in modern Western societies and contributes to the theorizing of the public sphere. In this way, then, these writings can be linked.

10 The reference here is to Gitlin, *The Twilight of Common Dreams*.

11 Bruce Robbins, "Introduction: The Public as Phantom," in *The Phantom Public Sphere*, ed. Bruce Robbins (Minneapolis: University of Minnesota Press, 1993), viii.

Mary Ryan, Elizabeth Brooks-Higginbotham, and Geoff Eley have compellingly noted, the truth is that the public spheres of past societies were
notable for a number of significant exclusions: those in the working class,
women, Native Americans, African Americans, Latino/as, and members of
other marginalized social groups were usually excluded from the official public spheres of past societies and were overlooked in discussions on public
matters.[12] Nevertheless, there is some truth to the conclusion that the valuation of public life—the concern for the quality of our lives together as a social
whole—has received a lower priority in our time. Moreover, it is also true that
the task of cultivating a public orientation has become more difficult today
due to the increase of social antagonism, the fracturing of progressive energies, the deterioration of a spirit of solidarity, and the present postmodernist
philosophic allegiance to micronarratives. Even so, it is pointless to attempt
to pinpoint previous flowering publicness; the truth is that the attainment of
publicness remains an unfulfilled task in history. It remains, however, an ideal
worthy of our aspiration.

The fact that the ideal of publicness has historically remained elusive in
social practice should not detract from our efforts to achieve a sense of social
wholeness that acknowledges yet traverses differences and helps to advance
the cause of social equality. The concept of the public, in spite of the contemporary "passion for difference,"[13] continues to be indispensable for those
who remain committed to a vision of better racial and ethnic relations in our
society and to the actuation of an overarching emancipatory project. If there
is some reluctance on the part of a discerning few in our society to see the
idea of publicness melt conclusively into the air, as Bruce Robbins percep-
tively notes, "the cause may not be vestigial piety so much as the fear that we
cannot do without it." Robbins writes,

> In radical struggles over architecture, urban planning, sculpture,
> political theory, ecology, economics, education, the media, and pub-
> lic health, to mention only a few sites among others, the public has

---

12 See Joan Landes, *Women and the Public Sphere in the Age of the French Revolution* (Ithaca,
N.Y.: Cornell University Press, 1988); Mary P. Ryan, "Gender and Public Access: Women's Politics
in Nineteenth Century America," in *Habermas and the Public Sphere*, ed. Craig Calhoun
(Cambridge, Mass.: MIT Press, 1992), 259-88; Elizabeth Brooks-Higginbotham, *Righteous
Discontent: The Women's Movement in the Black Baptist Church*, 1880-1920 (Cambridge: Harvard
University Press, 1993); and Geoff Eley, "Nations, Publics, and Political Cultures: Placing
Habermas in the Nineteenth Century," in Calhoun, ed., *Habermas and the Public Sphere*, 289-339.

13 See Henrietta Moore, *A Passion for Difference: Essays in Anthropology and Gender*
(Bloomington: Indiana University Press, 1994).

long served as a rallying cry against private greed, a demand for
attention to the general welfare as against propertied interests, an
appeal for openness to scrutiny … an arena in which disenfranchised
minorities struggle to express their cultural identity, a code word for
socialism. Without this discursive weapon, we seem to enter such
struggles inadequately armed.[14]

The significance of the concept of a public, as Robbins captures in this
statement, exists in its capacity to shore up the liberating potential that exists
in discursive interaction and emancipatory sociopolitical association as a
means of putting pressure either on states, markets, corporations, or greedy
individuals when these obstruct both the democratic fulfillment of citizens
and the possibilities for a more just social order. Surely, in a time such as ours,
marked as it is with rising socioeconomic inequality, heightened racial and
cultural group tensions, rampant individualism, and political balkanization,
the need for a public perspective that can sustain and harmonize the struggles for justice mentioned by Robbins has become conspicuously apparent.
Yet, we have placed much too low a priority on the ideals of social solidarity
and a shared public life, and on the development of the sorts of overarching
integrative visions and broad discursive analyses that could harmonize the
interests of diverse and currently fragmented constituencies in our society.
This trend should be troubling to liberationist and/or progressive individuals
living in this country, and indeed to all American citizens, because it seems as
if "our common destiny is more pronounced and imperiled precisely when
our divisions are deeper."[15] Therefore, we need more intellectuals who are
willing to "go public" with their thoughts by putting forward overarching
visions and broad analyses that seek to grasp, bind, and transform the social
whole. We must develop analyses and discourses that assume an orientation
that is publicist, and are capable of cultivating in society a public disposition.

However, this quest requires first that we identify and reckon with certain
dynamics that hinder the advancement of a public disposition in society.
Theologian Linell Cady offers some assistance when she studies one of the
modern-day developments that impedes a proper valuation of public life in
the United States: a shift in the value attached to public and private life,
owing to the legacy of the Western Enlightenment, that has led to an
enchantment with the private spheres of life and a devaluation of public life.
Cady's basic claim is that the desire for connectedness, and the appreciation

---

14 Robbins, "The Public as Phantom," x.
15 West, *Race Matters*, 8.

of the commonweal or public space, has been weakened in this country by a gospel of individuality that has its roots in the Western Enlightenment's liberal ideology. Her tracing of this development and its effect on the valuation of publicity in our society merits some consideration.

LIBERALISM, INDIVIDUALISM, AND THE ECLIPSE OF THE PUBLIC

Linell Cady, one of the contemporary theologians who has most methodically examined the possibilities and tasks of a public-oriented theology, believes that the public sphere is valued less today than it was in premodern times. In her major work on public theology, *Religion, Theology, and American Public Life,* Cady argues that in contrast to contemporary values, the ancient Greeks esteemed the public sphere much more than the private. They, for instance, envisioned the private exigencies and associations connected to private life, whether these had to do with self-concern, the household, family, or work, as matters that belonged to the domain of necessity. The public sphere, however, was viewed by them as the domain of authentic freedom, and participation in the life of the *polis* (that realm wherein the common bond among diverse people and virtual strangers occupying shared space in a broad political community was consistently negotiated) was considered to be not only an intrinsic good but also the ultimate end for which humans were created.

To her credit, Cady does not romanticize Greek civilization. She points out, for instance, that the Greek public sphere actually excluded the vast majority of the populace—women, slaves, residing noncitizens—and that Greek civilization was marked by practices that modern societies would find reprehensible. Cady's purpose, then, is not to idealize Greek life, but rather, to emphasize, by comparison, the low priority that we presently place on our public life. "Whereas the Greeks associated the public world with the exercise of freedom," Cady laments, "we are far more likely to consider freedom facilitated in the private sphere."[16] Now, she suggests, we invest private life with all of the dignity that was once reserved for public life. In a way, as Cady explains it, the private has changed places with the public in contemporary life.

Indeed, Cady is well aware that the private and the public spheres are always interrelated and that to speak of them as separate would, therefore, be misleading. Our private lives—our work, families, friendships, living communities, and even our cultural locations—are greatly affected by broader public affairs: law, political institutions, economic trends, societal dynamics and relations, and so forth. Conversely, public life is influenced by what

16 Cady, *American Public Life,* 7.

transpires in the private realms of life. As Robert Bellah and his associates have observed, "A minimum of public decency and civility is a precondition for a fulfilling private life." On the other hand, however, "To engage successfully in the public world, one needs personal strength and the support of family and friends."[17] Hence, the private and the public spheres of life are dialectically related, and the neglect of one will, in time, lead to the impoverishment of the other. Cady acknowledges this dialectical relationship in her work. Her fear, however, is that many American citizens have come to ignore it. She believes that we, unlike earlier societies, generally have accorded the private realm most of our attention and respect at the expense of our willingness to care for the quality of our lives together as a social and national public.

Cady attributes this shift in thinking and valuation to the wide-reaching effect that the modern Western liberal conception of human nature and society has had on contemporary life. Although this conception helped Western societies to deal with the crisis of authority and the sectarian strife engendered by the religious wars of the sixteenth and seventeenth centuries, and although it has served invaluably to emancipate human and social thought from the chains of uncritical submission to tradition, she suggests that the secular liberal framework invented by the Enlightenment thinkers has also served to generate a radical individualism, an enchantment with private life, and an ahistorical understanding of reason that has eventually served to constrict the meaning of public life.

"Basic to philosophic liberalism," Cady states, "is the assumption that human beings are radically autonomous creatures who are driven by their desires to pursue their own self-interest."[18] Human beings, according to this modern liberal anthropology, are self-made and self-dependent individuals who exist ontologically prior to society and to their relationships to others. In modern liberalism, this atomistic understanding of human *being* is usually joined with a conception of the self as egoistic. Modern liberal theory, then, posits a representation of the human as a socially unsituated self that seemingly drops from the sky ready-made—one that does not have intrinsic need of relationality and is biologically disposed to narcissism and conflict with others.

When applied to society, this modern liberal anthropology has given privilege to a conception of the social realm as a reality that comes into existence only through the voluntary contract of individuals, and to an

---

17 Bellah et al., *Habits of the Heart*, 163.
18 Cady, *American Public Life*, 10.

understanding of politics as merely a matter of protecting and maximizing individual interests.[19] Society, therefore, is little more than a collection of individual free agents that has no intrinsic value in and of itself. "All society," as Thomas Hobbes once put it, "is either for gain, as for glory; that is not so much for love of our fellows, as for love of ourselves."[20] Entry into civil society is to be esteemed only for its utilitarian worth—that is, because it helps to harness the worst excesses of human self-interest and therefore allows individuals to secure the possession of material, emotional, and intellectual goods. A body politic, then, is an artifice that exists because of human selfishness and whose purpose is to further promote it. Cady interprets the implications of liberalism's understanding of social and political life this way:

> Society, according to this view, is not based upon any substantive agreement about the "public good." Indeed, insofar as individuals are naturally disposed to seek their personal interests, there *is* no consensus about the good. Nor need there be, according to liberalism. The most desirable society is one that, as far as possible, maximizes the freedom of individuals to secure their private ends.[21]

Cady claims that the effects of the liberal understanding of human nature and society on contemporary life, particularly in the United States, have been considerable. She suggests that the radical individualism fostered by liberal ideology has proven to be detrimental to our ability to valuate public life in three central ways. First, it has served to weaken the sense of and desire for connection between the self and the other in society. Second, it has encouraged a one-sided enchantment with private life that values being in private— alone with ourselves, family, and intimate friends—as an end in itself, and thereby has weakened the desire to value those bonds of association in the *respublica,* where we must live in the "company of strangers."[22] Third, it has promoted an overly idealized understanding of reason and publicness that tends both to strip public life of its diversity, by reducing the individual to a

---

19 For studies that trace the influence of modern individualism on contemporary forms of sociologies and politics, see John Hall, *Liberalism: Politics, Ideology and the Market* (Chapel Hill: University of North Carolina Press, 1988); Iris Marion Young, *Justice and the Politics of Difference* (Princeton, N.J.: Princeton University Press, 1990).

20 Thomas Hobbes, *De Cive*, ed. Sterling P. Lamprecht (New York: Appleton-Century-Crofts, 1949), 24.

21 Cady, *American Public Life*, 10.

22 See Parker J. Palmer, *The Company of Strangers: Christians and the Renewal of America's Public Life* (New York: Crossroad, 1981).

least common denominator of personhood and ignoring the cultural particularities of citizens, and to downplay the social inequalities that may
exist in the public at large.[23] Taking issue with these three liberal tendencies, and the implications that they hold for the theorizing of the public
sphere, Cady argues,

> The public is not a collection of contextless or narrative-free selves—
> a lowest common denominator of personhood. Nor is the public
> exercise of reason one that transcends the historical location of these
> selves. The public is the all-encompassing community of persons
> who come together to debate and evaluate the effects of their associ-
> ational life. From this perspective, then, the public is, in an important
> sense, not fully realized. We currently have too many barriers to the
> full and equal participation of persons in shaping a communal life.
> The public must be created through the overcoming of narrow and
> distorted communication.[24]

Although the overarching ethos of the United States certainly has been
informed by other philosophical and ethical traditions that have served to
temper a virulent individualism, such as biblical faith and classical republicanism, Cady believes that these have been decreasing in influence in the
twentieth century. "As a result," she argues, "their tempering of the liberal
strain in the dominant ethos has lessened in recent decades, leaving, increasingly, a stark version of liberalism as the primary mythic framework for interpreting social, economic, and political life."[25] The point of Cady's critique of
classical liberalism is not to negate the value of individuality, but rather, to
call attention to the dangers of a limitless individualism and to the need for
equilibrium between individuality and connectivity in a democratic society.
She does not argue, therefore, that American citizens should cease to value
individualism; instead, Cady calls for some parity in the valuation of private
and public life.

---

23 See Cady, *American Public Life*, 6-17. For critiques of the liberal model of the public
sphere that help to bear out Cady's arguments, see Iris Marion Young's criticisms of John
Rawls's liberal conception of justice, and of liberalism's ideal of impartiality and the civic public, in *Politics of Difference*, esp. 15-38, 96-121; and Nancy Fraser's critical reflections on Jurgen
Habermas's idea of the public sphere in her article "Rethinking the Public Sphere: A
Contribution to the Critique of Actually Existing Democracy," which first appeared in Calhoun,
ed., *Habermas and the Public Sphere*, 109-42.

24 Cady, *American Public Life*, 16.

25 Ibid., 70.

Cady points out that concern in our contemporary society over the loss of what America's founding figures referred to as "public virtue"—the disposition to work toward the improvement of the commonwealth—has fueled a recent interest in notions of community and the possibility of a greater role for religion in public life. Indeed, Cady believes that this development is inspiring because it shows that not all Americans have become so self-interested as to ignore the public good. She also finds the interest in a more public role for religion a refreshing and worthy occurrence. But Cady does express concern with some of the ramifications of this recent interest. She rightly points out, for instance, that the stress on community found within the recent promotion of forms of communitarianism contains some serious shortcomings that can make it as problematic for the cultivation of a broad public disposition as is the radical liberalism that it seeks to overcome. First of all, communitarianism has tended to remain committed to the same logic of localism that liberalism endorses, because its emphasis mainly has been on local, homogenous, geographical enclaves rather than on the wider pluralistic society and body politic. Moreover, although it offers some important correctives to the individualist bent of classical liberalism, communitarian ideology often winds up creating a debilitating dichotomy between community and society that hinders the cultivation of a generalist or integrative perspective that grasps and cares for the state of the social whole. It also has tended to emphasize notions of moral consensus as well as narrow, cohesive, and homogenous associations—an inclination that makes it more akin to the generation of forms of tribalism and nationalism than to an all-embracing public sensibility. Whereas classical liberalism tends to deify the atomistic individual and the rights-bearing rebel, communitarianism's penchant has been to idolize local affiliation, homogeneous intimacy, and the clan.

The political danger of communitarianism is that it can just as easily be marked by exclusion as by inclusion, because its inclination is to absorb, assimilate, and monopolize diversity. The ideal of community often is employed in discriminatory fashion to mark off the exclusive territory of a particular group by excluding "others" whose foreignness or nonconformity makes them different from the group's insiders. Cady makes the point this way: "Focus upon community can all too easily become a self-legitimizing strategy that justifies concern for 'us' at the expense of 'them' who stand outside the community."[26]

Cady similarly expresses concern over the recent undiscerning calls for public religions. She rightly warns that certain forms of religion can serve to

---

26 Ibid., 151.

exacerbate the problems of our public life, either by promoting rather than
tempering the individualizing tendencies of the wider culture and/or by
introducing sectarian viewpoints that are more conducive to bigotry than to
the embracing of pluralism and solidarity. Troublingly, some of the calls
made for a more public religion are voiced with majoritarian overtones that
seek to impose certain values or religious viewpoints on all others in the public sphere. Hence, Cady suggests that pleas for a public form of religiosity
should not be aimed at giving any type of religion a public voice. Instead, she
claims that these should be concerned with the self-transformation of religion: "the 'theological retreading' of religion so that it may again contribute
to the sustenance and critique of the commonweal."[27] In this sense, what real-
ly is required, according to Cady, is a "public theology," which implies critical
reflection upon and, ultimately, transformation of religion. And the substantive aim of such a public theology, she suggests, should be to facilitate an all-
embracing moral vision that elicits a recognition of and commitment to the
common life that we share nationally, globally, and even cosmically, and that,
in this way, serves to temper the radical individualism that pervades our contemporary American society. Cady says it this way:

> A public theology seeks to elicit a recognition of and loyalty to a
> common public life that is more than a collection of autonomous
> individuals. By focusing upon the intricate and extensive interde-
> pendence that mark human and cosmic life, it seeks to temper the
> radical individualism of the liberal ethos through identification with
> a wider common life. By cultivating this sense a public theology seeks
> to sustain, deepen, and transform the common life that has been
> obscured and deformed within the liberal framework.[28]

Cady certainly does well in alerting us to the corrosive effects that an
unrestrained form of individualism may have on our ability to conceptualize
a shared public life. Her sociocultural analysis, however, rests on the assumption that the fundamental obstacle to the generation of an inclusive public
disposition in our American society is the mythology of classical liberalism.
But there are other profound forces, such as corporate capitalism and racism,
that militate against the cultivation of a public disposition in the United
States. The culture- and identity-based political imaginations presently
favored by the most salient emancipatory social movements of our time,

---

27 Ibid., 21.
28 Ibid., 71.

although important for the advancement of integral justice, often also serve to undercut the possibility and desirability of a public perception. Americans currently live in a world that places many pressures on their sense of connectedness, particularly to those who exist beyond the boundaries of their immediate families and cultural and ethnic groups. Unfortunately, these issues receive scant attention not only in Cady's work but also in the wider literature on public theology. The corrosive effects of corporate capitalism and racism on the activation of a public disposition in our society, and the implications of the rise of identity politics, however, should not be ignored.

CAPITALISM VERSUS THE CULTIVATION OF A PUBLIC PERCEPTION

In a market-driven social order such as ours, where meaning, value, and survival have more and more come to revolve around the buying and selling of commodities, it is indeed difficult to cultivate the ideals of publicness, solidarity, and the sense that *we are all part of one garment of destiny*. The emergence and recent global expansion of capitalism have increasingly fostered not only an egoistic market mentality that hinders the valuation of noble public goals, but also a widening gap in the distribution of wealth that has forced many to concentrate their efforts on making a decent living. What we are presently confronted with in the United States, after our long history of a market-driven economy and culture, is an unequal and fragmented society wherein more than one-third of the overall wealth in the country is held by 1 percent of the population, and two-thirds by the richest 10 percent; wherein the majority of the population is experiencing either wage stagnation or sheer poverty and, therefore, dwindling hopes for a decent standard of living; wherein Americans live isolated from each other because of vast class and economic differences; and wherein the ideals of solidarity, substantive democracy, and visions of an alternative to the present social order are fast receding.[29]

---

29 According to Lynn Karoly's 1993 study, family income inequality was greater in the 1990s than at any previous point in the last half-century. Recent economic indices also reveal that after having grown steadily between 1940 and 1970, when the modern American middle class was created following the manufacturing boom generated by warfare in Europe, the earnings of the typical nonsupervisory, private sector American worker declined by about 15 percent in the 1990s. According to sociologist Reynolds Farley, then, two major economic trends mark the last two decades: smaller paychecks for most and an increase in socioeconomic inequality. For these statistics, and a more in-depth analysis of them, see Reynolds Farley, *The New American Reality: Who We Are, How We Got Here, Where We Are Going* (New York: Russell Sage Foundation, 1996); Lynn A. Karoly, "The Trend in Inequality among Families, Individuals, and Workers in the United States: A Twenty-five Year Perspective," in *Uneven Tides: Rising Inequality in America*, ed. Sheldon Danziger and Peter Gottschalk (New York: Russell Sage Foundation, 1993), 19-97.

The entrenchment of capitalism in our moment of history, as both an economic and a cultural system, has compelled many to curtail their ambitions for greater distributive justice. On the one hand, the few who are truly wealthy and have profited from the upward distribution of wealth and goods in our society usually have little or no desire to entertain thoughts of a more just public sphere, because they benefit from the exploitation and misery of the greater society. On the other hand, those who are poor or are members of the increasingly wearied middle class understandably find it difficult to muster up the energy to consider a broader public vision or good and to participate in the public decisions that fundamentally affect their lives, because so much of their effort is being spent either trying to secure a more decent living or just trying to survive.[30] "The result," as Cornel West observes, "is lives of what we might call 'random nows,' of fortuitous and fleeting moments preoccupied with 'getting over.'"[31]

In addition to all of this—the creation of vast economic and social inequality; the generation of a large underclass and an exclusive economic elite; the fragmentation of communities along class and economic lines; and the cynicism that these have engendered among the vast majority of the nation's citizenship—the market-driven mentality fostered by present-day capitalism also has managed to weaken our social ability to cultivate non-market values such as love, care, service, commitment, friendship, solidarity, spirituality, and justice. We are left with an overall culture of consumerism that is more conducive to cold-hearted individualism, hedonistic self-indulgence, and competition than to the cultivation of a public vision marked by the prioritization of the quality of our lives together.

The deindustrialization and the internationalization that have taken place over the last few decades simply have exacerbated these problems and also have made it even more difficult to institute democratizing measures. There also has been a recent shift in the employment sector. The sort of

---

30 For a picture of the plight of the poor in this country, see especially Peter Rossi, *Down and Out in America* (Chicago: University of Chicago Press, 1989). For an examination of the plight and weariness of the American middle class, and its social effects, see Katherine S. Newman, *Falling from Grace: The Experience of Downward Mobility in the American Middle Class* (New York: Random House, 1988); idem, *Declining Fortunes: The Withering of the American Dream* (New York: Basic Books, 1993); Arlie R. Hochschild, *The Second Shift: Working Parents and the Revolution at Home* (New York: Viking Books, 1989); Barbara Ehrenreich, *Fear of Falling: The Inner Life of the Middle Class* (New York: Pantheon Books, 1989); and Juliet B. Schor, *The Overworked American: The Unexpected Decline of Leisure* (New York: Basic Books, 1991).

31 West, *Race Matters*, 10.

low-skilled manufacturing jobs that once paid decent middle-class wages, and once provided many people with an economic stepping-stone, have been gradually disappearing as a result of the emerging emphasis being placed on high-skilled, information-based employment and because corporations increasingly have opted to exploit the cheaper labor markets in Mexico, Asia, and other parts of the world in order to increase their profits. Economic and employment indices establish that 1.5 million manufacturing jobs were lost in the 1980s, and that industrial-based employment had fallen by another 7 percent during the first three years of the 1990s, signaling the possible loss of hundreds of thousands more production-type jobs.[32] As routine production work has either moved overseas or disappeared altogether, many blue-collar American workers have been left to compete for minimum-wage, low-bene-fit jobs in the service sector. Census bureau statistics bear this trend out: just as 1.5 million lower-middle-class-wage jobs in manufacturing were being lost in the 1980s, 3.8 million new minimum-wage jobs in retail or in services appeared during the same time span.[33] The fastest growth in recent employ-ment has been, therefore, in jobs that pay under $5.00 per hour and offer few or no benefits—the sort of jobs exemplified by employment in fast-food restaurants or at check-out counters. This happenstance has simply com-pounded the maldistributive effects of capitalism by widening the income gap between high-skilled and low-skilled labor, and often by fostering either unemployment or seasonal part-time employment and, therefore, poverty.

Although blue-collar workers from all groups have suffered from these economic changes, industrial restructuring has especially affected members of historically racialized and disadvantaged cultural and ethnic groups that have not been afforded the opportunities to pursue higher education in this country. Without the benefits of higher education, many of these persons wind up as permanent economic proletarians. Hence, these economic changes not only have led to a widening of the income gap, but also have served to aggravate the conditions of social inequality in our nation.[34] Moreover, they also have served to increase social antagonisms and to crys-tallize a racial divide that further fragments our society, by causing members of distinct disadvantaged groups to see each other as competitors for dwin-dling economic opportunities rather than as potential political allies, and by

---

32 See Farley, *The New American Reality*, 64-107.

33 Cited in Farley, *The New American Reality*, 91, 101. For more statistical analysis to this effect, see John Kasarda, "Industrial Restructuring and the Changing Location of Jobs," in *State of the Union: America in the 1990s*, vol. 1, ed. Reynolds Farley (New York: Russell Sage Foundation, 1995), 215-42; James R. Wetzel, "Labor Force, Unemployment, and Earnings," in Farley, ed., *State of the Union*, 243-67.

fostering conditions whereby members of the predominantly white affluent or middle-class community, because of increases in poverty-induced urban crime, feel increased pressure to insulate themselves from the poor and working-class members living in the inner cities.

Before capitalism became largely postindustrial and global, industrial unions and community-oriented programs were at times able to mitigate some of the rapacious tendencies of corporate America, either by limiting labor exploitation, controlling wage disparity, or pressuring for corporate commitment to local communities. But these sorts of restraints have lost much of their effectiveness because the move toward a high-tech postindustrial economy has limited the power of industrial unionism, and the globalization of the labor market has allowed American corporations to dodge demands for community involvement. Moreover, the usual governmental attempts to counter the maldistributive effects of capitalism—making income taxes more progressive, raising taxes on capital gains, enacting prounion legislation, raising the minimum wage, and so on—have had very limited success. The deindustrialization of America coupled with the internationalization of capital and labor, then, has paved the way for an even more predatory mode of capitalism that generates further inequality, permits community deterioration in many neighborhoods, obliterates nonmarket cultural values, and frustrates the actualization of a substantive egalitarian vision.[35]

Those of us who remain committed to the theorization and actualization of a more just social order must face up to a dual challenge. On the one hand, if we are to facilitate the advancement of a public perception in our society,

---

34 For studies that pursue the polarizing social effects of the recent economic restructuring trends in the United States and/or their effect on particular racialized and disadvantaged groups, see William Julius Wilson, *The Truly Disadvantaged: The Inner City, the Underclass, and Public Policy* (Chicago: University of Chicago Press, 1987); idem, *When Work Disappears: The World of the New Urban Poor* (New York: Alfred A. Knopf, 1996); Bennett Harrison and Barry Bluestone, *The Great U-Turn: Corporate Restructuring and the Polarizing of America* (New York: Basic Books, 1988); Andrew Sum and Neal Fogg, "The Changing Economic Fortunes of Young Black Men in America," *The Black Scholar* (March 1990): 47-55; and Rebecca Morales and Frank Bonilla, eds., *Latinos in a Changing U.S. Economy: Comparative Perspectives on Growing Inequality* (New York: Russell Sage Foundation, 1993).

35 For more on the process of economic deindustrialization, the dynamics of rising socioeconomic inequality, and the consequences, see Bennett Harrison and Barry Bluestone, *The Deindustrialization of America: Plant Closing, Community Abandonment, and the Dismantling of Basic Industry* (New York: Basic Books, 1982); Maury B. Gittleman and David R. Howell, *Job Quality, Labor Market Segmentation, and Earnings Inequality: Effects of Economic Restructuring in the 1980s* (New York: Jerome Levy Economics Institute, 1992); Sheldon Danziger and Peter Gottschalk, *America Unequal* (Cambridge: Harvard University Press, 1995); Danziger and Gottschalk, eds., *Uneven Tides*; and Jeffrey Madrick, *The End of Affluence: The Causes and Consequences of America's Economic Dilemma* (New York: Random House, 1995).

which is imperative for the implementation of broad-based progressive social activism, then we must contend with the ravages caused by, and individualist temptations presented by, our present capitalist economic and cultural order. On the other hand, the goal of redistributive justice calls for broad-based mobilization and, therefore, the facilitation of a public disposition that may engender progressive activism on many fronts. In this way, then, the fruition of cultural as well as distributive social justice and the promotion of a public sensibility are deeply interrelated. Although the prospects for the advancement of a public perspective and the fulfillment of a more just socioeconomic order may seem unpromising at present, I believe that the seeds for the possible fruition of both exist in the present weariness and dissatisfaction felt by so many in our nation.

RACISM, THE RISE OF IDENTITY POLITICS, AND THE SIGNIFICANCE OF A PUBLIC DISPOSITION

The overarching and integrative sense of the public needed for social solidarity and change is imperiled not only by the individualistic impulses of liberalism and capitalism, but also by the continued existence of racism. Racism has always been a corrosive problem in our nation, and it continues to be so. Indeed, some of our institutional arrangements and practices continue to operate under implicit, and at times explicit, racist assumptions. This is evidenced by, for example, the fact that the unemployment rate remains twice as high for African Americans and other minority groups than for whites; that individuals of color who apply for mortgages are much more likely to be turned down by lenders than are whites with similar financial credentials; that the poverty rate among racialized minority families is in some cases more than twice as high as it is for white families; that lawsuits claiming employment discrimination continue to be filed and won; and that the economic disparities between whites and members of other groups are not declining in our nation.[36] Moreover, as William Julius Wilson observes,

---

36 On the socioeconomic disparities existing between nonwhite and white groups, see the analyses and comparisons of the 1980 and 1990 census provided by Farley, *The New American Reality*, esp. 208-71, 334-55. For more on existing socioeconomic disparities among U.S. groups, particularly comparing African American and/or Latino indices to those among Anglos, see Gregory DeFreitas, *Inequality at Work: Hispanics in the U.S. Labor Force* (New York: Oxford University Press, 1991); Andrew Hacker, *Two Nations: Black and White, Separate, Hostile, Unequal* (New York: Charles Scribner's Sons, 1992); Joan Moore and Racquel Pinderhughes, eds., *In the Barrios: Latinos and the Underclass Debate* (New York: Russell Sage Foundation, 1993); John Yinger, *Closed Doors, Opportunities Lost: The Continuing Costs of Housing Discrimination* (New York: Russell Sage Foundation, 1995); Danziger and Gottschalk, *America Unequal*; and Dalton Conley, *Being Black, Living in the Red: Race, Wealth, and Social Policy in America* (Berkeley: University of California Press, 1999).

"Affirmative action programs are under heavy assault, and broad public sympathy for those minority individuals who have suffered the most from racial exclusion has waned."[37] Hence, although racial attitudes reminiscent of the Jim Crow era may have become less visible, and although some legitimate gains have been made in the public sphere, racial and cultural discrimination has by no means disappeared. In fact, in some ways it has gone underground, in the form of subtle cultural racism, making it even more difficult to interpret and combat.[38]

Certainly, the economic anxiety and the cultural deterioration experienced in our times help to deepen our racial divide. In a time of growing economic insecurity such as ours, when the downward trend in wages has lowered the incomes of working-class citizens, when so many workers are insecure about their employment status, when so many are overworked, and when more and more Americans sense that their long-term economic prospects are bleak, racial antagonisms become even greater. During such moments, people tend to become more susceptible to simplistic and divisive ideologies that deflect attention away from the complex sources of their problems and also encourage persons and groups to turn on each other instead of to coalesce in finding answers to problems that affect us all and that are, in fact, the result of intentional political choices being made outside of our immediate communities. The task of combating racism becomes even more difficult and complex under such circumstances. Yet it is imperative that we struggle against the existence of racism in our midst, because, if unabated, its cancerous effects will continue to eat away at our social fabric and will frustrate any of our attempts to vitalize our shared public square. As an essential step in this struggle against racism, we must develop new frameworks and discourses capable of linking issues of race to the broader public good.

In the introduction to his wonderful book *Race Rules*, Michael Dyson asks the rhetorical question "Why another book on race?" Answering his own

---

37 William Julius Wilson, *The Bridge over the Racial Divide: Rising Inequality and Coalition Politics* (Berkeley: University of California Press, 1999), 11.

38 For a commentary that throws light on forms of cultural racism, see Wilson, *Racial Divide*, esp. 11-43. For a good discussion on cultural deprivation theories, see Kenneth B. Clark, *Dark Ghetto: Dilemmas of Social Power* (New York: Harper & Row, 1965); Oscar Lewis, "The Culture of Poverty," in *On Understanding Poverty: Perspectives from the Social Sciences*, ed. D. P. Moynihan (New York: Basic Books, 1968), 167-200; Nicholas Lemann, "The Origins of the Underclass," *Atlantic* 257 (June 1986): 31-61; and Lawrence Bobo, James R. Kluegel, and Ryan A. Smith, "Laissez-Faire Racism: The Crystallization of a Kinder, Gentler, Antiblack Ideology," in *Racial Attitudes in the 1990s*, ed. Steven A. Tuch and Jack K. Martin (Westport, Conn.: Praeger, 1997), 15-42.

question, Dyson responds that the justification for yet another book on race is that we, as a nation, "haven't learned our lessons."[39] Indeed, Dyson is correct. We, as a nation, have not yet sufficiently owned up to the ugly reality of racism, nor have we appropriately responded to its continued existence in our midst. Unfortunately, even some of our most perceptive commentators on race relations misunderstand and underestimate the complications inherent in our present racial divide because they often constrict discourse on racism to a simplistic "black and white" framework. This sort of bipolar racial epistemology ignores the rich racial and cultural diversity that exists in our nation, and it disregards the way in which other racialized, and culturally oppressed, groups also suffer the effects of racism. More disturbing still, this reflective and discursive myopia discourages formation of the sort of multiracial coalition required to combat racism and material inequality, because it creates the illusion that racism is something that concerns only the African American and Anglo communities. As Latino theologian Harold Recinos rightly observes, the establishment of a new framework of racial discourse for the American national identity "requires recognition that race matters in more than Black and White."[40] Although certainly it has afflicted African American history in a very particular manner, racism affects, and has acted upon, many other racialized and disadvantaged ethnic and cultural groups in the United States as well. It surely has had a pervasive impact on Latinos and Latinas. Above all, racism affects everyone's well-being, and it must, therefore, be confronted by all, regardless of race, ethnicity, culture, economic status, or gender.

The political imagination and the discursive frameworks that have prevailed in liberationist and progressive sectors during the late twentieth century in the United States, which have revolved around notions of identity, difference, cultural domination, and group recognition, have not yet appropriately addressed the way in which these above-mentioned axes of false consciousness and oppression intersect to complicate the achievement of social justice. Nor have they sufficiently recognized the manner in which these "multiple jeopardies"[41] illuminate the need for the cultivation of a public disposition in society and in our modes of discourse.

---

39 Michael Eric Dyson, *Race Rules: Navigating the Color Line* (New York: Vintage Books, 1997), 7.

40 Harold J. Recinos, *Who Comes in the Name of the Lord? Jesus at the Margins* (Nashville: Abingdon Press, 1997), 29.

41 See Deborah King, "Multiple Jeopardy, Multiple Consciousness," *Signs* 14, no. 1 (1988): 42-72.

In the post–World War II era we have witnessed in the United States an impressive proliferation of differentiated liberationist and progressive activisms that have been guided either by a culture- and identity-based political imagination or by a politics of difference. Most of the endeavors labeled as identity politics or the cultural politics of difference, which have been advanced especially by African American, Latino/a-Chicano/a, feminist, gay, and lesbian theorists, have rightfully sought to defend existing identities, end forms of cultural domination, and win recognition for group particularities that have been devalued or minimized by the mainstream culture. In other words, they have aimed to target, protest, and remedy existing forms of injustices. Thus, the pursuits attached to the discourse of identity and difference reflect, in the words of Craig Calhoun, legitimate "struggles, not merely gropings,"[42] and as such, they contribute to the quest for and theorizing of social justice. Among other salutary contributions, the discourse of identity and difference that has been en vogue among leftists has refreshingly brought attention to the plurality that is a basic property of the human condition, to experiences of injustice that have long been disregarded in society, and to some of the circumstances of an inequitable polity. It also has profitably demanded that theory attend to culture. To this extent, it must be taken seriously as *a contributing component* of a comprehensive emancipatory political project in the United States.

Nevertheless, my sense is that few proponents of the discourse of identity and difference—and this must include most liberationist and progressive U.S. theologians—have sufficiently scrutinized the limits and consequences of their mode of discourse. Well-intentioned and necessary as they are, these theologies have often failed to truly grapple with at least five salient problems. First, identities must constantly be constructed and renegotiated by individuals or groups within concrete interactions and social relations, and are, therefore, not always produced purely by acts of individual volition. Second, an identity- or difference-based politics requires, if it is to carry the potential of expanding *social* justice, the development of "a critical theory of recognition that identifies and defends *only* those versions of the cultural politics of difference that can be coherently combined with *a social politics of equality*."[43]

---

42 Craig Calhoun, "Social Theory and the Politics of Identity Social," in *Social Theory and the Politics of Identity*, ed. Craig Calhoun (Cambridge, Mass.: Blackwell, 1994), 21.43 Nancy Fraser, *Justice Interruptus: Critical Reflections on the "Postsocialist" Condition* (New York: Routledge, 1997), 12 (italics added).

43 Nancy Fraser, *Justice Interruptus: Critical Reflections on the "Postsocialist" Condition* (New York: Routledge, 1997), 12 (italics added).

Third, claims for the recognition of individual or group identities and difference, if they are to carry broad meaning and the capacity to gain recognition by the general public, inevitably must be placed both within a field of shared relevance, such as a polity, and within a common ethical frame of reference that highlights the basic humanness and equal moral worth of every person. Fourth, the discourse of identity and difference has tended to focus on symbolic culture and on cultural politics, to the neglect of political economy and the consideration of social issues such as the relations between groups in society. Fifth, the group activisms that prevail in our present sociopolitical landscape, under the sway of the logic of identity and difference, generally have tended to turn inward toward their own concerns and separate causes, thereby obscuring the impulse toward coalition—toward action on many fronts for social justice. Few liberationists and progressives have recognized the need for modes of discourse and activism that can exemplify a public disposition—one that would be inclined to connect the cultural politics of identity and difference to a broader social politics of liberation and to search for the possibilities of social arrangements that could harmonize diverse emancipatory interests in the struggle for freedom and justice.

As a result of this salient "postsocialist"[44] political vision, we have seen a propagation of separate and distinct circumscribed struggles for justice that at times gain their advocates localized victories, usually in the symbolic or discursive realm, but at other times come into conflict with each other, leading to a political balkanization and often leaving intact the broader power structures that generate the disadvantages that occasioned their need in the first place. Ironically, therefore, although the leftist discourse of culture, identity, and difference is proposed as a revolutionary and transformative social praxis, in actuality it has remained simply an "oppositional" discourse that at best responds partially and transiently to the conditions of injustice in society, and at its worst serves to eclipse the theorizing of broad social justice and coalitional activism.

Theorists of justice, such as liberation theologians, must keep a key factor in mind when they are developing their discourses and pursuing their activistic commitments: the realization that the attainment of "integral"

---

44 Nancy Fraser aptly uses this term to reflect critically on the general parameters within which leftist political thought has moved, especially in the wake of 1989 (i.e., following the alleged delegitimization of socialism after the collapse of the Berlin Wall). I mention these in note 63 of chapter 2 of the present volume. For Fraser's use of this term, and a full explanation of the notions it conveys, see *Justice Interruptus*, esp. 1-8, 11-39, 173-88.

social justice,[45] particularly in a pluralistic, stratified, and fragmented society such as ours, depends greatly on our ability to cultivate deep feelings of social solidarity with a broad constituency in society—the kind of solidarity that may result in collaborative political activity. More deeply, however, this kind of solidarity requires a public disposition: the disposition to think of oneself as part of a social whole; to care for the quality of our lives together as a society; to cooperate with others of different experiences in seeking common goals. There cannot be significant social movements for justice— the kind that could foster substantive transformation in society—in the absence of a holistic public disposition that makes connections, alliances, and coalitions desirable and possible. Without a public disposition we may achieve nuanced categories of positionality in the linguistic and symbolic order, we might even gain some level of affirmation for our culturally defined groups, and we certainly will occasion many well-intentioned yet encumbering forms of provincialism and narrow particularism, but we will not affect much social and structural change. Progressive and liberationist theologians who want to help remedy social injustices should, therefore, seek to cultivate in society a public disposition. This means, first, that our theological discourses must themselves adopt an orientation that is publicist. And this, in turn, implies cultivating some skeptical distance from the fashionable left-wing logic of localism that, whether in the name of deconstruction, postmodernism, or cultural difference, unintentionally discourages the kind of overarching integrative thinking and speaking that may inform and impel the emancipatory coalitional activisms that the different demands for justice require today.

---

45 I use the expression "integral" social justice here to promote the idea that the ultimate commitment of liberationist and progressive thinkers should be to a comprehensive, integrative, emancipatory "sociopolitical" project that is attentive to the demands for recognition and redistribution in society, and, in this way, may be of aid to the diverse struggles for justice taking place among the public. My sense is that although liberation theologies in the United States have been concerned with, and have implicitly aimed to further, social justice, their understanding of injustice and justice has principally been cultural and symbolic rather than social in scope. As a result, injustices rooted in the political and economic structure of society have not received as much *careful* attention in our theologies. Another result has been insufficient contemplation of the possibilities for emancipatory social arrangements that could transform identities and structures, harmonize the interests of diverse and currently fragmented constituencies, and, in this way, benefit the social whole. Hence, I believe that we need thought forms that can couple cultural struggles to a broader social politic of liberation.

ACTIVIST COALITIONS, PUBLIC DISCOURSE, AND THEOLOGY

It would be naive to think that our visions and discourses can in and of themselves transform the worlds we inhabit; the task of social transformation requires agency and mobilization. Development of discourse is but a partial requirement for the progressive reshaping of our social realm, but it is a crucial one. Discourses do have influential power, and, therefore, consequences. Hence, they must be taken seriously. Precisely for this reason we must critically examine our discourses in order to decipher their practical implications and relevance for broad social change. The demands for justice in our times call for discourses that can move beyond the theorization of difference to the theorization of the interstitial sites of interaction, interconnection, and exchange that may exist *between* our different spaces of identity and struggle. This discursive move does not mean that we need to ignore questions of particular identity and difference within our theologies. It does require, however, that we highlight in them the things that persons and groups have in common—their common problems, aspirations, hopes, and humanity, as well as the possibilities that may exist for interaction—at least as much as we examine the space of specific cultural and ethnic identity and difference. If we fail to recognize what is held in common among us, as well as the potential space of relational interaction that could unite our different struggles for justice, then we can emphasize only that which divides us. Because the current prospects for the furthering of justice in its multiple forms markedly hinge on our abilities to promote broad-based alliances of struggle across differences, our liberatory theological discourses need to concentrate on the promotion and facilitation of coalitional activism.

All too often, the term "coalition" is loosely employed to mean simply an aggregate, or collection, of separate political components or constituencies that may happen to come into contact in the social realm. But coalition building requires some degree of forethought and intention. "It requires," in the words of Jerry Watts, "the concerted intent on the part of individuals and groups of individuals to link themselves together for reasons of pursuing an end that could not in all probability be attained if these disparate groups did not pool their resources."[46] In effect, the existence of meaningful political coalitions presupposes prior bargaining and strategic promotion. It is in this respect that our discourses can make a difference: they can serve to promote

---

46 Jerry G. Watts, "Blacks and Coalition Politics: A Theoretical Reconceptualization," in *The Politics of Minority Coalitions: Race, Ethnicity, and Shared Uncertainties*, ed. Wilbur C. Rich (Westport, Conn.: Praeger, 1996), 40.

the building of coalitions of struggle across racial, gender, class, and religious lines. This task involves the possession of a discursive public disposition (i.e., the desire to understand oneself as part of a potentially wider public; to broadcast one's discourse into ever widening arenas; to couple issues of local cultural politics to a comprehensive, emancipatory, sociopolitical project; and to emphasize solidarity and connection). It also involves a willingness to persuade persons and groups to focus on the interests that they hold in common, and to highlight the broad benefits that would accrue from multiracial and multifront political coalitions to all persons who are struggling economically or culturally in our society.

In this vein, we can begin by making explicit to historically subordinated persons and groups in society, who generally have lacked the power to single-handedly influence the political process, that they stand a much better chance of generating the political muscle needed to ease their varied burdens by considering cooperation with others. This means that "minority intellectuals" must be willing to outline the need and basis for emancipatory multiracial, multifront, coalitional activism, which, in turn, implies *solidarity with all of one's potential allies* in the struggle for social justice. Correspondingly, this involves attracting the attention and support of people and interests outside of one's own ethnic, cultural, or religious community of struggle in order to foster broad-based coalitions and alliances.

But we should also emphasize that it is not only members of racial minorities and disadvantaged ethnic or cultural groups in society who stand to gain from the political empowerment that coalitions may engender. The fact is that, along with African Americans, Latinos, Asians, and Native Americans, many whites in our nation also have experienced an increase in economic insecurity and the varied stresses on family and communal life that stem from these. Moreover, the social inequities, antagonisms, and pathological consequences—unemployment, poverty, criminal activity, social outrage—that result from inequality affect all Americans in one way or another. Hence, although the most powerful motivation for group action might come from the broad economic insecurity that has resulted from recent national and international economic changes, the existence of racism, sexism, and cultural prejudice in our nation should also alarm not just those who disproportionately suffer their effects, but all U.S. citizens, because the divisions and stratifications that result from them undermine the conditions of equality, justice, substantive democracy, social cohesion, and overall quality of life in America. Therefore, all who are concerned with the effects of socioeconomic and cultural inequality in our nation, and all who remain committed to the ideals of equality, justice, and democracy, should be supportive of efforts to generate broad-based political coalitions. And the purpose of these coalitions would be to counter those cultural, political, and economic practices of exclusion that violate the democratic fulfillment of persons or groups in society, and to put pressure, including voting and consumer pressure, on both public and corporate leaders to adopt policies that reflect the interests of ordinary people.[47]

Certainly, if political coalitions are to generate the kind of public pressure that might facilitate social change, they must attract and energize a wide enough constituency to make a difference in the public decision-making process. Furthermore, they must accomplish this goal within a social context marked by a proliferation of different activisms that at times engenders impasse. It follows, then, that our theological discourses must somehow navigate across racial, cultural, gender, and religious lines to cultivate holistic social arrangements that may harmonize the interests of diverse constituencies and, in this way, facilitate the possibilities for social change.

A central question arises here: How can theological discourse best attract the attention and concern of a wide audience in the broad terrain of civil society, and how can it best facilitate the building of coalitions of struggle across the many differences existing in our public? The sort of public theology I am calling for involves development of a mode of theological address that is first of all pragmatic and historicist rather than dogmatic. Public theology (1) is primarily concerned to respond to the salient issues of the moment in a given context rather than to develop systematic doctrinal treatises or static dogmas; (2) aims to constructively engage secular others as well as others with differing religious backgrounds rather than to impose the values of a particular religion on the public sphere; and (3) seeks to employ religious narrative and imagination as a source that brings people together to regenerate democratic possibilities rather than as a means to set at odds religious identities. Therefore, public theology requires a pragmatic and historical consciousness that shifts attention away from first principles, self-evident truths, and epistemic foundations to the everyday, down-to-earth historical effects, fruits, and consequences of our beliefs and courses of action in a given age and context.

---

47 My description of the goals of coalition building here is partly inspired by William Julius Wilson's arguments in *The Bridge over the Racial Divide*. Note, however, that the twofold aim of multiracial political coalitions that I suggest integrates a sensitivity to claims for multicultural recognition more openly than does Wilson's project. My desire within the arena of theological discourse is to *couple* matters of recognition to a comprehensive and emancipatory sociopolitical project.

It follows that a public theology should engage in forms of open inquiry and persuasion that do not lapse into authoritarian, parochial modes of argumentation or find their substantiation in "local reservations of spirit"[48] or cryptic revelatory messages. It must demonstrate the courage to employ critical intelligence, to face up to the inescapable fallibility of human thought and talk without succumbing to sophomoric relativism or wholesale skepticism, and to pursue the difficult trek of open and reasonable dialogue in civil society. In this sense, theology enters public life not to assert itself, but rather, to participate in the remedying of social injustice and, thus, to create a better society.

My promotion of a pragmatic and historicist theological discourse that uses the language of reason and rights in the public sphere, rather than the language of piety, confessionalism, or religious dogmatism, does not imply that theology must relinquish its distinctiveness as "theo-logos" or that theologians must decontextualize themselves from their particular religious traditions in order to speak for a general public. Indeed, if a public theology is to be theological at all, it must in some way draw on the insights of a particular religious tradition. But, as Linell Cady aptly observes, there is a difference between "a theology which is dogmatically bound to a tradition and one which is deeply informed by a tradition but which critically appropriates and extends that tradition."[49] The former kind of theology usually involves or requires either an unquestionable appeal to past authorities or an unquestioned reliance on specific texts or dogmas as strictly authoritarian. And its concern and focus is commonly to espouse the exclusive claims or identity of a given religious tradition in order to ensure the continuance of historic religious orthodoxy. The latter type of revisionist-constructive theology roots itself in a tradition, its categories, concepts, narratives, and images, but is willing to challenge, expand, and revise that tradition in light of the critical questions raised by the modern and, now, postmodern world. And it does so not because it fetishizes critical intelligence or because it belittles tradition or history, but rather, because it wishes to interpret, reconstruct, and appropriate a religious tradition in such a way that it can contribute anew to our human quest for meaning in the lived moment and also respond to new occasions and duties in a transformative manner. The constructivist or revisionist theologian begins admittedly with a specific tradition of faith but both acknowledges the open-textured and dynamic quality of that tradition and seeks to make manifest its meaning in nonexclusive ways that are responsive to the

---

48 See Tracy, *The Analogical Imagination*, 13.
49 Cady, "Public Theology," 206.

perceived needs and challenges of the time at hand, willing, as the occasion mandates, to reconstruct that tradition.

This last type of theology holds much more salutary potential for public discursive engagement than does a dogmatic theology. The problem with a dogmatic theology is that it lends itself much too easily to forms of religious fanaticism, exclusive claims-making, narrow-minded discourse, rigid orthodoxies, and inconsiderate, authoritarian impositions of values that can serve to short-circuit civil discourse and to engender divisions rather than rapport in the broader, pluralistic terrain of civil society. A dogmatic theology also runs the risk of having limited relevance, attracting the attention of those who share similar convictions and already stand within a theological circle but not beyond it. A public theology has to respectfully engage with, and compellingly speak to, secular others as well as persons of differing convictions in the general social public in order to facilitate the sorts of pluralistic civic collaborations needed for restorative and transformative nation-building.

Is there room in the sort of public theology that I am espousing for particular Christian insights and convictions? Certainly. But we must remember that, unlike perhaps the systematic and/or practical church theologian, who speaks mainly to persons who already stand within his or her theological circle, one of the tasks of a public theologian is to speak about the meaning of a religious tradition in terms that make sense to, and elicit a response from, people who do not share his or her theological convictions.[50] And the public theologian's ultimate concern is not to impose either a set of particular moral values or a religious position on others in the public sphere, but rather, to appropriate his or her particular religious worldview in such a way that it may contribute, alongside other faiths and persuasions, to the engendering of a sense of the public that fosters mutual respect, social accountability, and emancipatory civic activity in our nation. As Robin Lovin indicates, "Public theology, then, must live in the tension between its tasks of interpreting particular religious worldviews and transforming public life, but it must also conduct a dialogue between faith and world in a way that demonstrates the possibility of *public* theology."[51] A pragmatic and historicist theology that

---

50 Three exemplary thinkers who operated as Christian public theologians and/or philosophers in this manner, appropriating the symbolic resources of their religious heritages in a way that captivated the conscience of persons who did not necessarily share their religious commitments, were Martin Luther King Jr., Reinhold Niebuhr, and John Courtney Murray. I believe that in the present moment Cornel West is also offering a living example of this possibility.

51 Robin Lovin, "Response to Linell Cady," in *The Legacy of H. Richard Niebuhr*, ed. Ronald F. Thiemann (Minneapolis: Fortress Press, 1991), 136.

employs a constructivist or revisionist methodology, rather than one that is dogmatic and/or confessional, is better suited to negotiate this tension.

Public theology must add to its pragmatist and historicist orientation a prophetic dimension—one that envisions the religious imagination as a potential source that can help us to respond to historical tragedy and hypocrisy in a hopeful, rather than fatalistic or naively optimistic, manner. The Judeo-Christian prophetic tradition, which stretches back at least three thousand years, was always a form of sociocultural analysis and criticism motivated by an emancipatory, all-embracing, religious and moral vision. In contrast to the priestly religious tradition, which has nearly always tended to be otherworldly or complacent with the earthly status quo, the prophetic tradition has been characterized by its social, historical, moral, and ameliorative impulse. Its aim is always to confront the hard reality of tragedy, evil, and needless suffering caused by human agency, human limitations, and human existential angst, while at the same time promoting the possibility of human progress and creative social living. Prophetic discourse is thus a form of tragic and critical thought or speech in that it confronts individual and collective experiences of evil, bringing to bear relentless criticism on those individual practices or social arrangements that foster unnecessary suffering. It is also, however, a form of romantic and hopeful thought or speech in that it does not devalue human power, is motivated by compassion, views history as open-ended and receptive to new possibilities, and promotes utopian energies that can yield personal and social change for the better. In the words of Cornel West, prophetic discourse "wrestles with despair yet never allows despair to have the last word."[52]

Although prophetic discourse is by nature critical, at times even rebellious, it is also marked by a constructive universal consciousness that exudes a love for the larger picture. In making connections across lines and barriers, prophetic discourse actually hopes to enter the zone occupied by centralizing powers within the public arenas of citizen discourse and association in order to make a difference there. As Walter Brueggemann describes it, "Prophetic speech brings to the center a radically different perspective than that which dominates the imagination of the center; but it refuses to go away or be treated as the voice of the bizarre other."[53] The prophet, in this sense, speaks with the accents of an alter ego that successfully addresses us from inside even while challenging us with a dissenting message. Although the prophet's spirit opposes rather than accommodates any oppressive status quo, the prophet is nevertheless actively involved in society, seeking constantly to change and expand

---

52 Cornel West, *Restoring Hope: Conversations on the Future of Black America*, ed. Kelvin Shawn Sealey (Boston: Beacon Press, 1997), xii.

53 Walter Brueggemann, *The Prophetic Imagination* (Philadelphia: Fortress Press, 1978), 90.

minds, break down stereotypes and reductive categories that limit human thought and communication, and organize or harmonize social arrangements across lines of difference in the interest of greater social justice. Prophetic speech is, therefore, neither separatist nor parochial. Nor is it shy about entering and engaging the center. Rather, it emphasizes human connection, highlights the interdependence of all of our futures, and speaks the truth to power with authority and love. From these characteristics, we can conclude that the prophetic intellectual is one who is willing to build both on the best work that academics, experts, analysts, and pundits may make available, as well as on forgotten, abandoned, or subordinated histories and knowledges in order to illuminate the unsuitability of the present for many as well as a vision of what could and ought to be possible in our world.

In these days of inequality, suffering, sociopolitical fragmentation, cynicism, and fashionable conservatism, there is a definite need for prophetic discourse—discourse that can call for moral renewal, condemn oppression anywhere and everywhere, and energize those all-embracing human relationships that can help to sustain our emancipatory struggles against unnecessary tragedy. A public theology that aspires to social relevance in this manner must incorporate an element of sociocultural criticism, using historical, social, political, and cultural analyses to develop thoughtful accounts of the situation in which we find ourselves as a nation. But it must also project a regenerative vision that is broad enough to bring different persons, different kinds of liberationists and progressives, together in the public realm to collaborate for a greater social good. Despite the impressive proliferation of liberationist and oppositional theologies that we have seen during the last two decades, and the generation of progressive fronts of struggle in some areas of the general populace, my sense is that not enough people are articulating a broad enough emancipatory vision that could forge the sorts of solidarities necessary for regenerating meaningful liberatory possibilities. Hence, we are in need of *prophetic* public theologies, imbued with a sense of holism, that can transcend the space of self or specific identity and difference to engage the broader social context, and thus revitalize the populist sentiment and coalitional energy that the demands for justice require in our time.

Finally, theologians who wish to effect publicness in their writings and speech must adopt, without oversimplifying issues or losing profundity, an accessible style of reflection that a general audience of thoughtful people might understand. As Linell Cady points out, "Theology has, for the most part, become a specialized area of expertise, unintelligible to those outside"[54] the

---

54 Cady, "Public Theology," 203.

discipline. But a public theology, precisely because of its aim to enter the broader terrain of citizen discourse and association, must by necessity seek to communicate with a wide and diverse audience. This implies making use of language that, although thoughtful and distinctive as "theo-logos," is lucid and as far as possible free of technicality or jargon. In a sense, public theology must be *interdisciplinary*, appropriating the insights of science, philosophy, sociology, cultural studies, and critical theory, among others, to devise relevant theological discourse for a broad social public, and also be *dediscipliniz-ing*, refusing to be tied down to a specialty and the imposed restrictions or expectations of a profession or guild.

Given the emphasis placed on professionalization and specialization in the post-Enlightenment era, particularly in the intellectual milieu, it is understandable that theologians feel great pressure to write treatises that can appear to be scholarly to colleagues in other academic disciplines. Unfortunately, theology, as it is, is marginalized within the academy because it is often not deemed to be a legitimate, reasonable, or empirical discipline of study worthy of a place in university and college settings; its proper place is considered to be the theological seminary, and its proper role only that of preparation for the ministry. Hence, theologians must continue to respond to these historical and institutional pressures or biases in their writings by producing discourse that is intellectually sound, well versed, comprehensive, properly nuanced, and pragmatically relevant.

Nevertheless, theology must also face up to its broader cultural marginalization beyond the academy. Theology rarely has much of an impact in the public realm, whether to inform the lives of persons in the broader realm of civil society, beyond the confines of the church or seminaries, or to influence public discourse, or to prompt fellow citizens to take public action on behalf of greater social justice. The task confronting those theologians who aspire to operate as public intellectuals, rather than merely as academic intellectuals, is, therefore, to strike a fruitful balance in their writings and speech between intellectual profundity and public rhetorical accessibility.[55] Our theologies have failed to make an impact on the broader public because they generally have lacked a public disposition, sociopolitical relevancy, discursive ingenuity, and, therefore, the ability to speak across local, cultural, racial, and gender

---

55 I believe that the writings of Cornel West, who is a philosopher, cultural critic, and, in my opinion, presently America's preeminent public intellectual, and of Justo González, a renowned church historian and Latino theologian, offer excellent examples of learned and profound works that are accessible in communicative character to a general, educated public. See, for instance, West, *Race Matters*, and Justo González, *Mañana: Christian Theology from a Hispanic Perspective* (Nashville: Abingdon Press, 1990).

lines. But theological discourse might fulfill these requirements and still fail as *public* discourse if it is understandable only to an exclusive circle of theologians or academics. Theology that aspires to publicness must operate as public address. And the fact is that technical, jargon-filled discourse normally fails as public address because it is inaccessible to a wide enough audience. Hence, if theology is to become public discourse, and if theology is to attract wide segments of the population with a compelling message that facilitates emancipatory alliances across differences, it will have to adopt a style of reflection that, although erudite, profound, well informed, and nuanced, is accessible and valuable to a general audience of thoughtful people—to the public.

Thus, liberationist and progressive theologies that aim to promote social justice must seek to become public theologies—discourse that couples either the language, symbols, or background concepts of a religious tradition with an overarching, integrative, emancipatory sociopolitical perspective in such a way that it movingly captures the attention of a broad audience and promotes the cultivation of a concern for the quality of our lives together in society. Theologians can succeed in this effort by (1) moving beyond the theorization merely of specific cultural and ethnic identity and difference to the theorization of the interstitial sites of interaction, interconnection, and exchange that may exist between our different spaces of identity and struggle; (2) embracing a pragmatic and historicist orientation that makes use of religious narrative and imagination as a source to bring people together and to regenerate democratic possibilities rather than as a means to set at odds religious identities; (3) taking a prophetic stance that brings to bear relentless criticism on those individual practices or social arrangements that foster inequality and unnecessary suffering and also displays a universal consciousness that exudes a love for the larger picture; and (4) adopting, without oversimplifying issues or losing profundity, an accessible style of reflection that a general audience of thoughtful people might understand. Without this sort of public disposition and perspective, our theologies might achieve nuanced categories of positionality in the linguistic and symbolic order, and they might even gain some level of affirmation for our culturally defined groups or religious communities, but they will effect little social and structural change. In short, their ameliorative and liberating potential will be truncated in the broader public realm.

In the next chapter, the final chapter of this book, I call attention to my conviction that a public perspective does not require that categories of locational specificity, like cultural identity and difference, be abandoned, but rather, that they be supplemented and placed within a more comprehensive emancipatory sociopolitical imagination and discursive framework. I do this by looking into the possibility and significance of "subaltern counter*public*" communication and contestation for the construction of Latino/a theologies of liberation.

For though the common world is the common meeting ground of all, those who are present have different locations in it.

—Hannah Arendt[*]

The choice is not between a Latino/a identity versus a generic Americanness with no substantive content, but rather to understand how we can choose both Latino/a identity and a larger substantive identity for all who live in the United States. We ... need to think of ourselves—and understand ourselves—as full players in formulating a new national consciousness... Such a concept does not simply side with difference against universality or vice versa, but attempts a reconfiguration.

—Linda Martin Alcoff[†]

As the "nature"of postmodern social oppression presents itself in a more highly sophisticated, differentiated, and confusing manner, there is a greater necessity for members of subordinate groups to incorporate a differential mode of oppositional consciousness in order to build expanding alliances of struggle.

—Antonia Darder[‡]

The agency necessary for ethical and political change begins in ... the human capacity to reflect upon the meaning of our actions in relation to larger systems of the social order.

—Susan Friedman[§]

---

[*] Hannah Arendt, *The Human Condition* (Chicago: University of Chicago Press, 1958), 57.

[†] Linda Martin Alcoff, "Latina/o Identity Politics," in *The Good Citizen*, ed. David Batstone and Eduardo Mendieta (New York: Routledge, 1999), 108-9.

[‡] Antonia Darder, "The Politics of Biculturalism: Culture and Difference in the Formation of *Warriors for Gringostroika* and *The New Mestizas*," in *Culture and Difference: Critical Perspectives on the Bicultural Experience in the United States*, ed. Antonia Darder (Westport, Conn.: Bergin & Garvey, 1995), 11.

[§] Susan S. Friedman, *Mappings: Feminism and the Cultural Geographies of Encounter* (Princeton, N.J.: Princeton University Press, 1998), 64.

INTRODUCTION

In their eagerness to present theology as a form of public discourse, many in the theological community recently have taken to attaching the label of "public talk" or "public discourse" to just about any mode of theology that makes some sort of reference to society or to some of its problems. This propensity is lamentable, and can prove to be misleading, because it strips the concept and quality of publicness of its real meaning, distinctiveness, and analytical utility.

Certainly, a theology that aspires to a public quality must focus on the state of current affairs in a given society. But there are other tasks and qualities that define public thought and discourse. First of all, thought and discourse that aspire to publicness must elucidate the significance of the concept of the public, and must clarify the theoretical and practical benefits that can result from the adoption of a "public" orientation. Second, public thought and discourse are characterized not merely by the mention of social issues but by the provision of overarching visions and systemic, broad social analyses based on a keen sense of the numerous inequities faced by many in society. The ultimate goal of public thought and discourse must be to grasp and transform the social whole, not just a local social sector or group, and to cultivate care for the quality of our lives together. This in turn implies an ability to connect particular local group interests to some concept of public interest, all while being able to convince others of the broader implications of particular group interests, needs, and concerns. It also implies that public thought and discourse must display an all-embracing moral emphasis and ameliorative impulse that exhibits compassion for those who suffer unjustly, is mindful of and abhors all modes of injustice, and yearns for forms of resistance and struggle that can make a difference in society. Third, given the social fragmentation we face in our civic realm and the splintering of progressive and emancipatory movements in our time, contemporary public thought and discourse must demonstrate an integrative perspective that can harmonize the liberation and progressive struggles for justice of currently fragmented constituencies in order to facilitate alliances and coalitions across racial, cultural, gender, class, and religious lines. Therefore, the fundamental role of public thought and discourse is to capture the attention of a wide and diverse audience with a moving and harmonizing emancipatory message that can promote the cultivation of those modes of love, care, concern, and courage required both for individual or particular group fulfillment and for broad-based, broadly benefiting social activism. Theologies that do not exhibit these qualities, and do not aim to support these holistic and emancipatory visions, should not be labeled "public."

The concept of the public,[1] and the ideal of publicness in discourse, certainly encapsulates a "universalizing" emphasis. The subject of the public sphere, and the aspiration for publicness in discourse,[2] need not, however, be confused with a yearning for the return to a fallacious theory of universality devoid of specificity. To put it plainly, the theorizing of public space and discourse does not require that we forget about our particular social and cultural locations or that we disregard matters of culture, identity, subjectivity, and difference; rather, it requires that we return to them in a newly spatialized way—one that plays up the liberating possibilities that inhere in those interstitial sites of interaction, interconnection, and exchange "in between" differences in our society. When seen in this light, a theory of public space and of discourse can allow both for the recognition of particular community or group concerns and needs and for the utopic hope of comprehensive and equitable social justice.

---

1 Throughout this book, I align my conception of the public sphere with a discursive model of the public. That is to say, what I have in mind when I refer to the concept of the public is specifically the public arenas of citizen discourse and association in that institutionalized realm of civic political interaction that often is labeled "the realm of civil society." For an explanation of this particular view of the public, see Nancy Fraser, *Justice Interruptus: Critical Reflections on the "Postsocialist" Condition* (New York: Routledge, 1997), esp. 69-98. Fraser observes that "this arena is conceptually distinct from the state; it is a site for the production and circulation of discourses that can in principle be critical of the state." It is also, she notes, "conceptually distinct from the official-economy; it is not an arena of market relations but rather one of discursive relations, a theater for debating and deliberating rather than buying and selling" (p. 70). This particular theory of the public is especially indebted to the groundbreaking views originally elaborated by Jurgen Habermas, *The Structural Transformation of the Public Sphere: An Inquiry into a Category of Bourgeois Society*, trans. Thomas Burger and Frederick Lawrence (Cambridge, Mass.: MIT Press, 1989). For an analysis of distinct theories of the public, see Seyla Benhabib, "Models of Public Space: Hannah Arendt, the Liberal Tradition, and Jurgen Habermas," in *Habermas and the Public Sphere*, ed. Craig Calhoun (Cambridge, Mass.: MIT Press, 1992), 73-98.

2 Here I specifically have in mind the question of the potential public character of discourse. Hence, I must clarify that there are in fact two interrelated, yet distinct, topics taken up in this chapter: first, the theorizing of the public realm of civil society; and second, the theorizing of the nature or character of public discourse within the civic public realm. Whenever I use the "public" as a noun, I am referring to the general arena of citizen discourse and association in society that often is labeled "the realm of civil society." Throughout this work, I have employed the adjective "public" or the phrase "quality and/or ideal of publicness" to denote four particular reflective and discursive traits: (1) the disposition to enter into, highlight the potentiality of, and influence the public arenas of citizen discourse and association in the broader social public; (2) the demonstration of an overarching and integrative analytical perspective that seeks to grasp and transform the social whole rather than merely a segment of that whole; (3) the desire to identify and link many different emancipatory activisms through the facilitation of coalitions of struggle; and (4) the ability to attract and energize a wide and diverse populace willing and able to take principled public action on behalf of greater social justice.

Two general directions have been pursued in the theorizing of "the public." One has been marked by some dubious features of modern thought and, therefore, makes no provision for the consideration of specific identities and status differentials in society. The other direction, that of "subaltern counter-*public*" discourses, does make such provision. In this final chapter, I sketch the discursive implications of the theory of subaltern counter*public* communication and contestation for the construction of Latino/a liberation theology, suggesting that it can help to expand the vision of that theology by connecting its aspirations with those of public discourse.

DIVERSITY, EQUALITY, MULTIPLE PUBLICS, AND INTERPUBLIC RELATIONS IN THE PUBLIC SPHERE

Modern and contemporary social and political theory generally has tended to theorize the concept of a "public sphere" in restrictive and troublesome terms, often neglecting the consideration of cultural specificity, race, gender, and inequality when it comes to interpreting the conditions for and possibilities of public arenas of citizen discourse and association. "In conformity with the modern idea of normative reason," Iris Marion Young observes, the concept of the public in sociopolitical theory and practice has often stood for "a sphere of human existence in which citizens express their rationality and universality, abstracted from their particular situations and needs."[3] Hence, whether construed within the framework of classical civic republicanism, liberalism, or even more recent models such as Jurgen Habermas's public sphere theory, the concept of the public frequently has been theorized in terms that seem hostile to cultural difference, and that do not sufficiently scrutinize the discursive and practical implications of social inequality: the public sphere often has been construed in revisionist historiographies, as well as in social and political theories, as a discursive and associational arena in society in which interlocutors can, indeed should, set aside characteristics such as differences in birth or culture and speak to one another *as if* they were social, cultural, political, and economic peers, while discussing matters of "public concern," "common interests," and/or the "common good."[4]

---

3 Iris Marion Young, "Impartiality and the Civic Public: Some Implications of Feminist Critiques of Moral and Political Theory," in *Feminism as Critique: On the Politics of Gender*, ed. Seyla Benhabib and Drucilla Cornell (Minneapolis: University of Minnesota Press, 1987), 73.

4 For a work that elucidates and endorses an interpretation of the public that pursues the path of civic republicanism, see William M. Sullivan, *Reconstructing Public Philosophy* (Berkeley: University of California Press, 1986). For an examination of liberal models of the public and Jurgen Habermas's discursive model of the public, see Benhabib, "Models of Public Space," esp. 81-98.

Modernity's dubious fascination both with an ahistorical, universal mode of reasoning and with rational consensus has affected public sphere theory in still another way: it has induced most theorists to confine the theorizing of public life to a single, overarching public sphere of citizen discourse. This penchant has, in turn, led to an idealization of the bourgeois, mainly white and masculinist, public sphere of past societies; the assumption that the emergence of additional competing publics of discourse in society necessarily signals fragmentation and the corrosion of democracy; and the discrediting of other nonbourgeois public spheres of discourse that express the particular concerns, interests, and needs of members of subordinated social groups.

A conception of the public that builds on these assumptions meets, however, with various practical and theoretical limitations that must be questioned, especially when one is taking into consideration the existing conditions of pluralism and stratification in a society such as that of the United States. First, as it pertains to the idealization of a normative and universal mode of reasoning, we should note that theories of the public that stress the bracketing of cultural particularity usually assume, as Nancy Fraser observes, "that a public sphere is or can be a space of zero-degree culture, so utterly bereft of any specific ethos as to accommodate with perfect neutrality and equal ease interventions expressive of any and every cultural ethos."[5] But this assumption ignores two facts. This assumption overlooks the fact that the reasoning of those who inhabit the public discursive arenas of society will reflect, and will be influenced in some way by, the particular grids of their cultural traditions and life experiences, so that the public realm can never be a space of zero-degree culture where one can expect to witness the operation of universal reasoning. More disturbing, this assumption also neglects the fact that cultures and identities rarely have been equally valued in societies, especially those that have been marked by systemic inequality: "In stratified societies, unequally empowered social groups tend to develop unequally valued cultural styles. The result is the development of powerful informal pressures that marginalize the contributions of members of subordinate groups both in everyday life contexts and in official public spheres."[6] In sum, then, the idealization of the public sphere as an arena of collective deliberation and discursive exchange where citizens can and should express a universal mode of rationality abstracted from their particular histories, situations, and needs serves only to conceal the conditional quality of all human reason and the

---

5 Fraser, *Justice Interruptus*, 79.
6 Ibid., 79.

fact that cultural oppression has been, and continues to be, a reality in most societies. Instead of opting to circumvent the contributions of cultural histories, and instead of disregarding the dynamics of cultural oppression, theorists of the public should recognize both that the actualization of a democratic discursive public sphere entails, indeed relies on, openness to the simultaneous presence of different perspectives, histories, and cultures in society, and that lurking behind what parades as the universal there is always some disguised form of cultural particularism. In short, rather than evading the reality of culture, we must take culture and cultural oppression seriously in our theories of the public.

Second, regarding the assumption that interlocutors speak to each other in the public realm *as if* they were peers, past and present societies have, in fact, generally been marked by forms of structural inequalities that have caused status differentials among persons and social groups. Given the multiple inequalities—cultural, political, and economic—that have actually reduced the quality of life for many, and that have engendered real-life power differentials in the discursive, political, and economic realms of society, it is not just presumptuous but actually dangerous to conceive of the public sphere as a realm where interlocutors could or should discuss policies and issues affecting everyone *as if* social, cultural, and economic inequalities did not exist. Instead of purporting to ignore and bracket the existence of these inequalities, a conception of the public sphere should both be attentive to and seek to eliminate them. In the words of Nancy Fraser,

> We should be led to entertain serious doubts about a conception of the public sphere that purports to bracket, rather than to eliminate, structural social inequalities. We should question whether it is possible even in principle for interlocutors to deliberate *as if* they were social peers in specially designated discursive arenas, when these discursive arenas are situated in a larger societal context that is pervaded by structural relations of dominance and subordination.[7]

Third, as to the idealization of a single, official public sphere, the official public spheres of past societies were commonly marked by a number of significant exclusions. Women, slaves, children, laborers, and noncitizens—in other words, the majority of the population—usually were denied entry into and, therefore, participation in the public realms of society. Precisely because of such exclusionary practices, members of these and other subordinated

---

7 Ibid., 79.

social groups historically have found it propitious, indeed necessary, to develop alternative publics. Hence, there has never been only one public discursive sphere in modern societies: the bourgeois public never was *the* public. On the contrary, as Nancy Fraser observes, "Virtually contemporaneous with the bourgeois public there arose a host of competing counterpublics, including nationalist publics, popular peasant publics, elite women's publics, black publics, and working-class publics."[8]

Given the rich diversity that is basic to the human condition, and the important need in society for alternative discursive publics that can counteract the different forms of exclusions, oppressions, and inequalities prevalent in civil society, it is requisite that one question accounts that see public life as confined to a single, official sphere of public discourse. Theories of the public, perhaps particularly those that are unequivocally motivated by an emancipatory impulse, must be concerned with the reality and implications of diversity, of power differentials among persons and groups, and of the existence of systemic relations of dominance and subordination that affect the cultural, discursive, economic, and political structures of society. Mindful of these realities, an adequate theory of the public should allow for the inevitability and suitability of multiple, particularistic discursive publics in society. In short, a theory of the public that attends to the implications of power differentials and allows for a multiplicity of public discursive spheres in society is preferable to one that falls into a reverie of a single overarching public sphere.

In light of these challenges and exigencies, various thinkers have pluralized and expanded the concept of the public sphere to make room for what we may call "subaltern counter*publics*"[9]—that is, for "parallel discursive arenas where members of subordinated social groups invent and circulate

---

8 Ibid., 75.

9 Oskar Negt and Alexander Kluge's pioneering critique of Jurgen Habermas's interpretation of the public provided the groundwork for the notion of alternative public spheres of discourse in civil society, and for talk of counterpublics. See Oskar Negt and Alexander Kluge, *Public Sphere and Experience: Toward an Analysis of the Bourgeois and Proletarian Public Sphere*, trans. Peter Labanyi, Jamie Owen Daniel, and Assenka Oksiloff (Minneapolis: University of Minnesota Press, 1993). The expression "subaltern counterpublics" has particularly been proposed by Nancy Fraser to signal the oppositional character of those public discursive arenas developed by members of subordinated social groups. She constructs this designation by taking the term "subaltern" from Gayatri Spivak's work and combining it with the term "counterpublic," which is used by Rita Felski. See Gayatri Spivak, "Can the Subaltern Speak?" in *Marxism and the Interpretation of Culture*, ed. Cary Nelson and Larry Grossberg (Chicago: University of Illinois Press, 1988), 271-313; Rita Felski, *Beyond Feminist Aesthetics* (Cambridge: Harvard University Press, 1989). For Fraser's use of the expression "subaltern counterpublics," see *Justice Interruptus*, esp. 80-85.

counterdiscourses, which in turn permit them to formulate oppositional interpretations of their identities, interests, and needs."[10]

If we take the idea of subaltern counter*publics* seriously, then we can establish a helpful distinction between the broader public realm of civil society, which can be designated as the more comprehensive, all-inclusive arena of citizen discourse and association in society, and the different, more limited and specific, discursive public spheres that inhabit the larger civic public and that encapsulate the particular expressive idioms, identities, and concerns of culturally defined social groups. Within this framework, we can advance an understanding of the public of civil society as that comprehensive arena in which members of different, more limited local publics can talk across lines of cultural and other areas of diversity to deliberate about their common affairs as a body politic. Correspondingly, this view of the broader civic public realm allows for the existence of a multiplicity of local discursive publics where members of particular social groups, including members of historically subordinated and disadvantaged groups, can circulate specific interpretations of their identities, interests, and needs that can in principle be critical of the ethnocentrism, varied forms of exclusion, misrepresentation, and inequalities that exist in society. In this way, then, the broader civic public realm is never culturally neutral or devoid of local specificity, because it allows for a plurality of perspectives and culture-specific expressions, as well as for diverse discursive contestations that may emerge in response to exclusions and marginalizations in civic life. Yet, although this view of the public presupposes a plurality of perspectives, it permits us to envision the civic public realm as a space where collaboration among the distinct public spheres of social groups may occur in order to regenerate the sort of participatory interaction that can bring coalitional civic pressure to bear when official policies threaten to violate the democratic fulfillment of those living in a society. Hence, the idea of subaltern counter*publics* elucidates the possibility of a more comprehensive arena of discourse and association in which more limited, yet significant and contextually specific, public spheres infused with diverse values, identities, cultural styles, and context-specific needs can coexist and, when necessary, unite for the common good. From the vantage point of this conceptual framework, we can think of the public sphere as "the structured setting where cultural and ideological contestation or negotiation among a variety of publics takes place."[11]

---

10 Fraser, *Justice Interruptus*, 81.

11 Geoff Eley, "Nations, Publics, and Political Cultures: Placing Habermas in the Nineteenth Century," in Calhoun, ed., *Habermas and the Public Sphere*, 306.

The idea of subaltern counter*public* spheres of discourse has enormous analytical usefulness, particularly for theorists who are members of a subordinate group and for critical theorists overall. It allows for the expansion of the concept of the civic public beyond a single, official discursive public sphere, and allows for the theorizing of a polymorphous public realm made up of multiple, at times overlapping and even competing, arenas of discourse. More deeply, however, the idea of subaltern counter*publics* can function as a theory of discourse that could help us to negotiate the relationship between the requisites of public discourse and the recognition of specific social identities. The underlying assumptions of the concept of subaltern counter*public* discursive spheres serve to encourage us to hold together a commitment to the advancement of a comprehensive emancipatory project of social equality and a commitment to the ennoblement of a localist emancipatory project that aims to defend embattled identities, end cultural domination, and win specific recognition. In this way, the concept of subaltern counter*publics* can serve not only to expand the theorization of the broader civic public realm, but also to provide a theoretical basis for the development of liberatory public discourses that can connect legitimate localist aspirations for cultural justice and identity recognition to a more holistic, broad-based, emancipatory political project that seeks to grasp and transform the social whole. In short, it can function as a theory of public discourse that helps us to connect our theories of and struggles for cultural justice to a comprehensive theory of social justice, allowing for the integration of cultural theorizing and social theorizing and for the ennoblement of a coalitional politic of liberation. It is, thus, an idea that merits the consideration of critical theorists of justice.

The sensibility and/or postulation that underlies the concept of subaltern counter*publics* is central to the arguments that I have been making in this book. Throughout this study I have vehemently promoted the significance of a public disposition for liberationist and progressive theological discourses that aspire to be availing of social justice. This has led me to highlight the importance of, and indeed the urgent need for, overarching emancipatory visions and broad analyses that can navigate beyond the confines of the local—of identity, culture, and difference-based group politics—in order to energize both the programmatic thinking and the pluralistic collaboration necessary for regenerating concrete liberating possibilities in our society. Correspondingly, I have used the concept of the public and/or the notion of publicness to promote a concern for the quality of our lives together in society; to call Latino/a theologians in particular and liberationists and progressives in general beyond a commitment *centrally* to partial or particular group interest; and to promote holistic, programmatic, coalitional efforts. I have promoted such a perspective because I firmly believe that without a commitment to a wider sense of human solidarity, and without a commitment to the envisioning and energizing of social arrangements that can harmonize the interests of diverse liberationist and progressive constituencies through the building of broad-based coalitions, our emancipatory discursive praxis will fail to accomplish any significant changes in the sociopolitical arena. Ultimately, the success of our intellectual and practical struggle for greater justice, whether in the symbolic order or in the broader structuring of society, hinges on our ability to forge in society a sense of solidarity and our ability to facilitate emancipatory alliances across racial, cultural, gender, class, and even religious lines. This task calls for the building of discourses that can transcend the space of local signification and concern to reflect upon the meaning of our actions in relation to larger systems and blocks of the social order. As I have stressed previously, this task calls for forms of thought and speech that dare to be socially broad, integrative, holistic—in short, public in orientation.

Nevertheless, even as I have played up the possibility and desirability of comprehensive thinking, and even as I have highlighted the theoretical and practical limitations of a discourse centered on matters of local identity, culture, and difference, I have also insisted upon the need for and significance of particular struggles to defend embattled identities, end cultural domination, and win recognition. I have argued that for discourses that are organically linked to subordinate groups that have been deprived of recognition, respect, and equal treatment in the wider society, it has indeed been necessary to focus on the construction of distinctive local, ethnic, cultural, and group identities in order to counter forms of either cultural, ethnic, racial, gender, or sexual injustice. Acknowledging that identity-, culture-, or difference-based discourses are rooted, for the most part, in legitimate demands for greater participation in democratic life, I have argued that we should not dismiss those movements associated with a paradigm of the recognition of identity and difference, but rather, that we should understand the conditions and reasons that lead to their existence even as we attempt to move beyond their linguistic and political frameworks.

Thus, my project has been marked throughout by a dialectic that has sought to strike a balance between, on the one hand, a commitment to an overarching emancipatory project that seeks to grasp and transform the social whole and, on the other hand, a yearning to remain mindful of the specific interests and needs of subordinate social groups such as Latino/as. And my attempt to maintain these commitments in a fruitful balance stems from my belief that they should not be viewed by critical thinkers as diametrically opposed or as exclusive alternatives. The choice for Latino/a theologians and scholars, "minority" intellectuals, and critical theorists overall is not either a circumscribed identity or, as Linda Martin Alcoff puts it, "a generic Americanness,"[12] either a politics of cultural and difference recognition or a social politics of equality, either an identity politics or a coalitional politics. Rather, the assignment is to be attentive to these varied, yet crosscutting, interests all at once: we need to develop new critical, holistic perspectives that can more clearly connect the exigencies of cultural theorizing and identity politics to the exigencies of social theorizing and broad-based mobilization for justice. We must develop theoretical, discursive, and activistic frameworks that can appropriately balance a concern for the defense, reconstruction, and nourishment of unjustly embattled local identities with a concern for the building of broader political alliances—for the sake not only of group, but also of general social emancipation.

Much of my interest in the concept of the public, particularly one that allows for the existence and significance of alternative subaltern counter*public* discourses, lies with the capacity that I see in it to frame the question of cultural and identity politics as well as the question of a broader social politics of liberation. A conception of the public sphere that allows for the necessity of counter*public* discursive sites is capable of encompassing the concerns of local cultural and identity politics (e.g., the defense and reconstruction of particular embattled racial, ethnic, gender, sexual, and other culturally defined identities; the achievement of recognition and justice in the symbolic order; the realization of critical local-group consciousness and grassroots organization) and also the concerns related to the actuation of a comprehensive social politics of equality (e.g., the end of exploitation; the achievement of economic redistribution; the realization of broad-based social movements through pluralistic collaboration).

To speak of the public sphere under the rubric of the concept of subaltern counter*publics* is to stress a site of discursive and associational interaction that allows for the free expression of diverse values, identities, cultural styles, and particular histories, and also for alliances in a collective struggle for social change and, thus, equality. In this way, then, the concept of the public is able to incorporate the consideration of diversity, culture, identity, and specific experiences in the same way that the politics of identity and cultural difference can. But, unlike the conceptualization of political claims-making that undergirds the politics of identity and difference, which is prone both to notions of separateness and to enchantment with a logic of localism, it is

---

12 Alcoff, "Latino/a Identity Politics," 108.

more obviously open to the need for continuous formation of self and of group; dialogical and political interaction with other classes and culturally defined groups; and coalition building across difference. As Bruce Robbins puts it, a conception of the public that is open to the notion of subaltern counter*public* discourses invokes culture and identity "but does so with more emphasis on actions and their consequences than on the nature or characteristics of the actors."[13] It is, therefore, a theoretical category that is more amenable to the theorizing of the liberating potential that exists not only *in* but also *between* the differences that mark our distinct social identities, and, therefore, to the promotion of coalitions based on a solidarity of difference.

The concept of subaltern counter*publics* is advantageous for the development of emancipatory discourses and activism in yet another manner: it can help critical thinkers to avoid the insularity that unfortunately has marked and undermined most contemporary critical discourses and political activisms since the 1970s. The notion of the public that undergirds the concept of subaltern counter*public* communication and contestation presupposes a desire for publicness—for wide relevance, for the attraction of an ever widening audience, for intercultural communication, for translocal interest, for mutuality, for common concern, and for concerted action. Although it accommodates distinct social identities and a plurality of perspectives, the sense of publicness that underpins the idea of subaltern counter*publics* calls for persons and groups to interact discursively and politically as members of a wider public, understanding themselves as part of a broader social whole to which they are equally responsible. In this way, it serves to discourage ethnocentrism, intellectual parochialism, and separatism, highlighting instead our interdependence and promoting a sense of solidarity and wholeness. Consequently, the concept can help us to counter the marginalization of public interest and the common good that has intensified in our times. As Peruvian American Suzanne Oboler observes, civic-mindedness has eroded to the point that "it now seems natural that the burden and responsibility" of opposing specific violations of rights and failures of respect lies solely with the members of the victim's group "rather than with the national society as a whole."[14] "To interact discursively as a member of a public—subaltern or otherwise—" as Nancy Fraser puts it, "is to aspire to disseminate one's discourse into ever-widening arenas."[15] It is

---

13 Bruce Robbins, "Introduction: The Public as Phantom," in *The Phantom Public Sphere*, ed. Bruce Robbins (Minneapolis: University of Minnesota Press, 1993), xvii.

14 Suzanne Oboler, "It Must Be a Fake: Racial Ideologies, Identities, and the Question of Rights," in *Hispanics/Latinos in the United States: Ethnicity, Race, and Rights*, ed. Jorge J. E. Gracia and Pablo De Greiff (New York: Routledge, 2000), 135.

15 Fraser, *Justice Interruptus*, 82.

also to care about the quality of our lives together in society, which in turn implies caring deeply about the well-being of the social whole, the well-being of members of all other groups, as well as the well-being of our own groups. Thus, the concept of subaltern counter*publics* opens up possibilities for the creation of discursive and associational public spaces in society where different liberationists and progressives may envision social arrangements that could link their diverse emancipatory interests in order to bring more power and pressure to bear on the society as a whole. In sum, then, the emancipatory potential of the concept of subaltern counter*public* discourse resides in its capacity to connect aspirations for local cultural justice to the aspiration for broad social justice and equality. In this way, it permits for the theorizing of a comprehensive, emancipatory discursive and political project that makes allowances for the significance of local group struggles for cultural justice—the defense of cultural identities, the contestation of modes of cultural domination, and the hope of gaining group recognition—yet transcends the confines of partial local group interest through the promotion of a conception of the general social good and the merits of broad-based mobilization.

COUPLING THE ASPIRATIONS OF LATINO/A THEOLOGY AND PUBLIC DISCOURSE

What is the significance of this discussion of the concept of subaltern counter*public* communication and contestation in the broader realm of civil society for U.S. Hispanic/Latino liberation theologies? This concept offers Latino/a theologians particularly, and liberation theologians in general, a heuristic device at the level of a theory of discourse that can help us to connect the cultural to the social in our theologies; to fuse our locational discursive and political interests to a broader, all-inclusive emancipatory political project, and thus to expand both the theoretical and practical relevancy as well as the liberating potential of our theologies. To put it simply, Latino/a theologians can and should conceptualize and construct their theologies as forms of subaltern counter*public* discourses.

It can legitimately be said that Latino/a theology has been a type of subaltern counterdiscourse because it has delivered colloquies that derive from and are attentive to the lived context of a subordinate group—Latino/as—and because it has put forward colloquies that oppose modes of exclusion, marginalization, misrepresentation, and other oppressions that have long circumscribed Latino/a fulfillment in the United States. And it has done so in the hope of recasting the identities, interests, and needs of Latino/as in an emancipatory manner. Yet, although it has performed as a subaltern counterdiscourse, Latino/a theology has not yet fully functioned as a public discourse—at least in the way that I have defined public discourse in this book. Although Latino/a theology, like U.S. liberation theology as a whole, has assumed the public character of theological reflection and has aspired to liberating public relevance, it has not yet fully displayed a discursive public orientation and, as a result, has not yet fully effectuated its potential public pertinence as a public theological discourse.

I say "not yet fully" because I am not suggesting in any way that Latino/a theology has thoroughly lacked public interest, nor am I suggesting that it has been completely devoid of public character as a discursive form. I am not claiming, for instance, that Latino/a theology has been a privatistic theology focused on matters of private, individual piety. On the contrary, as an expression of liberation theology, it is certainly not a theology that focuses on issues of religious devotion detached from social reality. Latino/a theology has always contained an implicit public character in the sense that it has sought to respond to social issues concerning the Hispanic/Latino condition in the broader U.S. society. Hence, my contention and concern is not that Latino/a theology has been a private, socially detached theology, but rather, that it has thus far generally been a locally based theology of liberation that has unintentionally truncated its potential public character and, therefore, broad social significance in several ways.[16]

Latino/a theology has unknowingly narrowed its public capability and wider sociopolitical relevance by generally neglecting discussions on civil society that have emerged recently in the United States—discussions that seemingly have shifted the discursive context of our liberatory discourses by placing greater emphasis on forms of balkanization, fragmentation, and the loss of social and civil bonds in our society; by focusing mostly on the realm of particular culture and difference, on the internal space of "Latinidad," and not sufficiently on the need for broad-based social analysis and mobilization;

---

16 In this sense, then, the distinction that I am making is not between the public and private, but between the public and local. In other words, I do not use the term "public" to contrast some conception of the public-political sphere with the private-intimate sphere of our life-worlds, but rather, to make a distinction between partial or provincial thinking or interest and holistic or programmatic socially based thinking or interest. As I have argued throughout this book, I believe that critical theorists of justice, such as Latino/a theologians, must seek to rediscover the possibility and desirability of overarching thinking and broad analysis that may reflect on and seek to transform the social whole for the sake of the social whole. This implies analyzing and opposing all of the multiple and crosscutting inequities that affect not only our culturally defined social groups, but also other suffering persons and groups in our society. It implies, in other words, "other interest" or a conception of "public interest" that can transcend the boundaries of our local habitus.

by advancing an understanding of injustice that is mainly cultural rather than socioeconomic, surrendering, in the process, the conceptualization of a comprehensive emancipatory project that appropriately connects the theorizing of cultural justice to the theorizing of social justice;[17] and by failing to develop and promote a socially binding discourse that can connect the various struggles for justice of our Hispanic communities both to the similar struggles of other subordinated groups and to the progressive sensibilities of other constituencies in our society.[18] The result of these four tendencies is a

---

17 Whether by design or not, Latino/a theologians generally have exhibited an understanding of injustice that is mostly cultural, rather than socioeconomic, in their theologies. Hence, injustices rooted in the political and economic structure of society—such as, in the words of Nancy Fraser, "exploitation (i.e., having the fruits of one's labor appropriated for the benefit of others); economic marginalization (i.e., being confined to undesirable or poorly paid work or being denied access to income-generating labor altogether); and deprivation (i.e., being denied an adequate material standard of living)"—have not received sustained attention in most Latino/a theologies. Instead, most Latino/a theologians have devoted much of their attention to injustices that are rooted in social patterns of representation, recognition, and interpretation-such as, again in Fraser's words, "cultural domination (i.e., being subjected to patterns of interpretation and communication that are associated with another culture and are alien and/or hostile to one's own); nonrecognition (i.e., being rendered invisible by means of the authoritative representational, communicative, and interpretative practices of one's culture); and disrespect (i.e., being routinely maligned or disparaged in stereotypic public cultural representations and/or in everyday life interactions)." In sum, Latino/a theologians thus far have opted to focus more on the contestation of assimilationist tendencies—the discovery, defense, and reconstruction of local Latino/a cultures and identities—and the achievement of recognition for Latino/a cultural difference than on broad-based social analysis or redistributive justice. As I noted in chapter 2, this inclination is perceptible in the recurring use of, and significance attributed to, the concepts of mestizaje and popular religion in Latino/a theology—concepts that lend themselves more to cultural than social theorizing. Yet, because Latino/as suffer injustices that are traceable to both political economy and culture simultaneously, because others in society similarly suffer injustices that are traceable to both political economy and culture simultaneously, and because the achievement of concrete liberating possibilities within the realms of both political economy and culture depends on the activation of a broad-based political movement for justice that can bring different liberationists and progressives together, I suggest that Latino/a theologians should give equal attention to cultural and distributive injustices and should seek to connect the problematic of recognition and the problematic of redistribution within a comprehensive sociopolitical project for justice that promotes coalition building. In short, Latino/a theologians should grant the exigency for cultural change and the exigency for socioeconomic change equal consideration, searching for a critical stance that is appropriately bivalent. For more on the distinction between cultural and socioeconomic understandings of injustice that I cited above, see Fraser, *Justice Interruptus*, esp. 11-39 (the quotes used above come from pp. 13 and 14 of that work).

18 U.S. Hispanic/Latino theology has emphasized the importance of a collaborative spirit, a motivating impulse that even has been named and given prominence as a theme in itself: *teologia en conjunto* (collaborative or joint theology). The emphasis is on doing theology in

decreased capacity to respond to and influence public discourse; an insufficient scrutiny of distributive justice issues and of the need for an adequately comprehensive social theory that can connect the local to the public; a diminished ability to attract the attention and the support of people and interests outside of Latino/a communities; and, thus, a reduced ability to facilitate and nourish the kinds of social arrangements that can engender broad-based political coalitions across racial, cultural, ethnic, gender, class, and religious lines.

A theology that aspires to transformative social relevance, as Latino/a theology does, should seek to provide the religious or spiritual basis for the integration of the struggle for equality and justice into broader spheres of everyday life, and also should aspire to disseminate its discourse to ever widening arenas of discussion and association in the broader realm of civil society. The task of both Latino/a liberation and of broader social liberation requires, perhaps especially in our trying and fractious times, the articulation of a broad and integrative vision that can attract the attention of a large and diverse audience, and can bring together different liberationists and

---

cooperation with other Latino/a theologians as a communal exercise, and also in dialogue with one's community of faith. Although this is a noble and important proposition, I note that this emphasis unfortunately has been limited thus far to "intradialogue" and "intracollaboration" among Latino/a theologians only, and has not yet made sufficient allowances for dialogue and collaboration with other discursive communities of struggle. Hence, the specific form in which Latino/a theologians have elaborated the idea of *teologia en conjunto* does not promote "intergroup dialogue and collaboration" with, for instance, African American, Native American, Asian American, progressive Anglo feminist, and other leftist or progressive theologians. I believe that the concept should be expanded to promote and nurture discursive practices that bind together our local community's struggle for justice with those of other marginalized ethnic groups, subordinated groups, and progressive constituencies in the United States. In short, I submit that *teologia en conjunto* also should stand for doing theology *en conjunto*—in collaboration—with these other groups. This is precisely the sort of vision and undertaking that Anthony Pinn and I have sought to initiate and encourage between Latino/a and African American theologians in *The Ties That Bind: African American and Hispanic American/Latino(a) Theologies in Dialogue*, ed. Anthony B. Pinn and Benjamín Valentín (New York: Continuum, 2001). For works that define *teologia en conjunto* within Latino/a theology, see Ana María Pineda, "Pastoral de Conjunto," *New Theology Review* 3, no. 4 (1990): 28-34; Justo González, *Mañana: Christian Theology from a Hispanic Perspective* (Nashville: Abingdon Press, 1990), esp.28-30; José David Rodríguez and Loida I. Martell-Otero, introduction to *Teologia en Conjunto: A Collaborative Hispanic Protestant Theology*, ed José David Rodríguez and Loida I. Martell-Otero (Louisville: Westminster John Knox Press, 1997), 1-10; and Luis Pedraja, "Guideposts along the Journey: Mapping North American Hispanic Theology," in *Protestantes/Protestants: Hispanic Christianity within Mainline Traditions*, ed. David Maldonado Jr. (Nashville: Abingdon Press, 1999), esp. 136-37.

progressives to work toward meaningful social change and, thus, toward the improvement of the quality of our lives together. In order to be faithful to and meet the demands of such a comprehensive emancipatory discursive enterprise, Latino/a theology should engage in more serious efforts of social theorizing even as it continues to reexamine and develop modes of cultural theories and critiques. Along these lines, it should seek to acknowledge, analyze, and oppose all of the many and crosscutting inequities that afflict not only Latino/as but also many other suffering persons and groups in our society. Latino/a theology also should be willing to traverse the boundaries of group knowledge and interest in order to envision and articulate a social ontology that can more tangibly enable relationships across local personal and group difference and particularity. To put it differently, Latino/a theologians should seek to cultivate and evince the political imagination to build personal and political bridges with leaders, intellectuals, and persons of other social groups, willing to reach out to different kinds of leftists, progressives, and socially concerned persons with an emancipatory message of coalition building and radical democracy.

The important point here is not that the examination of specific identity recognition and formation, and the defense and maintenance of particular cultural traditions, should be disregarded by Latino/a theologians, for such matters remain crucial for Latino/a liberation, and indeed they should remain important for any general theory of justice. The importance of these is refreshingly captured in the theology of mestizaje presented by Virgilio Elizondo and in the hermeneutics of popular religion tendered by Orlando Espín. What is crucial, however, is that these categories and issues be linked to some conception of a public good and to a public perspective that may better help us to grasp and critically reflect on the transformation of the social whole, that may better help us to analyze the conditions for a comprehensive emancipatory political project that can integrate claims for cultural and identity recognition with a social politics of redistribution and a politics of coalition, and that may better help us to attract the attention of a larger audience in the hope of prompting it to take public action on behalf of the enhancement of the quality of our lives together.[19]

---

19 I must point out that public theology unfortunately has been generally inattentive to or disregarding of the particular local needs of historically disadvantaged groups in U.S. society. Legitimate claims for the recognition of difference; local group concerns regarding gender, sexual, and racial-ethnic injustice; local struggles to end existing forms of cultural domination; and the critique of actual existing democracy being vocalized by members of subordinated social groups—these have not received fair hearing in most expressions of public theology. Along these lines, it is also necessary to note that many who discuss public theology have tended to shy

I firmly believe that a liberatory discourse that hopes to be availing of a reinvigorated social justice movement in our present society—one that may generate meaningful social change and democratic possibilities for all—will have to find theoretical and political mechanisms that can integrate the legitimate interests of cultural justice and identity politics with the interests of a comprehensive social politics of liberation, equality, and coalition building. Given the multiplication of social antagonisms and the fracturing of utopian energies that we have seen in recent times, it is imperative that theorists of justice seek to cultivate, evince, and promote such a holistic and integrative perspective in their discourses.

Accordingly, the task of liberation for critical theorists such as Latino/a theologians, who are located within the context of historically subordinated and disadvantaged groups, is presently bivalent. On the one hand, social and local change requires the building and nourishment of our particular communities and communal identities. This implies attention to the particular interests and needs of our local group, and it also implies in many cases attention to the defense and/or reconstruction of embattled local identities, the end of cultural domination, and the achievement of recognition. Thus, we certainly have occasion for the continuing expression and affirmation in our

---

away from the liberationist commitments and perspectives being promoted by liberation theologians, such as Latino/a theologians. Public theology must not dismiss, however, the concerns, needs, and interests being voiced by such theologies that come from the perspective or contexts of subordinated social constituencies. At the core, theologians of "publicness" concern themselves with the possible betterment of American society, understood as the advancement of a broader common good. I cannot fathom how theologians of publicness can speak with integrity about this possibility without seriously taking into account the standpoints of the least advantaged in society. This includes seriously considering the way in which many persons and groups in the United States, especially non-Anglo groups, consistently suffer from injustices that are traceable to culture. As I see it, if one seeks to renew a nation's social vision, one must attend to the voices, concerns, needs, and visions of those who have been marginalized. Hence, even as I call upon liberationist theologies, such as Latino/a theology, to consider the idea of publicness that is being discussed among theologians of public life, I call upon public theology to take into account the specific local concerns, interests, needs, visions, and liberationist commitments being vocalized by those theologies that derive from subordinated social groups in our society. For a work in public theology that noticeably downplays the issues noted above and that openly reacts against liberationist commitments promoted by liberation theologians, see Robert Benne, *The Paradoxical Vision: A Public Theology for the Twenty-First Century* (Minneapolis: Fortress Press, 1995). Even within some works on public theology that stem from a more liberal-progressivist stance, this inattentiveness to the specific concerns of historically disadvantaged groups, and this apprehensiveness toward liberation theologies, can be detected. See, for instance, Ronald Thiemann, *Constructing a Public Theology: The Church in a Pluralistic Culture* (Louisville: Westminster John Knox Press, 1991), and even Linell Cady, *Religion, Theology, and American Public Life* (New York: State University of New York Press, 1993).

Latino/a theologies of what Virgilio Elizondo calls "the radical meaning and potential" that inheres in our particular mestizo/a identities;[20] for the continuing analysis of the way in which, according to Orlando Espín, fundamental Hispanic/Latino cultural values "have found their place in and their medium of dissemination through popular religion";[21] for the continuing unearthing of what Jeanette Rodriguez has called Latino/a "cultural memory";[22] and for the continuing theorization of what many of us have labeled *lo cotidiano*— the quotidian, or the particular everyday experience of Latinos and Latinas in the United States.[23] On the other hand, social and local change, especially in the United States today, requires the building and nourishment of wider communal bonds among the subordinated groups and among the distinct progressive constituencies of a given society. And this in turn implies attention to the larger web of shifting social and political relations that transcends the space of the self, of particular culture and identity, and of our everyday local habitus. It also implies attention to the intricacies involved in creating public spaces so that, as Latina theologian Ada María Isasi-Díaz puts it, "the unfolding of the kin-dom of God can become a reality"[24] in our society.

Moving beyond the contours of an identity- and culture-based localist political discourse does not mean, then, that we ignore questions of identity within our theologies. The questions of who I am and of who we are as an ethnic group should always be pertinent to our theological construction. The task of self-definition is especially pertinent and critical within a context that has consistently worked to deny one's selfhood and the formation of a collective communal identity—particularly when one is non-Anglo. Nevertheless, identity formation also requires a high level of attention to the broader matrices of location that form the context of one's self and group. And the fact is that the different justice demands of our time—whether traceable to culture, social structuring, or political economy—call for solidarity with other groups and progressive constituencies for the purposes of

---

20 See especially Virgilio Elizondo, *Galilean Journey: The Mexican-American Promise* (Maryknoll, N.Y.: Orbis Books, 1983), 16-18, 100-102; idem, *The Future Is Mestizo: Life Where Cultures Meet* (Bloomington, Ind.: Meyer Stone Books, 1988), 38-45.

21 Orlando Espín, *The Faith of the People: Theological Reflections on Popular Catholicism* (Maryknoll, N.Y.: Orbis Books, 1997), 103.

22 See Jeanette Rodriguez, "Sangre llama a sangre: Cultural Memory as a Source of Theological Insight," in *Hispanic/Latino Theology: Challenge and Promise*, ed. Ada María Isasi-Díaz and Fernando F. Segovia (Minneapolis: Fortress Press, 1996), 117-33.

23 For a good overview of the employment of *lo cotidiano*—the everyday experience of Latinas— as a theological source within Hispanic/Latino theology, see Ada María Isasi-Díaz, *Mujerista Theology: A Theology for the Twenty-First Century* (Maryknoll, N.Y.: Orbis Books, 1996), 66-73.

24 Isasi-Díaz, *Mujerista Theology*, 106-7.

building effective political coalitions. This in turn creates the need for distinctive theological discourses that can travel translocally and transculturally even while engaging the needs of the particular communities that we speak from and that define us. Toward this goal, I suggest that Hispanic/Latino theologies need to become discourses that can offer constructed knowledges of the self, local communities, and world that can empower women and men to actualize an integral, inclusive, and equitable vision of human solidarity.

Certainly, as individuals and particular ethnic communities living in the United States, we all have differences, and we must account for these in order to keep at bay harmful notions of homogenization that undermine particular self-defining narratives. However, we also must acknowledge that often our distinct ethnic and cultural groups can share, and indeed have shared, some parallel and even common stories, struggles, hopes, visions, and journeys. In order to allow for social change through emancipatory coalition building, we must acknowledge and highlight these continuities and common interests in our Hispanic/Latino theological discourses at least as much as we examine the space of specific identity and cultural difference. Perhaps in this way we might be better able to create a solidarity of difference that, while acknowledging and respecting our differences, may bring more significant collective power to bear on the society as a whole for the betterment of the quality of our lives together.

Perhaps in this way we might also be better able to "experience God moving within, *between*, and among us."[25] In thinking about God and in seeking to experience something of God's immanent transcendence, we must make way for the idea, potentiality, and requirement of far-reaching connectivity. The imaginative meditations and distillations of interpreted experience presented to us in the Hebrew Scriptures and in early Christian literature abound with references to the primacy of interconnection and relationality when speaking about God and the *imago dei* in human nature. Whether when conceiving of God's central nature or quality; when tendering a picture of the connection between God, humanity, and the whole of creation; when putting forward a covenantal or a prophetic theology that calls on humans to be God's people by practicing solidarity and justice; or when offering assurances of God's continued presence among us in Christ, the Judeo-Christian Scriptures advance an understanding of God that emphasizes connection, affiliation, and interdependence and that discloses God's primary work as that of bringing us together. The God presented to us in Scripture is ostensibly a

---

25 I borrow this phrase from Carter Heyward, *Our Passion for Justice: Images of Power, Sexuality, and Liberation* (New York: Pilgrim Press, 1984), 11 (italics added).

God who is connected to humanity and creation, a God who knows no bounds, a God who constantly is crossing over between and among us, looking to help us to burst free of particular locations in order that we may be better able to build bridges, make connections, and fabricate solidarities among ourselves that could, in turn, engender social justice.

Scripture's relational portrayal of God offers possibilities for reflection on our tasks as justice-seeking theologians; for meditation on our connection to others who are different from us, whether on account of geography, race, ethnicity, culture, religion, class, gender, or sexual orientation; and for the theological promotion of emancipatory multiracial political cooperation in our fragmentary and fractious times. Within this rendering is the possibility of appreciating differences, realizing and valuing our common humanity, and also the hope for moving others toward God's holistic justice. If God is the ultimate source of right relation and, thus, of justice, and if our potentiality as creatures of God is best realized in the salutary connections and relationships we may work up, nourish, and maintain, then our yearning should be to "hold onto God until you and I touch, until we are able to realize our power in intimate and immediate relation"[26] across the boundaries of difference.

This is precisely the longing that Isasi-Díaz expresses in her reflections on the "kindom of God." Besides doing away with the sexist, elitist, and hierarchical connotations conjured up by the term "kingdom," her theological reconstruction of the Judeo-Christian concept of the kingdom of God along the lines of "kinship" helps us both to envision God as the source of wide-embracing connectivity and to ascribe importance to the common humanity that ultimately links us all. The concept of the "kindom of God," as Isasi-Díaz explains it, suggests that "when the fullness of God becomes a day-to-day reality in the world at large, we will all be sisters and brothers—kin to each other; we will indeed be the family of God."[27] Insofar as it is the kindom of God, and insofar as this kindom appears as a fulfillment of God's initiative in *lo cotidiano*—the day-to-day reality of human history—the symbol privileges a God who at once makes a relational commitment to humanity, calls us into mutuality with each other, and is available to us as our source of solidarity. Insofar as it is a kindom comprised of humans, the symbol stresses the basic humanness that connects and equalizes each of us.

Isasi-Díaz's theological construct conveys two other important sensibilities. First, it is marked by an energizing hope. That is, Isasi-Díaz's notion of

---

26 Again, I borrow from Carter Heyward, *The Redemption of God: A Theology of Mutual Relation* (Lanham, Md.: University Press of America, 1982), xviii.

27 Isasi-Díaz, *Mujerista Theology*, 103.

the kindom of God visualizes with hopeful anticipation the actualization of an integral and inclusive vision of human community and solidarity. And it also looks to God as a source for human mutuality. But this theological hope should not be mistaken for either optimism or passivity. "Optimism," as Cornel West puts it, "adopts the role of the spectator who surveys the evidence in order to infer that things are going to get better"; hope, by contrast, "enacts the stance of the participant who actively struggles against the evidence in order to change the deadly tides of wealth inequality, group xenophobia, and personal despair"[28] that impede the actualization of solidarity and justice in the world. Isasi-Díaz's notion of the kindom of God is marked by the latter responsiveness, rather than the former. That is, it is characterized by an activistic hope that stresses human striving. Thus, it does not transfer responsibility and possibility for historical change to God's doing; rather, it envisions God's agency as taking place in history and, therefore, within our human efforts to ensure mutuality. The kindom of God, in this sense, is a historical project "that takes form and shape according to the actions of the oppressed and their 'friends'" in the here and now. "Liberative actions born out of commitment to mutuality, therefore, are not only glimpses of the future but eschatological actions making parts of the future present now."[29] Given the fashionable neoconservative leanings that serve to erode utopian visions in our time and the nihilism that saps working-class and underclass communities of their subversive energies, and given the fact that the traditional bearers of hope in our society, such as political movements and mainstream churches, are in decline and disarray, we certainly can make use of such a "blood-drenched hope" to revitalize our activistic energies for the work of social change that must be done.

Second, Isasi-Díaz's construct of the kindom of God accepts human difference even as it relativizes it. The language of kinship that she employs, after all, does not insist upon identicalness. The unity that it aspires to is not based upon homogeneity; it is founded on reciprocity. Thus, the kindom of God says yes to the fact of human diversity. What it insists upon, however, is the negotiation of difference. Mindful of human diversity and of the dangers that accompany assimilationist reasoning, it nevertheless challenges us to journey across the boundaries of difference in order to occasion solidarities of difference that may, in turn, advance the goal of social justice.

---

28 Cornel West, *Restoring Hope: Conversations on the Future of Black America*, ed. Kelvin Shawn Sealey (Boston: Beacon Press, 1997), xii.

29 Isasi-Díaz, *Mujerista Theology*, 100.

Our times call for the construction of relational theologies. Those interested in what Chicana literary critic Paula Moya calls "the possibility of cross-cultural communication"[30] for the purpose of fostering emancipatory public activity should particularly have a vested interest in the construction of such theological programs. We can pretend that our current particularist, identity- and culture-based theologies of liberation will somehow produce a liberationist movement that will raise the living standards for Latino/as and members of other social groups, and will somehow bring to bear meaningful broad-based pressure on the unjust institutional structures of society, but the evidence thus far has been overwhelmingly to the contrary. After three decades of our discursive and activistic affiliation with the paradigm of identity politics and a cultural politics of difference, the poor have become poorer while the truly wealthy have become wealthier, racism continues to permeate institutional life, and cultural oppression and sexism continue to exist. Moreover, we have witnessed the fissuring of liberationist and progressive social movements—a happenstance that has somewhat dampened the willingness to envision social arrangements that could harmonize the interests of our diverse and currently fragmented local utopian energies and, thus, energize meaningful pluralistic political collaborations between our different group activisms. Clearly, then, we are in need of types of liberationist theological discourse that may be better able to evince and cultivate in society a healthy sense of the public, one that can foster the kinds of bonds of trust and mutual respect, broad social accountability, and utopian coalitional energies that we so desperately need.

In light of these challenges, I have called on Latino/a liberation theology to assume an orientation that is public. I have highlighted for Latino/a theologians the significance of a discursive outlook that critically reflects on the social whole rather than chiefly on the local realm of identity, symbolic culture, and subjectivity, and on the conditions for a comprehensive equitable human interconnectedness. Accordingly, I have called upon them to put forward overarching visions and broad analyses that may captivate the interest of a broad pluralistic social constituency beyond our culturally defined groups.

In discussing the exigencies of such a discursive outlook, and the multiple intersecting demands for justice that currently make its realization a necessity, I have suggested that the time has come for Latino/a theologians to transcend the boundaries of symbolic culture, local identity, and cultural

---

30 Paula Moya, "Cultural Particularity versus Universal Humanity: The Value of Being *Asimilao*," in Gracia and De Greiff, eds., *Hispanics/Latinos in the United States*, 87.

difference in their theologies, not by way of a thorough dismissal of these matters and categories, but rather, through a careful supplementation that more noticeably accounts for the multiple injustices suffered by Latino/as and other persons and groups, and that also plays up those potential interstitial sites of interaction, interconnection, and exchange in our society that may point to the possible harmonizing of social identities and political activisms for the purposes of furthering social justice. Through such an expansion of vision and such a fusion of horizons, we will be able to *go public* with our Latino/a liberation theologies on roads that we have not often traveled.

Selected Bibliography

Abalos, David. "The Personal, Historical, and Sacred Grounding of Culture: Some Reflections on the Creation of Latino Culture in the U.S. from the Perspective of the Theory of Transformation." In *Old Masks, New Faces: Religion and Latino Identities,* ed. Anthony Stevens-Arroyo and Gilbert Cadena, 143–72. New York: The Bildner Center for Western Hemisphere Studies, 1995.

Acosta-Belén, Edna. "From Settlers to Newcomers: The Hispanic Legacy in the United States." In *The Hispanic Experience in the United States: Contemporary Issues and Perspectives,* ed. Edna Acosta-Belén and Barbara R. Sjostrom, 81–106. New York: Praeger, 1988.

Acuña, Rodolfo. *Occupied America: A History of Chicanos.* 2d ed. New York: Harper & Row, 1981.

Aguirre, B. E., and Rogelio Sáenz. "A Futuristic Assessment of Latino Ethnic Identity." *Latino Studies Journal* 2, no. 3 (1991): 19–32.

Alarcón, Daniel Cooper. *The Aztec Palimpsest: Mexico in the Modern Imagination.* Tucson: University of Arizona Press, 1997.

Alcoff, Linda Martin. "Latina/o Identity Politics." In *The Good Citizen,* ed. David Batstone and Eduardo Mendieta, 93–112. New York: Routledge, 1999.

Almaguer, Tomás. "Toward a Study of Chicano Colonialism." *Aztlan: Chicano Journal of Social Sciences and the Arts* 1 (fall 1970): 7–21.

Anderson, Victor. *Pragmatic Theology: Negotiating the Intersections of an American Philosophy of Religion and Public Theology.* New York: State University of New York Press, 1998.

Anzaldúa, Gloria. Foreword to *This Bridge Called My Back,* 2d ed., ed. Gloria Anzaldúa and Cherríe Moraga, iv–v. New York: Kitchen Table/Women of Color Press, 1983.

———. *Borderlands/La Frontera: The New Mestiza.* San Francisco: Aunt Lute Books, 1987.

Aponte, Edwin D. "*Coritos* as Active Symbol in Latino Protestant Popular Religion." *Journal of Hispanic/Latino Theology* 2, no. 3 (1995): 57–66.

Appiah, K. Anthony. "The Uncompleted Argument: DuBois and the Illusion of Race." In *"Race," Writing, and Difference*, ed. Henry Louis Gates Jr., 21–37. Chicago: University of Chicago Press, 1986.

———. "The Multiculturalist Misunderstanding." *The New York Review of Books* 44, no. 15 (9 October 1997): 30–36.

Aquino, María Pilar. "Theological Method in U.S. Latino/a Theology: Toward an Intercultural Theology for the Third Millennium." In *From the Heart of Our People: Latino/a Explorations in Catholic Systematic Theology*, ed. Orlando O. Espín and Miguel H. Diaz, 6–48. Maryknoll, N.Y.: Orbis Books, 1999.

Arendt, Hannah. *The Human Condition.* Chicago: University of Chicago Press, 1958.

Barrera, Mario. *Race and Class in the Southwest.* Notre Dame, Ind.: University of Notre Dame Press, 1979.

Bean, Frank D., and Marta Tienda. *Hispanic Population of the U.S.* New York: Russell Sage Foundation, 1987.

Bellah, Robert, et al. *Habits of the Heart: Individualism and Commitment in American Life.* Berkeley: University of California Press, 1985.

Benhabib, Seyla. *Situating the Self: Gender, Community, and Postmodernism in Contemporary Ethics.* New York: Routledge, 1992.

———. "Models of Public Space: Hannah Arendt, the Liberal Tradition, and Jurgen Habermas." In *Habermas and the Public Sphere*, ed. Craig Calhoun, 73–98. Cambridge, Mass.: MIT Press, 1992.

Benne, Robert. *The Paradoxical Vision: A Public Theology for the Twenty-First Century.* Minneapolis: Fortress Press, 1995.

Bethell, Leslie, ed. *The Cambridge History of Latin America.* 11 vols. Cambridge: Cambridge University Press, 1984–95.

Bhabha, Homi. "The Third Space." In *Identity, Community, Culture Difference*, ed. J. Rutherford, 207–21. London: Lawrence and Wishart, 1990.

———. *The Location of Culture.* London: Routledge, 1994.

Bobo, Lawrence, James R. Kluegel, and Ryan A. Smith. "Laissez-Faire Racism: The Crystallization of a Kinder, Gentler, Antiblack Ideology." In *Racial Attitudes in the 1990s*, ed. Steven A. Tuch and Jack K. Martin, 15–42. Westport, Conn.: Praeger. 1997.

Bonino, José Míguez. *Toward a Christian Political Ethics.* Philadelphia: Fortress Press, 1983.

Bowser, Frederick S. "Colonial Spanish America." In *Neither Slave nor Free: The Freedman of African Descent in the Slave Societies of the New World*, ed. David W. Cohen and Jack P. Greene, 19–58. Baltimore: Johns Hopkins University Press, 1972.

Brooks-Higginbotham, Elizabeth. *Righteous Discontent: The Women's Movement in the Black Baptist Church, 1880–1920*. Cambridge: Harvard University Press, 1993.

Brueggemann, Walter. *The Prophetic Imagination*. Philadelphia: Fortress Press, 1978.

Cady, Linell E. "A Model for a Public Theology." *Harvard Theological Review* 80, no. 2 (1987): 193–212.

———. *Religion, Theology, and American Public Life*. New York: State University of New York Press, 1993.

Calhoun, Craig, "Social Theory and the Politics of Identity." In *Social Theory and the Politics of Identity*, ed. Craig Calhoun, 9–36. Cambridge, Mass.: Blackwell, 1994.

Carrión, Arturo M. *Puerto Rico: A Political and Cultural History*. New York: W. W. Norton & Company, 1983.

Chinchilla, Norma, Nora Hamilton, and James Loucky. "Central Americans in Los Angeles: An Immigrant Community in Transition." In *In the Barrios: Latinos and the Underclass Debate*, ed. Joan Moore and Raquel Pinderhughes, 51–78. New York: Russell Sage Foundation, 1993.

Chopp, Rebecca S. *The Praxis of Suffering: An Interpretation of Liberation and Political Theologies*. Maryknoll, N.Y.: Orbis Books, 1986.

———. "A Feminist Perspective: Christianity, Democracy, and Feminist Theology." In *Christianity and Democracy in Global Context*, ed. John Witte Jr. 111–29. Boulder, Colo.: Westview Press, 1993.

———. "Reimagining Public Discourse." In *Black Faith and Public Talk: Critical Essays on James H. Cone's Black Theology and Black Power*, ed. Dwight N. Hopkins, 150–64. Maryknoll, N.Y.: Orbis Books, 1999.

Chopp, Rebecca S., and Mark Lewis Taylor, eds. *Reconstructing Christian Theology*. Minneapolis: Fortress Press, 1994.

Clark, Kenneth B. *Dark Ghetto: Dilemmas of Social Power*. New York: Harper & Row, 1965.

Conley, Dalton. *Being Black, Living in the Red: Race, Wealth, and Social Policy in America*. Berkeley: University of California Press, 1999.

Danziger, Sheldon, and Peter Gottschalk. *America Unequal*. Cambridge: Harvard University Press, 1995.

Darder, Antonia. "The Politics of Biculturalism: Culture and Difference in the Formation of *Warriors for Gringostroika* and *The New Mestizas*." In

Culture and Difference: Critical Perspectives on the Bicultural Experience in the United States, ed. Antonia Darder, 1–20. Westport, Conn.: Bergin & Garvey, 1995.

Davis, Cary, Carl Haub, and JoAnne L. Willette. "U.S. Hispanics: Changing the Face of America." In *The Hispanic Experience in the United States: Contemporary Issues and Perspectives*, ed. Edna Acosta-Belén and Barbara R. Sjostrom, 3–55. New York: Praeger, 1988.

DeFreitas, Gregory. *Inequality at Work: Hispanics in the U.S. Labor Force*. New York: Oxford University Press, 1991.

DeJesús, Joy L., ed. *Growing Up Puerto Rican: An Anthology*. New York: William Morrow & Company, 1997.

Dewey, John. *The Public and Its Problems*. New York: Henry Holt & Company, 1927.

Díaz-Stevens, Ana María, and Anthony Stevens-Arroyo. *Recognizing the Latino Resurgence in U.S. Religion: The Emmaus Paradigm*. Boulder, Colo.: Westview Press, 1998.

Duany, Jorge. *Quisqueya on the Hudson: The Transnational Identity of Dominicans in Washington Heights*. New York: CUNY Dominican Studies Institute, 1994.

Dyson, Michael E. *Race Rules: Navigating the Color Line*. New York: Vintage Books, 1997.

Ehrenberg, John. *Civil Society: The Critical History of an Idea*. New York: New York University Press, 1999.

Ehrenreich, Barbara. *Fear of Falling: The Inner Life of the Middle Class*. New York: Pantheon Books, 1989.

Eley, Geoff. "Nations, Publics, and Political Cultures: Placing Habermas in the Nineteenth Century." In *Habermas and the Public Sphere*, ed. Craig Calhoun, 289–339. Cambridge, Mass.: MIT Press, 1992.

Elizondo, Virgilio. *Christianity and Culture: An Introduction to Pastoral Theology and Ministry for the Bicultural Community*. Huntington, Ind.: Our Sunday Visitor, 1975.

———. *La Morenita: Evangelizer of the Americas*. San Antonio, Tex.: The Mexican American Cultural Center, 1980.

———. "A Bicultural Approach to Religious Education." *Religious Education* 76, no. 3 (1981): 258–70.

———. *Galilean Journey: The Mexican-American Promise*. Maryknoll, N.Y.: Orbis Books, 1983.

———. *The Future Is Mestizo: Life Where Cultures Meet*. Bloomington, Ind.: Meyer Stone Books, 1988.

———. "Popular Religion as the Core of Cultural Identity in the Mexican American Experience." In *An Enduring Flame: Studies on Latino Popular Religiosity,* ed. Anthony Stevens-Arroyo and Ana María Díaz-Stevens, 113–32. New York: PARAL, 1994.

———. *Guadalupe: Mother of the New Creation.* Maryknoll, N.Y.: Orbis Books, 1997.

Espín, Orlando O. "Popular Catholicism among Latinos." In *Hispanic Catholic Culture in the U.S.: Issues and Concerns,* ed. Jay Dolan and Allan Figueroa Deck, 308–59. Notre Dame, Ind.: Notre Dame University Press, 1994.

———. *The Faith of the People: Theological Reflections on Popular Catholicism.* Maryknoll, N.Y.: Orbis Books, 1997.

Etzioni, Amitai. *The Spirit of Community: The Reinvention of American Society.* New York: Simon & Schuster, 1993.

Farley, Reynolds. *The New American Reality: Who We Are, How We Got Here, Where We Are Going.* New York: Russell Sage Foundation, 1996.

Felski, Rita. *Beyond Feminist Aesthetics.* Cambridge: Harvard University Press, 1989.

Flores, Juan. "Pan-Latino/Trans-Latino: Puerto Ricans in the New Nueva York." *Centro: The Journal of the Center for Puerto Rican Studies* 8, nos. 1/2 (1996): 171–86.

Fox, Geoffrey. *Hispanic Nation: Culture, Politics, and the Construction of Identity.* Tucson: University of Arizona Press, 1996.

Fraser, Nancy. *Unruly Practices: Power, Discourse, and Gender in Contemporary Social Theory.* Minneapolis: University of Minnesota Press, 1989.

———. *Justice Interruptus: Critical Reflections on the "Postsocialist" Condition.* New York: Routledge, 1997.

Friedman, Susan S. *Mappings: Feminism and the Cultural Geographies of Encounter.* Princeton, N.J.: Princeton University Press, 1998.

Fusco, Coco. *English Is Broken Here: Notes on Cultural Fusion in the Americas.* New York: The New Press, 1995.

García-Rivera, Alex. *St. Martin de Porres: The "Little Stories" and the Semiotics of Culture.* Maryknoll, N.Y.: Orbis Books, 1995.

Garrison, Vivian, and Carol Weiss. "Dominican Family Networks and United States Immigration Policy: A Case Study." *International Migration Review* 13, no. 2 (1979): 264–83.

Gates, Henry L., Jr. *The Signifying Monkey: A Theory of Afro-American Literary Criticism.* New York: Oxford University Press, 1988.

Gibson, Charles. *Spain in America.* New York: Harper & Row, 1966.

Gitlin, Todd. *The Twilight of Common Dreams: Why America Is Wracked by Culture Wars.* New York: Metropolitan Books, 1995.

Gittleman, Maury B., and David R. Howell. *Job Quality, Labor Market Segmentation, and Earnings Inequality: Effects of Economic Restructuring in the 1980s*. New York: Jerome Levy Economics Institute, 1992.

Goizueta, Roberto. *Caminemos con Jesús: Toward a Hispanic/Latino Theology of Accompaniment*. Maryknoll, N.Y.: Orbis Books, 1995.

Gómez-Peña, Guillermo. *Warrior for Gringostroika*. Saint Paul, Minn.: Graywolf Press, 1993.

Gómez-Quiñónez, Juan. "Notes on the Interpretation of the Relations between the Mexican Community in the United States and Mexico." In *Mexican/U.S. Relations: Conflict and Convergence*, ed. Carlos Vásquez and Manuel García, 417–39. Los Angeles: University of California Press, 1983.

González, Justo L. *Mañana: Christian Theology from a Hispanic Perspective*. Nashville: Abingdon Press, 1990.

González, Nancie. "Peasant Progress: Dominicans in New York." *Caribbean Studies* 10, no. 3 (1971): 154–71.

Gracia, Jorge J. E. *Hispanic/Latino Identity: A Philosophical Perspective*. Malden, Mass.: Blackwell, 2000.

Gracia, Jorge J. E., and Pablo De Greiff, eds. *Hispanics/Latinos in the United States: Ethnicity, Race, and Rights*. New York: Routledge, 2000.

Habermas, Jurgen. *The Structural Transformation of the Public Sphere: An Inquiry into a Category of Bourgeois Society*. Trans. Thomas Burger and Frederick Lawrence. Cambridge, Mass.: MIT Press, 1989.

Hacker, Andrew. *Two Nations: Black and White, Separate, Hostile, Unequal*. New York: Charles Scribner's Sons, 1992.

Hall, John. *Liberalism: Politics, Ideology and the Market*. Chapel Hill: University of North Carolina Press, 1988.

Hall, Stuart. "Ethnicity: Identity and Difference." *Radical America* 23, no. 4 (1990): 9–20.

Harrison, Bennet, and Barry Bluestone. *The Deindustrialization of America: Plant Closing, Community Abandonment, and the Dismantling of Basic Industry*. New York: Basic Books, 1982.

———. *The Great U-Turn: Corporate Restructuring and the Polarizing of America*. New York: Basic Books, 1988.

Hernández, Ramona, Francisco Rivera-Batiz, and Roberto Agodini. *Dominican New Yorkers: A Socioeconomic Profile*. New York: CUNY Dominican Studies Institute, 1995.

Hero, Rodney. *Latinos and the U.S. Political System: Two-Tiered Pluralism*. Philadelphia: Temple University Press, 1992.

Heyward, Carter. *The Redemption of God: A Theology of Mutual Relation*. Lanham, Md.: University Press of America, 1982.

————. *Our Passion for Justice: Images of Power, Sexuality, and Liberation.* New York: Pilgrim Press, 1984.

Himes, Michael, and Kenneth Himes. *Fullness of Faith: The Public Significance of Theology.* Mahwah, N.J.: Paulist Press, 1993.

Hobbes, Thomas. *De Cive.* Ed. Sterling P. Lamprecht. New York: Appleton-Century-Crofts, 1949.

Hochschild, Arlie R. *The Second Shift: Working Parents and the Revolution at Home.* New York: Viking Books, 1989.

Hodgson, Peter C. *Winds of the Spirit: A Constructive Christian Theology.* Louisville: Westminster John Knox Press, 1994.

Hollenbach, David. "Public Theology in America: Some Questions for Catholicism after John Courtney Murray." *Theological Studies* 37 (1976): 290–303.

————. "Theology and Philosophy in Public: A Symposium on John Courtney Murray's Unfinished Agenda." *Theological Studies* 40 (1979): 700–706.

Isasi-Díaz, Ada María. "Solidarity: Love of Neighbor in the 1980s." In *Lift Every Voice: Constructing Christian Theologies from the Underside,* ed. Susan B. Thistlethwaite and Mary Potter Engels, 31–40. San Francisco: Harper & Row, 1990.

————. *En La Lucha/In the Struggle: Elaborating a Mujerista Theology.* Minneapolis: Fortress Press, 1993.

————. *Mujerista Theology: A Theology for the Twenty-First Century.* Maryknoll, N.Y.: Orbis Books, 1996.

————. "Un poquito de justicia—A Little Bit of Justice: A Mujerista Account of Justice." In *Hispanic/Latino Theology: Challenge and Promise,* ed. Ada María Isasi-Díaz and Fernando Segovia, 325–39. Minneapolis: Fortress Press, 1996.

Isasi-Díaz, Ada María, and Yolanda Tarango. *Hispanic Women: Prophetic Voice in the Church.* Minneapolis: Fortress Press, 1992.

Jiménez, Alfredo, ed. *Handbook of Hispanic Cultures in the United States.* Vol. 2, *History.* Houston: Arte Público Press, 1994.

Jordan, June. *On Call: Political Essays.* Boston: South End Press, 1985.

Karoly, Lynn A. "The Trend in Inequality among Families, Individuals, andWorkers in the United States." In *Uneven Tides: Rising Inequality in America,* ed. Sheldon Danziger and Peter Gottschalk, 19–97. New York: Russell Sage Foundation, 1993.

Kasarda, John. "Industrial Restructuring and the Changing Location of Jobs." In *State of the Union: America in the 1990s,* vol. 1, ed. Reynolds Farley, 215–42. New York: Russell Sage Foundation, 1995.

Kaufman, Gordon D. *An Essay on Theological Method.* Atlanta: Scholars Press, 1979.

————. *In Face of Mystery: A Constructive Theology.* Cambridge: Harvard University Press, 1993.

————. *God-Mystery-Diversity: Christian Theology in a Pluralistic World.* Minneapolis: Fortress Press, 1996.

Keller, Catherine. *From a Broken Web: Separation, Sexism, and Self.* Boston: Beacon Press, 1986.

————. "Seeking and Sucking: On Relation and Essence in Feminist Theology." In *Horizons in Feminist Theology: Identity, Tradition, and Norms,* ed. Rebecca S. Chopp and Sheila Greeve Davaney, 54–78. Minneapolis: Fortress Press, 1997.

King, Deborah. "Multiple Jeopardy, Multiple Consciousness." *Signs* 14, no. 1 (1988): 42–72.

Klein, Herbert S. *African Slavery in Latin America and the Caribbean.* Oxford: Oxford University Press, 1986.

Korrol, Virginia Sánchez. "In Their Own Right: A History of Puerto Ricans in the U.S.A." In *Handbook of Hispanic Cultures in the United States,* vol. 2, *History,* ed. Alfredo Jiménez, 281–301. Houston: Arte Público Press, 1994.

Landes, Joan. *Women and the Public Sphere in the Age of the French Revolution.* Ithaca, N.Y.: Cornell University Press, 1988.

Lemann, Nicholas. "The Origins of the Underclass." *Atlantic* 257 (June 1986): 31–61.

Lewis, Oscar. "The Culture of Poverty." In *On Understanding Poverty: Perspectives from the Social Sciences,* ed. D. P. Moynihan, 167–200. New York: Basic Books, 1968.

Lippy, Charles. *Being Religious, American Style: A History of Popular Religiosity in the United States.* Westport, Conn.: Greenwood Press, 1994.

López, Adalberto. *The Puerto Ricans: Their History, Culture, and Society.* Cambridge, Mass.: Schenkman Press, 1980.

Lorde, Audre. "Age, Race, Class, and Sex: Women Redefining Difference." In *Out There: Marginalization and Contemporary Culture,* ed. R. Ferguson et al., 281–87. New York: The New York Museum of Contemporary Art, 1992.

Lovin, Robin. "Resources for a Public Theology." *Theological Studies* 40 (1979): 706–10.

————. "Social Contract or a Public Covenant?" In *Religion and American Public Life: Interpretations and Explorations,* ed. Robin Lovin, 132–45. Mahwah, N.J.: Paulist Press, 1986.

————. "Response to Linell Cady." In *The Legacy of H. Richard Niebuhr*, ed. Ronald F. Thiemann, 131–36. Minneapolis: Fortress Press, 1991.

Madrick, Jeffrey. *The End of Affluence: The Causes and Consequences of America's Economic Dilemma*. New York: Random House, 1995.

Maduro, Otto. "Liberation Theology." In *A Handbook of Christian Theology*, ed. Donald W. Musser and Joseph L. Price, 287–93. Nashville: Abingdon Press, 1992.

Martínez, Oscar J. "A History of Chicanos/Mexicanos along the U.S.-Mexico Border." In *Handbook of Hispanic Cultures in the United States*, vol. 2, *History*, ed. Alfredo Jiménez, 261–80. Houston: Arte Público Press, 1994.

Marty, Martin. *The Public Church*. New York: Crossroad, 1981.

————. *Religion and Republic: The American Circumstance*. Boston: Beacon Press, 1987.

McElroy, Robert. *The Search for an American Public Theology: The Contribution of John Courtney Murray*. Mahwah, N.J.: Paulist Press, 1989.

McFague, Sallie. *Models of God: Theology for an Ecological, Nuclear Age*. Philadelphia: Fortress Press, 1987.

Minha, Trinh T. "An Acoustic Journey." In *Rethinking Borders*, ed. John C. Welchman, 10–24. Minneapolis: University of Minnesota Press, 1996.

Moore, Henrietta L. *A Passion for Difference: Essays in Anthropology and Gender*. Bloomington: Indiana University Press, 1994.

Moore, Joan. "The Social Fabric of the Hispanic Community Since 1965." In *Hispanic Catholic Culture in the U.S.: Issues and Concerns*, ed. Jay Dolan and Allan Figueroa Deck, 6–49. Notre Dame, Ind.: University of Notre Dame Press, 1994.

Moore, Joan, and Racquel Pinderhughes, eds. *In the Barrios: Latinos and the Underclass Debate*. New York: Russell Sage Foundation, 1993.

Moraga, Cherríe. *The Last Generation: Prose and Poetry*. Boston: South End Press, 1993.

Morales, Rebecca, and Frank Bonilla, eds. *Latinos in a Changing U.S. Economy: Comparative Perspectives on Growing Inequality*. New York: Russell Sage Foundation, 1993.

Negt, Oskar, and Alexander Kluge. *Public Sphere and Experience: Toward an Analysis of the Bourgeois and Proletarian Public Sphere*. Trans. Peter Labanyi, Jamie Owen Daniel, and Assenka Oksiloff. Minneapolis: University of Minnesota Press, 1993.

Neuhaus, Richard J. *The Naked Public Square: Religion and Democracy in America*. Grand Rapids: Eerdmans, 1984.

Newman, Katherine S. *Falling from Grace: The Experience of Downward Mobility in the American Middle Class*. New York: Random House, 1988.

————. *Declining Fortunes: The Withering of the American Dream.* New York: Basic Books, 1993.

Novas, Himilce. *Everything You Need to Know about Latino History.* New York: Plume Books, 1994.

Oboler, Suzanne. *Ethnic Labels, Latino Lives: Identity and the Politics of (Re)Presentation in the United States.* Minneapolis: University of Minnesota Press, 1995.

Padilla, Félix. *Latino Ethnic Consciousness: The Case of Mexican Americans and Puerto Ricans in Chicago.* Notre Dame, Ind.: University of Notre Dame Press, 1985.

Palmer, Parker J. *The Company of Strangers: Christians and the Renewal of America's Public Life.* New York: Crossroad, 1981.

Paredes, Tito. "Popular Religiosity: A Protestant Perspective." *Missiology* 20, no. 2 (1992): 205–20.

Pedraja, Luis. "Guideposts along the Journey: Mapping North American Hispanic Theology." In *Protestantes/Protestants: Hispanic Christianity within Mainline Traditions,* ed. David Maldonado Jr., 123–39. Nashville: Abingdon Press, 1999.

Pineda, Ana María. "Pastoral de Conjunto." *New Theology Review* 3, no. 4 (1990): 28–34.

Pinn, Anthony B., and Benjamín Valentín, eds. *The Ties That Bind: African American and Hispanic American/Latino(a) Theologies in Dialogue.* New York: Continuum, 2001.

————. *Earth Bound: Toward a Theology of Fragile Cultural Memory and Religious Diversity* (working title). Minneapolis: Fortress Press, forthcoming.

Poyo, Gerald E., and Mariano Díaz-Miranda. "Cubans in the United States." In *Handbook of Hispanic Cultures in the United States,* vol. 2, *History,* ed. Alfredo Jiménez, 302–20. Houston: Arte Público Press, 1994.

Pratt, Mary Louise. *Imperial Eyes: Travel Writing and Transculturation.* London: Routledge, 1992.

Recinos, Harold J. *Jesus Weeps: Global Encounters on Our Doorstep.* Nashville: Abingdon Press, 1992.

————. *Who Comes in the Name of the Lord? Jesus at the Margins.* Nashville: Abingdon Press, 1997.

————. "Politics, Martyrdom, and Life Story: Salvadoran Refugees Speak a Word of Life in the United States." *Journal of Hispanic/Latino Theology* 5, no. 2 (1997): 5–21.

Robbins, Bruce. "Introduction: The Public as Phantom." In *The Phantom Public Sphere,* ed. Bruce Robbins, vii–xxvi. Minneapolis: University of Minnesota Press, 1993

Rodríguez, Jeannette. *Our Lady of Guadalupe: Faith and Empowerment among Mexican-American Women.* Austin: University of Texas Press, 1994.

———. *Stories We Live/Cuentos Que Vivimos: Hispanic Women's Spirituality.* New York: Paulist Press, 1996.

———. "Sangre llama a sangre: Cultural Memory as a Source of Theological Insight." In *Hispanic/Latino Theology: Challenge and Promise,* ed. Ada María Isasi-Díaz and Fernando F. Segovia, 117–33. Minneapolis: Fortress Press, 1996.

Rodríguez, José David, and Loida I. Martell-Otero. Introduction to *Teologia de Conjunto: A Collaborative Hispanic Protestant Theology,* ed. Jose David Rodríguez and Loida I. Martell Otero, 1–10. Louisville: Westminster John Knox Press, 1997.

Rossi, Peter. *Down and Out in America.* Chicago: University of Chicago Press, 1989.

Ryan, Mary P. "Gender and Public Access: Women's Politics in Nineteenth Century America." In *Habermas and the Public Sphere,* ed. Craig Calhoun, 259–88. Cambridge, Mass.: MIT Press, 1992.

Safa, Helen I. "Migration and Identity: A Comparison of Puerto Rican and Cuban Migrants in the United States." In *The Hispanic Experience in the United States: Contemporary Issues and Perspectives,* ed. Edna Acosta-Belén and Barbara R. Sjostrom, 137–50. New York: Praeger, 1988.

Said, Edward. *Culture and Imperialism.* New York: Viking, 1993.

———. *Representations of the Intellectual.* New York: Pantheon Books, 1994.

Schor, Juliet B. *The Overworked American: The Unexpected Decline of Leisure.* New York: Basic Books, 1991.

Sennett, Richard. *The Fall of Public Man.* New York: Vintage Books, 1978.

Silvestrini, Blanca G. "The World We Enter When Claiming Rights: Latinos and Their Quest for Culture." In *Latino Cultural Citizenship: Claiming Identity, Space, and Rights,* ed. William V. Flores and Rina Benmayor, 39–53. Boston: Beacon Press, 1997.

Spivak, Gayatri. "Can the Subaltern Speak?" In *Marxism and the Interpretation of Culture,* ed. Cary Nelson and Larry Grossberg, 271–313. Chicago: University of Illinois Press, 1988.

Stackhouse, Max. *Public Theology and Political Economy: Christian Stewardship in Modern Society.* Grand Rapids: Eerdmans, 1987.

Stevens-Arroyo, Anthony. "The Emergence of a Social Identity among Latino Catholics: An Appraisal." In *Hispanic Catholic Culture in the U.S.: Issues and Concerns,* ed. Jay Dolan and Allan Figueroa Deck, 77–130. Notre Dame, Ind.: University of Notre Dame Press, 1994.

Sullivan, William M. *Reconstructing Public Philosophy.* Berkeley: University of California Press, 1986.

Sum, Andrew, and Neal Fogg. "The Changing Economic Fortunes of Young Black Men in America." *The Black Scholar* (March 1990): 47–55.

Tanner, Kathryn. *Theories of Culture: A New Agenda for Theology.* Minneapolis: Fortress Press, 1997.

Thiemann, Ronald F. *Constructing a Public Theology: The Church in a Pluralistic Culture.* Louisville: Westminster John Knox Press, 1991.

————. *Religion in Public Life: A Dilemma for Democracy.* Washington, D.C.: Georgetown University Press, 1996.

Thomas, Sowell. *Ethnic America.* New York: Basic Books, 1981.

Tillich, Paul. *Systematic Theology.* Vol. 1. Chicago: University of Chicago Press, 1951.

Torres, María de los Angeles. "Transnational Political and Cultural Identities: Crossing Theoretical Borders." In *Borderless Borders: U.S. Latinos, Latin Americans, and the Paradox of Interdependence,* ed. Frank Bonilla et al., 169–82. Philadelphia: Temple University Press, 1998.

Tracy, David. "Defending the Public Character of Theology." *The Christian Century,* 1 April 1981, 350–56.

————. *The Analogical Imagination: Christian Theology and the Culture of Pluralism.* New York: Crossroad, 1981.

Trueba, Enrique T. *Latinos Unidos: From Cultural Diversity to the Politics of Solidarity.* Lanham, Md.: Rowman & Littlefield, 1999.

Valentin, Benjamin. "Nuevos Odres Para el Vino: A Critical Contribution to Latino/a Theological Construction." *Journal of Hispanic/Latino Theology* 5, no.4 (1998): 30–47.

————. "Strangers No More: An Introduction to, and Interpretation of, U.S. Hispanic/Latino Theology." In *The Ties That Bind: African American and Hispanic American/Latino(a) Theology in Dialogue,* ed. Anthony B. Pinn and Benjamín Valentín, 38–53. New York: Continuum, 2001.

Valle, Víctor, and Rodolfo Torres. "The Idea of *Mestizaje* and the 'Race' Problematic: Racialized Media Discourse in a Post-Fordist Landscape." In *Culture and Difference: Critical Perspectives on the Bicultural Experience in the United States,* ed. Antonia Darder, 139–53. Westport, Conn.: Bergin & Garvey, 1995.

Vasconcelos, José. *The Cosmic Race/La Raza Cósmica.* Baltimore: Johns Hopkins University Press, 1997.

Villafañe, Eldin. *Seek the Peace of the City: Reflections on Urban Ministry.* Grand Rapids: Eerdmans, 1995.

Watts, Jerry G. "Blacks and Coalition Politics: A Theoretical Reconceptualization." In *The Politics of Minority Coalitions: Race, Ethnicity, and Shared Uncertainties,* ed. Wilbur C. Rich, 35–51. Westport, Conn.: Praeger, 1996.

West, Cornel. *The American Evasion of Philosophy: A Genealogy of Pragmatism.* Madison: University of Wisconsin Press, 1989.

———. *Prophetic Reflections: Notes on Race and Power in America.* Monroe, Maine: Common Courage Press, 1993.

———. *Race Matters.* New York: Vintage Books, 1994.

———. *Restoring Hope: Conversations on the Future of Black America,* ed. Kelvin Shawn Sealey. Boston: Beacon Press, 1997.

Wetzel, James R. "Labor Force, Unemployment, and Earnings." In *State of the Union: America in the 1990s,* vol.1, ed. Reynolds Farley, 243–67. New York: Russell Sage Foundation, 1995.

Whitman, Walt. "The Spanish Element in Our Nationality." In *The Works of Walt Whitman,* vol. 2, ed. M. Cowley, 112–18. New York: Funk & Wagnalls, 1948.

Wilson, Kenneth L., and Alejandro Portes. "Immigrant Enclaves: An Analysis of the Labor Market Experiences of Cubans in Miami." *American Journal of Sociology* 86 (September 1980): 295–319.

Wilson, William Julius. *The Truly Disadvantaged: The Inner City, the Underclass, and Public Policy.* Chicago: University of Chicago Press, 1987.

———. *When Work Disappears: The World of the New Urban Poor.* New York: Alfred A. Knopf, 1996.

———. *The Bridge over the Racial Divide: Rising Inequality and Coalition Politics.* Berkeley: University of California Press, 1999.

Wood, Ellen M. *Democracy Against Capitalism: Renewing Historical Materialism.* Cambridge: Cambridge University Press, 1995.

Yinger, John. *Closed Doors, Opportunities Lost: The Continuing Costs of Housing Discrimination.* New York: Russell Sage Foundation, 1995.

Young, Iris Marion. *Justice and the Politics of Difference.* Princeton, N.J.: Princeton University Press, 1990.

———. "Impartiality and the Civic Public: Some Implications of Feminist Critiques of Moral and Political Theory." In *Feminism as Critique: On the Politics of Gender,* ed. Seyla Benhabib and Drucilla Cornell, 57–76. Minneapolis: University of Minnesota Press, 1987.

Zazueta, Carlos. "Mexican Political Actors in the United States and Mexico: Historical and Political Contexts of a Dialogue." In *Mexican/U.S. Relations: Conflict and Convergence,* ed. Carlos Vásquez and Manuel García, 78–104. Los Angeles: University of California Press, 1983.

Index